Good quotes p.7

Praise for *Transforming Grace*

"Anne Carr gives us a balanced introduction to feminist theological questions. Her Christian feminist theology seeks to build bridges not only between different feminist directions within Christianity, but also between Christian and post-Christian feminists. Indispensable reading for anyone interested in current feminist theology."
—Elisabeth Schüssler Fiorenza, author of *In Memory of Her: A Feminist Reconstruction of Christian Origins*.

"Although the patriarchal practices have driven women 'out of the church,' a determined group refuses to leave *and* refuses to be silent in the face of inadequate theological symbols, unjust practices, and untenable teachings. Carr combines her skills as a theologian with her experience in the women's movement to argue that the challenge and vision of women in the church is grounded on the Gospel itself, and that the 'radical' changes imagined by feminists are consistent with the Christian tradition at its finest."—Mary Jo Weaver, professor of religious studies, Indiana University, author of *New Catholic Women*

"The international women's movement has advanced often in recent decades with the guidance of the courageous voices of women raised in the Roman Catholic tradition. Here is one of those voices, calling the Christian church to be faithful to its own vision of justice as that vision is interpreted anew by the experience of modern women."
—Constance H. Buchanan, director of women's studies in religion, The Divinity School, Harvard University

TRANSFORMING GRACE

TRANSFORMING GRACE

Christian Tradition
and Women's Experience

Anne E. Carr

1817

Harper & Row, Publishers, San Francisco

New York, Grand Rapids, Philadelphia, St. Louis
London, Singapore, Sydney, Tokyo, Toronto

Grateful acknowledgment is made for the use of the following material: From *A Room of One's Own* by Virginia Woolf, copyright © 1929 by Harcourt, Brace, Jovanovich, Inc.; renewed 1957 by Leonard Woolf. Reprinted by permission (US rights) of Harcourt, Brace and Jovanovich, Inc. Reprinted by permission (excluding US rights) of the author's estate and The Hogarth Press. From "Coming of Age in Christianity: Women and the Churches" by Anne E. Carr, previously published in *The Furrow*. Reprinted by permission of *The Furrow*. From "On Feminist Spirituality" by Anne E. Carr, previously published in *Horizons*. Reprinted by permission of *Horizons*. From "The Church in Process: Engendering the Future" by Anne E. Carr, in *Women and Catholic Priesthood,* edited by Anne Marie Gardiner. Copyright © 1976 by Paulist Press. Reprinted by permission of Paulist Press.

FIRST HARPER & ROW PAPERBACK EDITION PUBLISHED IN 1990.

Library of Congress Cataloging-in-Publication Data

Carr, Anne E.
  Transforming grace.

  Bibliography: p.
  Includes index.
  1. Feminism—Religious aspects—Christianity.
2. Ordination of women. I. Title.
BT704.C38   1988   261.8′344   87-45692
ISBN 0-06-254824-7

ISBN 0-06-254870-0 (pbk.)
90 91 92 93 94 MCN 10 9 8 7 6 5 4 3 2 1

In Memory of
Marjorie Tuite, O.P.

Contents

Acknowledgments

I want to thank the many people who have helped me in the formulation of the ideas in this book and in the writing process. My religious community, the Sisters of Charity, B.V.M., has long provided a context of love, debate, and support for my conviction that the movement of women is indeed a transforming grace in our time. Betty Prevender, friend and editor, read most the original chapters and always provided needed criticism and encouragement. The Hyde Park Women's Faculty Group has been an ongoing source of support both in discussion of feminist theological issues and in the warmth of their collegiality, as have colleagues and students at the Divinity School of the University of Chicago and at the Harvard Divinity School's Women's Studies in Religion Program (1983–84). I especially thank Madeleine Boucher, Dawn DeVries, Mary Donahey, Werner Jeanrond, Carol Frances Jegen, Mary Knutsen, DeAne Lagerquist, Linda Lee Nelson, Anne Patrick, Susan Shapiro, Janet Summers, Terry Martin, and Mary Jo Weaver for their suggestions and help along the way. Michelle Harewood and Nathelda McGee did fine work in their production of the manuscript, as did Elena Procario in preparing the bibliography. And Justus George Lawler has been an able editor and friend. Thanks also to the editors of *Chicago Studies, The Furrow, Horizons, Listening, Theological Studies,* and the Paulist Press for the use of some material from earlier publications.

Introduction

The recent emergence—or perhaps explosion—of women's voices in the public realm of the church, in ministry, theology, and new forms of active leadership, has meant some troubling questions and significant reorientations of mind and heart for many women (and men) with regard to Christianity, especially Roman Catholic Christianity. Some women wonder, for example, whether their deep commitment to "feminism" as a broad perspective that honors and celebrates the dignity and full personhood of women is really consonant with a critical perception of Christianity. Others reverse the issue and hesitate to call themselves "feminist" because their religious commitment to Christianity is so deeply rooted, so central as a life orientation that any other cause, even that of their own dignity and freedom and of their daughters and grandmothers, must be measured against their primary Christian criterion.

These concerns are real and are rooted in the contradictions that women experience in relation to Christianity and the church. For example, while in some of its statements and policies the church has affirmed the dignity and equality of women and has urged that discrimination based on sex should be removed from every area of church and society, in other statements and practices the same church seems opposed to the cause of women as a dubious or even anti-Christian movement that threatens traditional Christian values, especially values connected with the home and family. The chapters that follow argue that there is nothing inherently contradictory about "Christian feminism" or "feminist Christianity." Rather, I maintain that Christianity and feminism are not only compatible but they are, in fact, integrally and firmly connected in the truth of the Christian vision. While feminism presents a challenge to Christianity today, it is a challenge that is a powerful grace in its call for the church to be faithful to its own transcendent truth, to the deepest meaning of its symbols, its great tradition, and the new experience of over half its faithful members.

True enough, there are those who maintain that the fundamental Christian symbols of God and of Christ, for example, are intrinsically patriarchal and thus damaging for women. There are also those Christians who believe and argue strenuously that espousal of the cause of women is destructive of Christian tradition, that is, not only destructive of traditional understandings of women's "place" in the church and society but of the intrinsic patterns of Christian revelation. But there are many Christian and Catholic women who, in their deepest self-understanding and experience, cannot accept either position but who know themselves as both Christian and feminist. These are women who struggle to integrate feminism with Christianity and who experience the feminist critique of Christianity as a new vision of the Christian truth, as an authentic grace offered to Christianity in our time. It is this ecumenical Christian experience that this book seeks to articulate as it addresses the central symbols of Christian faith and the implications of these symbols for Christian life and practice today.

The chapters in this book represent themes and issues that have emerged in the theological conversation about women and the church, or women and Christianity, over the last decade as these issues become more immediate and pressing concerns in the lives of Catholic Christian women. They represent, as well, a progression of thought from practice to theory and back to practice. The community of Catholic feminists (1) began its reflections with the question of the ordination of women in ministry, (2) moved to the broader theological issues relative to women and the church, and then (3) returned to questions of practice in a new focus on a Christian feminist spirituality for women.

While these chapters are obviously written from a Roman Catholic theological point of view, they are all cast in what I believe is a broader Christian and ecumenical perspective, for the Christian feminist experience cuts across denominational boundaries. Christian women, in working for and exploring the cause of women in Christianity, have discovered an ecumenical sisterhood that unites us in a common vision. It is my hope that critical reflection on our shared Christian symbols may be theologically and religiously helpful to persons and communities within the wider Christian family.

The chapters of the book consist of some materials that have been published in different journals and books. In order to make these available to a broader range of readers, they have all been revised and some new chapters have been added. Conversations with students and colleagues across the country lead me to suspect that there is a hunger for feminist theological reflection on the major symbols of Christian faith *from within the context of faith,* as these symbols are received, reformulated, and newly appropriated by Christian women and men who have internalized the feminist critique of Christianity as persuasive and true. My hunch is that the method of dialectical retrieval that is proposed and exemplified in this book in fact reflects and articulates the experiences of many thoughtful women and men who have appropriated that radical critique and yet choose to remain in the churches and to struggle for the transformation of Christian symbols for the church of the future.

In this context, it is important to note that all theology bears the imprint of its own time and place. Just as my perspective reveals its origin as white, academic, middle class, Western, and Catholic, and is only one voice in the wider feminist conversation, so too the theological views expressed here reflect a wider range of contemporary discussion about the themes explored. The movement of thought and practice in feminist theology, as in theology generally, is a community affair. Each voice in the conversation makes a contribution that is partial and indebted to those who have gone before. It remains for the community to debate and correct the views expressed here and to move the discussion forward.

I am grateful for the stimulating discussion and genuine conversation always provided by my faculty and student colleagues at the Divinity School of the University of Chicago and especially for the continuing encouragement of our dean, Franklin I. Gamwell. In addition, I benefited greatly from the student and faculty colleagueship provided by a year (1983-84) in the Women's Studies in Religion Program at Harvard Divinity School, under the able and spirited direction of Constance Buchanan.

1. Coming of Age in Christianity: The Women's Movement and the Churches

There is abundant evidence that the two successive movements in the West for the emancipation of women—the first in the nineteenth century, the second in the twentieth—have had a deep impact on women in the Christian churches. Whether that impact comes from the direct and organized action of women in the churches or as a ripple effect created by the secular women's movements, the self-understandings and roles of women in the churches have visibly shifted. Feminist or not, pro- or anti-ERA, Christian women think differently about themselves, operate more assertively as full citizens in the churches, and are increasingly recognized by their communities—as individuals and as a group—as a force to be reckoned with. This opening chapter explores some of the connections between the women's movement and Christianity, especially Christian feminism, in order to clarify some of its central concerns and practical implications for theology and for life.

Twenty years ago, there were few signs of a women's movement, either in society generally or in the churches.[1] But today there are strong and well-established organized groups of women within the churches whose goals are clearly feminist.[2] While their purposes vary and their views diverge on many issues, these groups work as one in their efforts toward the full participation of women at every level in the churches. These groups can be divided into "ministers" and "scholars" for purposes of discussion, although their work frequently overlaps, and some individuals are often members of both groups. In fact, it is characteristic of Christian feminism that both ministers and scholars work closely together. But they represent two different emphases that can be distinguished and described.

"Ministers" are those women whose focus is their work in the churches. In recent years women have moved into a variety of new ministries: on campuses, in prisons, hospitals, homes for the aged, in traditional parishes with new groups—groups of youth, married couples, women themselves, the elderly, the very poor or marginalized—in coalitions for social justice, and in the local and national offices of the churches. These concerns have led women to seek the more sophisticated education they need for effective ministry; in turn, they have brought their experience to bear on the academic work they are doing in colleges, seminaries, and universities. They have become politically astute about church structures and decision·making. They have recognized their secondary, auxiliary status as women and have worked to change structures, recognizing that certain interests (often unpopular ones) will be represented only when women themselves can participate in decisions about policy, finance, and institutional commitments. These women have become highly skilled professionals whose work with people has convinced them that they deserve an equal voice and full participation.

The "scholars" are those women whose work goes hand in glove with that of women in ministry but extends beyond the churches in its scope. These women are highly trained exegetes, historians, theologians, literary critics, psychologists, sociologists, anthropologists, etc., whose studies and experience have persuaded them of the depth of sexism in the churches as well as other institutions in our society. They have focused their research and writing on the situation of women and on the particular asymmetry in the understanding of male and female in the theoretical underpinnings of church life. Within the Christian framework, they have attended especially to the Bible, Christian history, and theological and ethical reflection in exposing the traditional, as well as contemporary, bias and limitation of role accorded to women in Christianity. These women have helped to produce much of the literature of Christian feminism that has appeared in the last fifteen years.

Working together, women ministers and scholars have begun the important work of formulating what has become a distinctive part of the theology of liberation. Like its black and Latin American counterparts, feminist theology begins with the concrete experience of women (consciousness raising), understands itself as a collective struggle for justice (sisterhood), and aims toward a transformation of church and societal structures consistent with the practical implications of the gospel. It proceeds through a critique of the underlying mythology or ideology that supports sexist or patriarchal structures, and is characterized by both action and reflection (praxis). The close connection between the ministers and the scholars has made for a vibrant movement (including a good deal of internal self-criticism and debate) that deeply stirs the personal and societal lives of women (and men) in the churches.

FEMINIST THEOLOGY

An examination of some major emphases in Christian feminist literature indicates the direction of the women's movement in the churches. Both logically and chronologically, its first task is *critique of the past*. Like parts of liberation theology with which it is allied, feminist theology has criticized aspects of the Christian tradition that denigrate women. Passages in the Hebrew Bible that associate the female with matter, chaos, and evil (especially the figure of the temptress Eve who led Adam to sin) and New Testament injunctions to women about silence in the Christian assembly and subordination to male "headship" underscore ancient patriarchal attitudes that legitimate notions of the inferiority and subordination of women. The words of the church fathers make the point of historical Christian misogynism clearly enough: Tertullian's view of women as "the devil's gateway," the "first deserter" of the divine law; Clement of Alexandria's observation that woman should be covered with shame when she thinks "of what nature she is"; and Augustine's exhortation that "in her the good Christian likes what is human, loathes what is feminine."[3] Thomas Aquinas's notions that "woman is defective and misbegotten," that "it is not possible in the female sex that any eminence of degree can be signified, for a woman is in the (natural) state of subjection" reflect the medieval tradition that kept women in a state of subservience.[4] Feminist theologians subject such opinions about women to the cold light of day and in the process keep alive the "dangerous memory" of women's historical oppression—dangerous because it is the very outrageousness of such assertions that fuels the movements of today.[5]

Second on the agenda of feminist theology is the *recovery of the lost history of women* in the Christian tradition. Work in this area has made it clear that women exercised significant leadership within almost all the Christian traditions and historical periods: as genuine apostles in the earliest Christian communities; as scholars and foundresses in patristic and medieval times; as socially archivist organizers in Catholic Reformation religious communities; as preachers in Quaker, sectarian, and evangelical circles; as religious and social reformers in nineteenth-century America.[6] The faith and tenacity of these religious leaders of the past have encouraged contemporary Christian feminists in their struggle for equality and have as well provided a series of surprising and inspiring role models.

A third aspect of feminist theology is *revisioning Christian categories* in ways that take seriously the equality and the experience of women. This broad rubric includes reformulations of the doctrine of God (no longer conceived in purely masculine images and concepts); of understandings of Jesus Christ (in ways that emphasize his humanity rather than his maleness); of the church, its ministry, and its ritual (as a community of equal partnership rather than one of male dominance).[7] An important example of such theological reconstruction begins with criticism of traditional Christian doctrines of sin and grace as cast exclusively in terms of male experience. Christian writers have been inclined to speak of sin as pride, self-assertion, and rebellion against God and of grace as the gift of self-sacrificial love. But in fact such categories relate more to the experience of men, in cultures that encourage them toward roles of domination and power. Women's temptation or "sin," conversely, relates to *lack* of self-assertion in relation to cultural and familial expectations, failure to assume responsibility and make choices for themselves, failure to discover their own personhood and uniqueness rather than finding their whole meaning in the too-easy sacrifice of self for others. Reinterpreted by feminist theologians, grace takes on a wholly different character as the gift of claiming responsibility for one's life, as love of self as well as love of others, as the assumption of healthy power over one's life and circumstances.[8] From this brief example it is apparent that feminist theology seeks to correlate the central and liberating themes of biblical and Christian tradition with the experience of women in the contemporary situation.[9]

It is important to distinguish mainline Christian feminism from two other religious approaches that have appeared on the recent scene: at one end of the spectrum, a strictly conservative point of view and at the other, a so-called revolutionary perspective. Conservative or fundamentalist Christian writers use biblical injunctions about women's subordination to discourage women from assuming fully adult roles in church and society and to encourage them to find "total womanhood" in subjecting themselves completely to their husbands' every whim.[10] This espousal of male leadership and rule, derived from a literal interpretation of certain biblical passages, is echoed in aspects of the Christian charismatic movement as well; thus the Bible and the Christian tradition are used by fundamentalist or conservative thinkers to criticize contemporary movements for the expansion of women's roles and options in both church and society. At the opposite "revolutionary" pole, radical feminist analysis is used to criticize the biblical tradition and the churches in a single-minded way that finds Christianity, its male God and savior figure, and its male-dominated structures hopelessly irredeemable. These feminists urge women to leave Christianity behind and to adopt a purely feminist spirituality, for example, Goddess worship or feminist Wicca (a form of witchcraft) in what sometimes seems to become a worship of their own inner experience.[11] The unself-critical exaggerations of both extreme positions serve to highlight the balance of what can be described as mainline Christian feminism, as well as the urgency of its message for the churches.

Mainline feminist activity and scholarship represents a sisterhood that crosses denominational boundaries. Traditional divisions, based on historic doctrinal differences, are often overcome among women who recognize a unique solidarity in their own traditions. On the one hand there is that aspect of biblical tradition that clearly understood women to be less than fully human, less than rational, that classed women with other possessions of men: slaves, herds, things. Women are conscious of New Testament themes that would silence them in the churches and subject them to the patriarchal traditions of Graeco-Roman society as these are carried over in the churches today. On the other hand, the same biblical tradition speaks of an exodus from slavery to freedom and represents a movement of liberation toward justice and equality. Here is the figure of Jesus, who broke the cultural taboo that forbade his speaking with women, who touched the woman with the polluting menstrual flow, who had women friends and disciples. Women take very seriously the baptismal formula of the early Christian movement that proclaimed "neither slave nor free, Jew nor Greek, male nor female, but all one in Christ Jesus" (Galatians 3:28) as a concrete political formula, still awaiting realization. The growing number of Christian feminists, both Protestant and Catholic, both women and men, are conscious of this dual religious heritage that extols male leaders, popes, reformers, and theologians and that has rendered nearly mute the story of women in the course of history. They use the liberating gospel message of equality, mutuality, and service—and their own experience—to criticize those elements in the tradition that capitulate to patriarchal norms. And they use the central biblical tradition of justice and equality to criticize sexist patterns and practices in culture and society.

NINETEENTH-CENTURY FEMINISM AND THE CHURCHES

Most of the insights of contemporary Christian feminism, elements of which have now filtered into the ranks of other church women who do not consider themselves feminist at all, are not really new. They were already being explored over a century ago in the first women's movement, which began before the American Civil War. Although the roots of the movement go back even further in both England and the United States, concerted work for the rights of women in this country began in the 1840s, particularly with the historic meeting for the rights of women at Seneca Falls, New York, in 1848. That meeting took place in a Methodist church, and the women who organized it—Elizabeth Cady Stanton and Lucretia Mott—

had met some years before at an antislavery meeting in London when an attempt to allow women to participate was voted down by the official male delegates. (The ministers were the most opposed.) While some of the women in the nineteenth-century movement eventually broke their ties with Christianity, others were active in promoting the cause of women within the churches, arguing for the admission of women to seminaries and to the ministry, as well as for suffrage. Some, like Anna Howard Shaw, were outstanding preachers. But all were inspired by fundamentally Christian notions of justice in their work for abolition, temperance, moral reform (the closing of brothels), and the rights of women. And many of these women took to the pulpit—when they were allowed—to advocate their cause.[12]

The initial vision of the nineteenth-century feminists was broad; it included reform of the structures of home and family, education and social life (including the physically inhibiting clothes of the era), work in a burgeoning industrial society, the church, and political participation. The writings of Elizabeth Cady Stanton demonstrate her awareness of the depth and extent of the women's issue. Gradually, however, the women's platform narrowed to the question of the vote. The rhetoric of these early feminists sometimes took on anti-negro and anti-immigrant tones, and they exploited the Victorian ideal of feminine purity as they struggled—and they struggled for nearly a century—to win support for women's suffrage. Historians today point out that by narrowing their focus to a single issue and by placing all their hope in the almost miraculous changes they thought would come about through the vote, nineteenth-century women lost their wider vision of change in all the aspects of women's lives. The vote for women was won in 1920, and the women's movement died.[13] It was another forty-some years before the question of women became a public issue again.

The Christian churches had a good deal to do with the demise of that wide-ranging early movement for the emancipation of women. Historian Ann Douglas argues that an alliance emerged in the mid-nineteenth century between northeastern Protestant clergymen and some middle-class literary women. Both groups had previously suffered a significant loss of social power—the clergy as an effect of disestablishment (the end of state support for religion) and the women because of their diminished economic status as paid labor moved out of the home and family setting. Douglas theorizes that the two groups attempted to regain social influence through the glorification and sentimentalizing of the "feminine" virtues. Together they justified the exclusion of women from the harsher realms of economic and political life by describing women's situation as one of special privilege, claiming women's freedom from corruption, and ascribing their higher morality and sensitivity to their more delicate emotions.[14] This romantic falsification—sometimes called the angel-in-the-house or pedestal myth, a denial of the fact that women are just as pragmatic, corruptible, selfish, and perverse as men—was promulgated both by the Christian churches and by women. It is an ideology that became a part of American mass culture and continues to be advocated by some church leaders and theologians and by women and men today who fear the Equal Rights Amendment, the ordination of women, or simply the increasing autonomy of women.

CONTEMPORARY FEMINISM AND THE CHURCHES

The twentieth-century women's movement has similar connections with, and splits from, the churches. The wider secular movement for the liberation of women and the struggle against sexism in institutional life (home, family, education, and the professions, industry, politics) was simultaneously joined in the 1960s by movement in the churches for the ordination of women and for expanded roles in ministry, seminary education, and decision making, participation, and power. Even those denominations that allow for the ordination of women (the United Church of Christ; the American Baptist Convention; the Presbyterians; the Methodists, who have several women bishops; two of the Lutheran synods; and the Episcopalians) still have difficulty in the acceptance of women in local congregations. This makes it clear to women in churches that still do not permit ordination, especially the Roman Catholic, that concentration on one issue will not effect the overall change desired. Women's equal participation in church life is recognized by feminists today to be connected to a cluster of issues, not all of which immediately appear to be related to the question of women in the church at all. Christian feminists today, in ways unlike their nineteenth-century sisters, point out the intimate connections between patriarchy and hierarchy, and between sexism, racism, and classism.[15] That is, they are aware of the subtle connections between the culture and the churces and are sensitive to the criticism that the movement for the liberation of women is a luxury in which only affluent, white, Western, middle-class women can afford to engage.

Thus the women's movement in the churches today is character-ized by a concern for sisterhood that reaches beyond parochial con-fines. While its scholars have analyzed the situation of women in minority communities and in the Third World, there is an acute awareness of the particularities of the situation, for example, of wom-en in black or Hispanic communities, and of the cultural and reli-gious differences entailed when one moves to the global question of women. A wider bonding has begun to take place, and women who are active in promoting the cause of women in church life are likely to be those involved in movements for peace and social justice, for racial equality, for solution of the world hunger problem, etc. Their work parallels, in analogous fashion but on a broader front, the work of nineteenth-century feminists for abolition, temperance, and moral reform. The wider social concerns of today's church women have brought them more solidly into national and local political life just as they have been active in bringing concerns for justice and equality into the life of the church. Thus there are significant coalitions of men and women working for the connected causes of justice in both church and society—with both understood today in global perspective.

Like some of their nineteenth-century prototypes, there also are women who, in the course of their struggle for full recognition in the church, have come to the point of departing from Christianity or from their individual churches. For some, the structures of the churches or of Christian theology have become so alienating that after a while they simply leave. Some women have moved from one church to another for the sake of ordination, and others have left the church entirely. Some find in feminism itself a spiritual home—a space of comfort, encouragement, creativity, acceptance—that is more inviting than traditional Christianity. Anger and frustration are a clear pattern in the consciousness raising that accompanies feminism; for some it becomes a further impetus for change, and for others it is the cause of a complete departure from Christianity itself.

THE CHRISTIAN FEMINIST AGENDA

For those feminist women who stay in the churches—and these are by far the greatest number—a series of issues on the agenda indicates the direction of the movement today, both in its ministerial and its scholarly work. Most of these issues have been raised in connection with the issue of ordination of women, which is an important focal symbol for all of them. But they are distinct concerns, not all of which are solved simply by acceptance of women for ordination.

The first issue, and the one most obvious to the churchgoer, is the question of language. Feminists in the church argue that language shapes experience as much as experience shapes language. Thus the repetition of prayers, hymns, and scriptural passages that consistently refer to Christians as "brothers" or "men" and to God as "he"—despite the protests of theologians who insist that God transcends sexuality—do inculcate an idea of God as male. While certain changes have been made to achieve a more inclusive language for the congregation ("men and women," "sisters and brothers"), the language used in reference to God presents more difficulty, enshrined as it is in the Bible and especially in the central New Testament designation of God as "father." Here the problem of Christian revelation, communicated historically in the language and symbols of a patriarchal culture, is acute. One cannot simply strip away the historical conditioning of the Bible as the record of revelation without altering its original content and meaning. Some have argued for the use of "father *and* mother," of God as "parent," or alternatively suggested balancing the use of "father" with a distinctively feminine language for Spirit (which in the Hebrew Bible is rendered in the feminine grammatical gender).[16] Others have insisted on the need to move away from parental images entirely,[17] given the psychological ambiguity revealed by the Freudian critique of religion, and by the later feminist critique of Freudianism.[18] Categories of friend and friendship have been suggested as more appropriate to both the Christian tradition and the contemporary cultural situation.[19] The question of linguistic usage in the churches is not a light one, not "mere semantics"; it is a serious concern with far-ranging implications for women who are increasingly sensitive to the way in which the language of the church reflects its awareness of more than half its membership and shapes the lives of its people.

That Jesus Christ was himself male is a less negotiable issue. There are those who claim that because of its male savior figure, the Christian churches have little to offer women. Yet mainline Christian feminists have fewer problems with the historic and symbolic figure of Jesus. For them he was a man who was amazingly free from the restrictions of the patriarchal culture in which he lived. He related to women in a human fashion that transcended the cultural limitations of his time and was sharply critical of those institutions—family, religion, society—that placed burdens on people and prevented their full human response to God. Jesus represents a model of humanity that can be emulated by both women and men. But Christian feminists do stress that the Christ of historical Christian faith was always understood primarily as human, not as male. Thus some feminist writers have pointed to the novelty and indeed the heresy of the formulations, for example, of the Vatican Declaration[20] that emphasize the maleness of Jesus. They insist that the ancient Christian formula "what was not assumed was not redeemed" by Christ either means that women are not fully human, baptized, and redeemed or that women are in fact fully represented in Jesus' humanity and thus eligible for any office or function in the church.[21]

Together with the question of male language, Christian feminists insist, church structures must reflect the equality of the sexes that the Christian message implies. Women have achieved fuller participation in the decision-making powers of many church bodies. For some churches, however, notably the Roman Catholic, equal participation is associated with ordination; women in this church continue to work toward that goal.[22] In Protestant communions where the ordination of women has been accepted, women are already experiencing the burdens and joys of fuller leadership. While not yet fully accepted on the local level, they are proving themselves competent in local congregations and are exercising their leadership at higher levels of the organizational life of the churches. These women are still the unusual figures, but they are becoming more common. In seminary life, women faculty are appearing, although not in numbers proportionate to women students. An informal survey would show that women in seminaries represent a third to a half or more in many student bodies, indicating the intentions of increasing numbers of women to find careers in church work. While some still envision themselves in the traditional work of education, others are preparing for tasks once performed only by men or in the new ministries mentioned earlier.

Other issues on the Christian feminist agenda are more subtle, concerning the underlying attitudes fostered by the churches and theology toward women and toward sexuality, with which women have traditionally been identified. Sexual stereotypes in which women are classified as passive, irrational, less organized, or incapable of intellectual work or leadership are often rooted in religious views difficult to dislodge. The ancient and medieval theologians set forth a series of dualisms in which women were said to represent matter as opposed to (male) spirit, body as opposed to soul, emotion as opposed to reason or intellect. Such dualisms, which split the wholeness of the human person, eventuated in the distinction in modern times between the softer virtues of home, the private realm, and the tougher virtues of the public realm of men, between "nature" and "culture." These views, often sanctified by the churches in official writings and sermons, support a split between the private and the public realms and a narrowly limited women's "place" within the wider male "world"—in which the home is a haven and the woman an angel who guards its doors against the harsh realities of business and politics.[23]

Christian feminists see such splits and stereotypes, still preached by the churches, as harmful for women, for men, and for society itself. They are subtly communicated to children from their earliest years, in home and church, with the result that from childhood they learn to view themselves according to categories that limit their horizons as persons. Add to this the peculiar identification of women with sexuality present in biblical and historical Christian views of women as temptress and seducer, and one finds the strange mix in modern cultures of the female sex object, with massive industries devoted to its enhancement, and the lingering fear of women familiar to psychiatrists and novelists. The grain of truth that is present in the stereotypes is often there because it is fostered in the attitudes held and reproduced by the culture itself,[24] attitudes often reinforced by religion and the churches.

PROJECTIONS FOR THE FUTURE

There is an important connection between the level of education among women and movements for the democratization of the structures of religious institutions.[25] American church women are quickly becoming as highly educated as their male counterparts. A class of female professionals is emerging which threatens, for example, the end of traditional volunteerism on the part of women, in the churches or in society generally. From a financial point of view, women who invest time and money in seminary education look for remuneration that is appropriate to their training and skills, and their various ministries have become highly specialized areas of expertise. Thus volunteerism in the churches is increasingly seen as exploitative and as unfair to those who seek to earn a living in their ministries. Women are becoming justifiably demanding about working arrangements, compensation, fair contracts—difficult issues to integrate with Christian ideals about *service* in the churches. The dilemmas created by this situation are apparent: increased bureaucracy, loss of the communal or familial character of the congregation on the one side but, on the other, fair employment practices, ministers whose level of educational sophistication is commensurate with that of their constituencies, first-rate programs, well-trained leaders. Careful planning needs to be done in the churches to insure the preservation of authentic Christian values—generous service, the gifts of time, energy, creativity—in a context of authentic justice for women.

Just as the secular movement for the rights of women is having a major influence on family life and the traditional roles of men as well as women, the involvement of women in the life of the churches will not necessarily mean holier or purer or more virtuous religious lives for individuals or congregations—only structures that are more just and adequate to the message of the Christian gospel. But Christian women are also clear in their understanding that human freedom and the ability to choose self-transcendence and to respond to the ideals of Christian love and service are deeply influenced by the cultural expectations and limits embedded in the institutional contexts of any society, including the churches.

Aware of the limitations on the range of options open to women in the past, mainstream Christian feminists—both scholars and ministers—see the church as a significant cultural force in forming the attitudes, self-understandings, and expectations of women—and of men—and of society itself. They are deeply conscious of the damage that the churches have done to women, in the theologies, the language, and the structures that have kept women in a narrowly defined "place." They are determined to change the churches, radically. They refuse to leave. Perhaps they are more revolutionary than those who have given up. They refuse to ignore the liberating, indeed revolutionary, message that the churches bear about the realm of justice, peace, and equality coming in the future but, as the gospel proclaims, even now being born among us.

I. THE SYMBOL
OF ORDINATION

2. The Church in Process: Engendering the Future

Ordination is an ambiguous symbol for many feminist women (and men) today. On the one hand, ordination is a central and profound symbolic focus for the lack of equality and mutuality in the church and of the equality which would enable women to share in governance, decision making, and sacramental life at every point. On the other hand, many have come to see the clerical priesthood, the distinction between clergy and laity, and the hierarchy as it is presently structured as precisely the wider problem in the church. Thus there is argument that the admission of women to the present clerical structure would not solve but only exacerbate the contradictions of the present shape of the church.

Nevertheless, the question of ordination to the priestly ministry represents an important symbol of the lack of the presence of women in the official life of the church, a symbol of women's exclusion from all significant decision making and practical policy formation, a traditional exclusion that is historically based on the inferiority and subservient status ascribed to them. Thus it is important to look at the question, both historically and symbolically, whatever one's opinion might be of the strategic value of the (however unlikely) admission of women to the Roman Catholic priestly ministry at the present time.

The symbol of ordination speaks clearly of the current status of women in the church. And to imagine the possible transformations that might occur were women to be admitted to priesthood is not merely a useless fantasy. In this chapter, I suggest a new way of thinking about the church as sacrament that might emerge if women were to be included in the future, a model of equality and mutuality that is fully inclusive. The following chapter probes theological issues and presuppositions that are entailed in the issue of ordination. Both chapters represent an important cognitive moment in the theological reflection that is part, but only a part, of the transformations that Christian women are experiencing today.

Voices calling for the ordination of women in the Roman Catholic church make it clear, despite authoritative advice to the contrary, that the issue will not disappear. The question is not peripheral to the major business of the church; for many women and men, it is central to the shape of Catholicism for the future. The urgency of these voices in all parts of the community challenges theology to present the evidence to the church and to call it to fidelity to its own message in its most visible expression, the structures of the church and its ministry.

In this effort, theology must conjoin two sources, the Christian tradition and common human experience, in a unified expression that is adequate and appropriate to both. It must be faithful to the Christian message as it is found in the New Testament and the living tradition of the church, especially the central religious affirmations of that message, and it must be responsive to the contemporary situation in which the gospel is proclaimed and witnessed.[1] Thus in this chapter I will correlate (1) the significance of the Christian tradition on the church and its ministry with (2) the experience of women, as reflected in the contemporary women's movement within and on the boundaries of the church. Women's experience has much to say to the church, as the church and its tradition have much to say to women, if (3) an authentic model of the church is to be engendered for the future.

There is some tension between these two sources for theological reflection. The Christian message, carried by the church's tradition, proclaims that in the life, death, and resurrection of Jesus, all humankind is redeemed in principle through the miracle of God's self-gift and word to all. In the sending of the Spirit, all are joined in communion such that the social distinctions of ethnicity, class, race, and sex are overcome. Equality, freedom in the Spirit, and love of one another are the hallmarks of the church, the one body of Christ, the People of God. In this communion women are told they share fully in the life of faith through Baptism. Nevertheless, the church has not, in its traditional practice, accepted women as sharing equally and fully in its life. Today, Christian women are no longer willing to gloss over this inconsistency between faith and practice. Thus there is a growing call for the recognition of women's full personhood and redemption in Christ in the important symbol of sacramental ordination.

In quite a different sense of the word *tradition* (that is, customs, *traditiones*), however, women are not considered suitable candidates for the ordained priesthood in the Catholic church. Women are expressly excluded from ordination in canon law, which reflects longstanding thought and practice in the church. The arguments given for the exclusion of women from the ordained ministry, as for their inferior status in the life of the church—that God is revealed in predominantly masculine imagery as father in the Scriptures; that Jesus is male, as were the apostles he chose; that women's role is different from (that is, subordinate to) the male role of leadership in the patterns of revelation; that the long history of the societal subjection of women as a class is the order of creation; that the ancient belief in the uncleanness and temptation of their sex makes women unfit for ordination—all have been questioned and refuted logically and theologically. God is not sexual; the significance of Jesus is not his maleness but his humanness; distinctions must be made between the symbolic function of the "Twelve" and the apostles of Jesus who were not all male; women's subordinate roles in the church have been shaped by social and political views of female inferiority and subjection; women's sexuality is not evil or unclean but good in the goodness of creation and sanctified in the sacramental life of the church.[2]

Nevertheless, members of the church are told to avoid discussion of the ordination of women because of "tradition." Yet they also know that *tradition* fundamentally means handing on the word of faith, indeed the reality of faith—the body of the Lord—in the preaching of the word, in pastoral service and liturgical expression.[3] They know that tradition is not a static past. And there are seeds for a new model of ministry that includes women fully, in the church's own understanding of the process by which tradition develops and lives, when this is joined with the new experience of Christian women today.

THE CHRISTIAN TRADITION

Our age is profoundly aware of development and change in every dimension of human experience. Contemporary people know in their very bones that this is not a static world, but a world of flux and relativity; consciousness of time and history pervades human relationships, politics, institutions, even the understanding of our deepest beliefs and values. Nowhere has the impact of this historical consciousness been felt more deeply than in the religious sphere where the formulas of faith and notions of the church, indeed their intrinsic meaning and truth, have been challenged and reformulated.

The challenge of history, however, has also been an opportunity for rebirth: witness the Second Vatican Council's efforts to read the signs of the times. Describing itself as an interior mystery that no human language can directly comprehend, the church used a variety of images, many of biblical origin, to express its own reality. Phrases like the "People of God" and "pilgrim church" became as familiar as the more extrinsic notions of "institution" and "society." According to Vatican II, the divine-human, visible-invisible church, the sacrament of Christ, is both interior mystery of communion and external sign of Christ's presence in the assembly of believers on their march in history toward the reign of God.[4]

The awareness of historical change that marked the church's self-understanding at Vatican II and its plural self-description was, to an extent, the result of historical studies of the church's doctrine and practice. For historians have demonstrated that many different models of the church were present in early Christianity and that these plural models issued in a variety of ministerial expressions.[5] Today there is awareness of this pluralism of models of the church in the various Christian traditions and within the historic Catholic communion itself. Each is, in a different way, expressive of the fundamental mystery of the church—the church as mystical communion, as sacrament of Christ and of the world, as herald of the gospel, as servant, according to Avery Dulles's now well-known list.[6] This variety makes clear that over the centuries, the church has always adapted itself to its times. Today, for example, the need is recognized for a democratized, declericalized, open church.[7] All of the models of the church represent changing expressions of the church's self-understanding as it adapts itself to new situations in its history.

The relationship of the church to its changing historical setting poses the thorny question of separating the relative from the absolute, peeling the onion, to use a conventional analogy. How far can the accretions of history be peeled from the core of truth? What changes can be allowed? The truth of the one Christian mystery is always embodied in human, temporal forms and simply is not available in its pristine essence.[8] So as one Catholic theological argument goes; if the church, that is, the *magisterium,* allows a change, then it is allowable, and this can then be recognized as a "theological development" under the inspiration of the Spirit.[9]

Women do not challenge this belief in the work of the Spirit. On the contrary, contemporary Christian women are deeply conscious of the way the Spirit breathes where the Spirit will. But they are also aware of another facet of historical consciousness, its dimension of freedom. Christians know that human freedom is the bearer of divine freedom in the world, that God's work is entrusted to the responsible and responsive freedom of limited, fallible women and men. The visible, human church must strive, freely and with increased consciousness of its own history, to be adequate to its invisible reality, the enduring mystery of Christ, and precisely in doing so to be adequate to the needs of its times. The revelation to which it witnesses is for *people,* in their here-and-now situation. Because so many older forms of cultural and social life are crumbling, the church can no longer depend on social and political forms developed in response to a past culture. It must find new forms appropriate to the present and future if it is to hand on its permanent message authentically and effectively to the coming age.[10]

That such free adaptation is in fact "traditional" is clear in the history of the ministry and the emergence of priesthood itself, for "no major Roman Catholic ministerial office in its modern form can be found in the New Testament—*pope, bishop* or *priest.*"[11] Rather, the

Scriptures describe a plurality of ministries in the church. There were the functions of apostles, prophets, teachers, evangelists, admonishers for the preaching of the gospel; the functions of deacons and deaconesses, of those who distributed alms or cared for the sick, of the widows who served the congregations; there were presiders, overseers, and shepherds who led. Each of these functions was understood in the early Pauline churches, for example, as a gift of the Spirit, a *share (clerus)* in the authority of the risen Lord, a charism or calling from God for service to the congregation.[12] There is evidence of at least three models of what we today would call priesthood, that is, leaders of the Eucharist, in the very early churches: the hierarchical (the apostles and the bishops or presbyters), the charismatic-prophetic (prophets and perhaps teachers), and the communitarian (natural or appointed leaders who presided in the absence of the apostles).[13]

According to the New Testament, there is only one priest and mediator, Jesus Christ. Never is the word *priest (hieros)* used for an individual who holds office in the church.[14] The entire People of God, all believers in fundamental equality and as a whole, constitute a royal priesthood. "All Christians are priests" in having direct access to God, in offering spiritual sacrifices, and in the preaching of the word. Likewise, Baptism, the Lord's Supper, and absolution are given to the whole church.[15] Some scholars have suggested that from a New Testament perspective the word *priest* should be dropped as an exclusive term for those who have specific ministries in the church because all believers are priests.[16] Others insist that the relatively late awareness of the Eucharist as a sacrifice accounts for the absence of the word *priest* in the New Testament and for the gradual emergence of the vocabulary of priesthood in relation to the Christian celebration.[17]

What about church office? Again, there is no word in the New Testament for office; rather, an ordinary nonreligious term is used, *diakonia,* ministry or service, as in serving at table.

Apparently Jesus himself had set a standard which was not to be put aside. It is characteristic that the same logion of Jesus about serving appears six times, in various forms, in the gospel tradition (controversy among the disciples, the Last Supper, the washing of the feet): the highest should be the server (table server) of all.[18]

Hence there is no office among the followers of Jesus constituted simply according to law and power, like that of state officials; nor is there any office that derives simply from knowledge and dignity, like that of scribes. This is not to deny authority in the church. But New Testament authority receives its legitimation from service and develops as a function of *leadership* in the congregation.[19] It derives fundamentally from the risen Christ through those commissioned by him to bear witness to the resurrection.[20]

Not all New Testament ministries are of equal importance. One group of charisms is more private in nature, others more public and permanent, and some are appointed. Most important are the apostles, witnesses of the Resurrection who received a personal commission from Jesus to proclaim the gospel and who spoke with his authority.[21] Beyond the apostles, upon whom the church is built in "apostolic succession," the most striking evidence is of a plurality of congregational structures. Paul's churches particularly appear to be "associations of free charismatic ministries." After Paul's death, however, when the expectation of an imminent parousia ended, a system of presbyter and overseer took effect that included a special calling to the ministry of leadership through the imposition of hands.[22]

Complicated developments in the post-apostolic era led to the presbyters becoming the sole leaders of the congregation, in contrast to the more charismatic prophets and teachers. The monarchical episcopate emerged in which the original collegiality of overseer and presbyter became that of one overseer with his presbyters and deacons.[23] As the church spread from the cities to the country, the overseer, who had originally been president of a congregation, became president of a whole church district or a diocese, in our terms, a bishop. This development was legitimate and functional and indicates that neither Jesus nor the apostles imposed any absolute forms of ministry.[24] The young churches freely adapted to their new situations in society as they attempted to maintain unity and preserve the authentic gospel message after the death of the original witnesses.

Yet it is important to note the increasing tendency toward institutionalization, uniformity, and toward a fixed structure of ministry in the presbyteral model. This was achieved through an increase in the power of one of the members and the decrease in the significance of other ministries, "by a greater emphasis on pastoral authority at the expense of the service of the word" that had had unchallenged priority in the earliest phases of New Testament ministry.[25] But because of the looser charismatic structure of the Pauline churches and the indication of several early models of eucharistic leadership, there is no reason for not allowing other routes to the ministry today. Rather, there is good argument for remaining open at least to all the possibilities that existed in the primitive churches. "The New Testament does not allow the canonization of one congregational structure alone,"[26] and while its own models need not be slavishly imitated, certain elements must endure even in radically different situations. One theologian suggests the ministry of leadership must (1) be a service to the congregation, (2) follow the norm of Jesus, (3) be faithful to the apostolic testimony, and (4) reflect a plurality of functions, ministries, and charisma.[27] Another suggests two: service of the word and service of unity, adding that "the forms and structures of these services are adaptable and can be changed as required."[28]

As early as the second century, ministerial forms took on the pattern of the Roman civil service, with the bishop as the civil head of a region and presbyters and deacons as lower officials. The medieval class of clerics later derived from a series of earlier changes: in the fourth century, the granting of special privileges, immunities, and titles; in the fifth, traditional clothing and monastic tonsure; in the sixth, the increasing requirement of celibacy; in the eighth, Latin as the clerical language, special training, and later the breviary.[29] Thus "sociological factors contributed to the rise of a special caste . . . . underlined by the privileges allotted them in civil law" and these "spiritual men" came to be understood as of a higher moral value than the laity, with which they were often seen in contrast rather than unity.[30] Theologically, this class of clerics was understood as distinguished by the single cultic power of offering the sacrifice of the Mass, to the diminishment of the New Testament centrality of preaching the word and of the priesthood of all believers in Christ's one priesthood.[31] Obviously, the historically conditioned character of these practical and theological developments cannot and has not been considered normative or irreversible. There is no strong argument against new structures of ministry that can be derived from the historical development of the priesthood or because of contemporary needs and changes.

This can be seen clearly when we compare two statements of the *magisterium* on the priesthood: the Council of Trent in the sixteenth century and Vatican Council II in the twentieth. The Catholic view of office was fixed at the Council of Trent, which emphasized a visible priesthood with exclusive powers in relation to the sacrifice of the Mass and penance, an indelible sacramental character, and the existence of a hierarchy of bishops, priests, and deacons.[32] These conciliar decisions confirmed the medieval priesthood, with its emphasis on the cultic powers of the priest, the Mass as a sacrifice, and the consequent overshadowing of the service of the word and the priesthood of the faithful, the ministry of all Christians.

As is well known, Vatican Council II returned to a New Testament viewpoint, even as it retained and enriched many traditional structures. While affirming an official priesthood in the church, it reunited the liturgical-cultic function of priesthood with the prophetic service of the word and pastoral leadership,[33] righting a balance of ministerial tasks that had been askew, not just since Trent, but since the second century. With the restoration of the diaconate as a permanent ministerial function, the Council underlined the diversity of ministries in the church.[34] Finally, when these views of ministry are aligned with the *Constitution on the Church* in its affirmation of the whole church as a People of God, of a collegial ministry of service in the priesthood of the entire community of believers, of the importance of the charismatic element in the church and of the local congregation[35]—there is evidence of a response to a new historical and cultural situation that is at the same time faithful to the original sources of the Christian message.

Trent and Vatican II demonstrate the church in process and the historical differences in the operative models of its own self-understanding. While Trent polemically intensified an institutional model against Protestant biblical notions, Vatican II, in a nonpolemic context, consciously returned to New Testament and patristic sources in its self-configuration. And newly aware of its own historical relativity, it produced the *Pastoral Constitution on the Church in the Modern World*, affirming that the human race is involved in a "new stage of history," "a true cultural and social transformation."[36] One commentator remarked at the time that the Council "had caught hold of the dominant truth of our time: human institutions are challenged either to renew themselves or to suffer slow but sure disintegration."[37] Part of the social and cultural transformation of which Vatican Council II spoke was the international women's movement, which from its inception had its voices in the church, voices raised in protest at the Council itself, which refused to allow a woman to read a paper before the assembly and which tried to bar women journalists from attending Council Masses or receiving Communion during its meetings.[38]

THE EXPERIENCE OF WOMEN

The cultural situation to which Christian tradition must be correlated today is the growing and questioning experience of women in the church. Like women in the general society, women in the church experience their own emergence into fuller personhood, central to which is an awareness of mutuality and equality with men, that seeks to overcome sexual stereotyping and generally passive roles for women. The message of Jesus, transmitted in the apostolic testimony, has taken on new power for women in the search for an expression of a full personhood that is adequate to women's experience of themselves and to women's cultural situation in society. The discovery of gifts and talents of intellectual, pastoral, and personal leadership has forged a variety of ministries in which women today express a new, yet very traditional, Christian charism. It is a call for service to the Christian congregation and the world that includes the experience of vocation to the sacramental ministry as well as to other ministries in the church. This experience of vocation on the part of women is traditional in that women have always been involved in the church's ministry. But while this tradition of female service is long, the record is sketchy and often unclear; the roles of women in the church for the most part seem to have reflected the subjected position of women in society.

Women are the recipients of a contradictory tradition, and the strange history of women's position in the church has been widely documented. This history is central to an understanding of the experience of Christian women today. In the Bible, for instance, there is a group of statements that proclaims women's equality in creation and redemption. Genesis 1:27 declares "God created man in the image of himself . . . . male and female he created them," an obvious statement of equality. Genesis 2, in which man's rib is the origin of women, is the account used by Paul and the tradition following him to justify the subordination of women. More significant for women, however, is the implication of equality in the words, "This at last is bone from my bones and flesh from my flesh"—where, in some interpretations, woman is described as the completion and even perfection of creation.[39] Genesis 3 tells of the curse and woman's subjection to men. But this subjection of women is presented as a result of sin and man is cursed too.[40] Galations 3:28, which has become the "women's text," indicates that indeed salvation, that is, restoration and reconciliation, have come: "All baptised in Christ, you have clothed yourselves in Christ, and there are no more distinctions between Jew and Greek, slave and free, male and female, but all of you are one in Jesus Christ."[41] A final text from Paul, 1 Corinthians 11:11–12, is especially interesting because it occurs in the middle of the statement about women keeping their heads covered and their creation as "the reflection of man's glory" and "for the sake of man": "However, though woman cannot do without man, neither can man do without woman, in the Lord; woman may come from man, but man is born of woman—both come from God." Following this statement of equality, the argument (about woman's head covering when she prophesies or prays in public) ends abruptly with Paul's assertion, "it is not the custom with us!"[42] This last phrase indicates an important distinction between theological affirmation and arguments derived from sociological conditions, from custom.

These texts from the Bible surround the Gospel stories of Jesus himself, an amazing record given the historical context. For the pattern is one of Jesus' disregard for the social inferiority and uncleanness of women. Jesus, against all social and religious custom, had women friends and helpers, discussed religious matters with Jewish women (who were forbidden to study the Torah), broke the blood taboo by acknowledging the faith of the woman with the hemorrhage, and broke the double taboo against talking to women in public and against Samaritans in the story of the woman at the well. Jesus' pattern, as portrayed in the Gospel stories, was inclusive of women and of other oppressed groups; it was radically countercultural.[43] And it was the pattern of the early Christian congregations, in which women played an active role in a variety of ministries.[44] This freedom for women, however, diminished as it became apparent in the church that the return of the Lord was not going to happen immediately and as the church forgot, or ignored, the theological equality of women in accommodating itself more permanently to its patriarchal cultural settings in Jewish and Hellenistic society.

Thus a new pattern of theological equivocation enters and endures throughout post-apostolic Christian history as the fathers and medieval theologians justify theologically the cultural and religious inferiority of women. There is a frank record of misogynism in the fathers of the church who identify women with sexuality and sin even as they recognize women's redemption in their glorification of virginity and lofty praise of Mary.[45] There is the record of the "equality of souls but inequality of sexes" in medieval theology, the title of an essay that concludes with the imperative for contemporary Christians to recognize that the categories underlying medieval theological and psychological accounts of sex are as time bound and relative as the dogmas of Aristotelian biology.[46] The author of this study detects the heart of Christian revelation enduring in the medievals' assertion of the moral equivalence of the sexes in marriage, never given full cultural expression but never quite lost. She warns against the acceptance *today* of an easy notion of "different but equal": "under every bush of 'complementarity' . . . espy a hierarchical cosmology and a rationalized subordination of women."[47] Finally, the historical-theological subordination (indeed humiliation) of women is intensified and given systematic legal status in canon law.[48]

In the church's "conquest" of the West it adopted the political power models of its culture. And while there are interesting exceptions indicating the theological equality of women (ordained deaconesses until at least the eleventh and perhaps the eighteenth century, women martyrs, saints, and abbesses whose spiritual and intellectual gifts caused male observers to remark that they had transcended their sex to become truly "men"), the uncritical acquiescence of the church to the cultural oppression of women was almost complete.[49] The most charitable interpretation is that it was also unconscious.

Today that interpretation is impossible. The position of women in secular society has shifted so radically that the church, in its public statements, has already taken notice. The *Pastoral Constitution on the Church* of Vatican II, for example, states that women have been "denied the right and freedom to choose a husband, to embrace a state of life, or to acquire an education or cultural benefits equal to those recognized for men." And it teaches that

with respect of the fundamental rights of the person, every type of discrimination, whether social or cultural, whether based on sex, race, color, social condition, language or religion, is to be overcome and eradicated as contrary to God's intent.[50]

Pacem in Terris adds that

it is obvious to everyone that women are now taking a part in public life. This is happening more rapidly perhaps in nations with a Christian tradition, and more slowly, but broadly, among peoples who have inherited other traditions or cultures. Since women are becoming ever more conscious of their human dignity, they will not tolerate being treated as inanimate objects or mere instruments, but claim, both in domestic and in public life, the rights and duties that befit a human person.[51]

Statements can be multiplied. Let us simply add the words of Pope Paul VI at the time of the International Women's Year in 1975:

What is most urgent is . . . to labor everywhere to have discovered, respected and protected the rights and prerogatives of every woman in her life—educational, professional, civic, social, religious—whether single or married.[52]

There official statements follow in the wake of the early modern popes' resistance to the inroads of the Enlightenment and of the industrial and medical revolutions on the traditional roles of women. With some exceptions, the modern church completely resisted the full equality of women. Women's place was in the home or in traditional religious life, and women's emancipation was construed as a result of the de-Christianization of modern society.[53] And yet, as *Pacem in Terris* notes, the secular emancipation of women took place first and more rapidly in Christian societies. Why? Could it be the message of the gospel, submerged in oppressive cultural forms, acted as a leaven in surprising ways? Many women believe this is the case, that the emergent call for their full humanity is not anti-family and anti-church, but arises precisely from the gospel itself preserved in the living tradition of the Christian community.

This is a serious issue not only for women who wish to remain Christian and Catholic but for authority in the church. Some feminists, as we have noted, maintain that the Christian churches are the ultimate bastions of female oppression, constituted by patriarchal systems and mythologies that are intrinsically misogynist. Patriarchy is so deeply embedded in Jewish and Christian traditions that both doctrine and practice are "beyond redemption."[54] Others claim that the substantive Christian truth can transcend its patriarchal forms and language. Among the latter are women who have moved into the church's plurality of ministries, who find their source of feminist hope in the story of Jesus and the message of the gospel, who experience their own liberation and call to the church's ministry as the action of grace.[55]

Women who are faithful to their own experience, to conscience and to common insight, have banded in a new sisterhood, a "fourth world." Those in the West see their relationship to other oppressed groups in the world and the consonance of joint demands for liberation, justice, and peace. They recognize, at the same time, that their oppression is not the same as that of others.[56] They know that they participate in the oppression of class and race even as they struggle against the oppression due to sex.[57] There is recognition therefore that women's issues are part of the whole web of social and political issues relevant to justice in the world. Women recognize further that, even in the West, sisterhood is torn by the issues of reproductive rights, radical separation, and anti-male hostility, that emancipation into new freedom is not without the loss of many old securities, that there is risk of isolation, loneliness, ridicule, further repression. Women ask what word the church has for them today and whether it can possibly mediate the gospel to women without their full participation in its decision making and its ministry.

Women know that their own experience as women has to be a fundamental source for reflection as they shape the future,[58] that "as in every liberation movement in history, the freeing of women must be principally the work of women" for "no oppressor willingly hands over his power (or what he thinks is power) to his restive vassal."[59] Will sisterhood be able to emerge into a community of women *and* men?[60] Or will serious women continue to drop out of the church and withdraw their energies because no support, no home is to be found there but only tokenism, half-way gestures, pious words in solemn assemblies of men? Many would agree with Mary Daly's earlier observation that "at this point in history the church is in the somewhat comical position of applauding women's legal, professional, and political emancipation in secular society while keeping them in the basement of its own edifice."[61]

Some maintain that answers to the dilemmas of women are indeed found in the Christian tradition, in its gospel of reconciliation, its prophetic and liberation thought, its affirmations of authentic religious transcendence. These are women and men who have urged the church, authorities and congregations alike, to think and act in new ways, to choose imagination over the violence of authoritarian structures of power, prestige, and caste.[62] They ask the church, its all-male hierarchy and its male-dominated structures, not just to permit thinking in new ways but to lead in this thought, to demonstrate that the power of the Christian gospel is strong enough to reverse the patterns of secular history where "no oppressor ever willingly handed over what he thinks is power." It seems that in heightened Christian consciousness of the past and responsibility for the future, an important option is imminent. The church can choose to affirm fully the personhood of women, or it can continue to equivocate in a way that is intolerable to women's human and Christian experience.

It is clear that the developing tradition of the church and its ministry should be correlated with the experience of contemporary women in such a way as to legitimize the ordination of women. The variety, flexibility, and charismatic structure of New Testament ministries offer ample precedent for the recognition of the pastoral service, the natural and charismatic leadership, and the service of the word that many women are already performing and for the calling many women experience to sacramental ordination. Conversely, the experience of women in the church—their liberation to fuller personhood—could be used to open up a richer image of the church and of its ministry, quite in continuity with the New Testament and the renewal initiated by Vatican Council II. The full affirmation of women's ministry would reverberate in the whole church, on men in the church, and on the church as a male institution, and church tradition could be more fully searched through the sacramental participation of women to illuminate the new Christian experience of women today.

AN AUTHENTIC CHURCH MODEL FOR THE FUTURE

Rather than a "theology of women" in which women are a special case, an oddity to be accounted for, the correlation of the church's tradition with the experience of women might result in a new understanding of the church as sacrament. As the sacrament of the incarnation of Christ into all of humankind, the church would fittingly express the mutuality of the human sexes and its service to both women and men by male and female ordination. If both men and women participated in all its ministries, it would be a fuller sacrament of the one priesthood of Christ in the whole People of God and of the apostolic witness of the message of Jesus to both men and women. It would be a clearer sacrament of the transformation of the priesthood from medieval clerical caste to the New Testament patterns of equality and mutuality that began to be reincorporated into church structures at Vatican Council II: the transformation of the clerical priesthood into a ministry of service, the uniting of liturgical expression to the ministry of the word, and the service of a unity in which there are no patterns of domination but the collegiality of all Christians in a plurality of functions. New routes to the ministry would thus be opened, uniting charismatic and communitarian leadership with appointed ordination. And the eschatological nature of the church would be more clearly signaled in today's society: the new order of things promised as the church moves in history toward the reign of God.

As sacrament of God's self-gift for the reconciliation of all persons, the church would embody the Christian message of equality, freedom, and love as a causally effective sign to itself and to the world. This sacrament would include the church as institution in a sign of its care for ordered and efficient planning in the organization of *all* its personnel, women and men, for pastoral action and for an effective and authentic mission founded on apostolic testimony. The institutional-legal side of the church would not dominate, however, but would signal and serve its mystery, the interior communion of men and women in Christ and the Spirit, a pilgrim people together in exodus toward the reign of God. Internally, it would sacramentalize its message in the preaching of the word, proclaiming the gospel in the variety of pastoral ministries and in the breaking of the bread and other liturgical gestures that flow from and move toward the eucharistic celebration, all shared by women and men. As such, it would be the sacrament of the word, proclaimer of the gospel to which it is bound, to the message and the God of Jesus Christ whose continuing revelation through the Spirit in history it does not control. Finally, it would be an authentic sign of the church as servant, not only lending its strength to the forces of healing and reconciliation in the world but *leading* in its prophetic determination to deal with the roots of injustice and oppression, rather than their symptoms. The church's criticism of policies and attitudes that deny the dignity of individuals and peoples, classes, races, and sexes would have the power of authenticity because it had seen carefully to justice in its own house.

Such a church would be a sacrament of its own tradition, of its fidelity to the gospel and to its times. It would be traditional in its concern for the authentic handing on of the word of the gospel to both women and men, and would signal this in its willingness to relinquish outdated forms, worldly securities, titles, honors, and prestige, the better to conform to the tradition of the poor and crucified Jesus.[63] It would be traditional in this larger sense by breaking with "traditions" as it has broken with them in the past—in reversing its stands on usury, persecution of heretics, the single reception of the sacrament of penance, the vernacular liturgy, slavery, war, racism, crusades against Moslem and Jew, democracy, modern science, philosophy, history, and biblical exegesis—and in developing a more sensitive conscience in areas where it clings to outmoded political forms and theological arguments. Going against traditional practice has been called for many times and is called for especially now in a church newly conscious of its sinfulness past and present, of the times it has sided with the rich and powerful over the poor and powerless, with vested interest over truth in scholarship. Tradition, like the word of God, is a two-edged sword; it can mean betrayal as well as handing on.[64] Lest it betray its own word of human equality, the church would reject its own misogynist traditions in which women are considered less than fully human, less than fully redeemed, as well as those symbolic traditions in which women are "glorified" as more than human but still denied full Christian personhood.

In this church, ministry would also be a sacrament, indeed a revelation of the church's faith and values.[65] Because it would include in its pastoral, liturgical, and social expressions a full representation of classes, races, and sexes, it would witness to its belief in "neither Jew nor Greek, slave nor free, male nor female." It would reveal ministry as service, especially with the powerless, and as oriented toward the fullness of its own life in word and sacrament. Signaling the importance of the variety of ministries in its liturgical life, it would at once make clear the importance of its sacramental life for all its ministries.[66] Recognizing that Christian salvation is essentially sacramental and that the service of the word is integral to the sacraments, none of its official ordinations would be closed, in principle, to any members of the priestly people engaged in the ministry of the word. The mutual involvement of men and women in the sacramental ministry would be an intrinsic sign of the service of unity required by the gospel.

Women today are already engaged in this ministry of the word and in pastoral service. They share in caring for the poor, the hungry, the sick, the elderly; they administer social service agencies, perform pastoral functions in parishes, prisons, on campuses; they teach children, young people, and adults and have joined their brothers in pastoral and theological reflection and in the preaching of the word; women counsel and give retreats. The assumption of these ministries by women reflects their status in secular society, where the emancipation of women has opened the educational and cultural opportunities closed in the past. The old theological arguments against the ordination of women, which rested on women's subjected position in society, women's ignorance, obviously do not make sense today. In the ancient world, only men could perform the functions of leadership because only men had the necessary education, authority, and mobility. Now, when the subjected, ignorant woman of the past has ceased to exist, at least in many parts of the world, when a new cultural environment means equally educated, mobile, theologically and pastorally competent women, there is no obstacle to prevent the official hierarchical church's recognition.[67]

Indeed, women's ministry is already recognized by the church, but only as an auxiliary service. Women are allowed to help, to volunteer, to work in very limited ways, to have limited representation in the decision-making bodies of dioceses and parishes and often are overworked and not adequately paid. As long as women are barred from full recognition and sacramental completion of the service they are already fulfilling, barred in fact from the liturgical functions usually assigned to eight-year-old boys, the language of the church is unfortunately clear in what it is saying to women and to the world about women. In the theology of sacrament, language clarifies the ritual action, which in turn infuses the words with deepened meaning. In the attempt to purify everyday language of sexist overtones, women recognize its power as reflector and shaper of attitudes and beliefs. They strive to purify religious language of the implications of patriarchal domination, to find new words for God. When the church's language, its gestures, and its actions become a real sacrament, sign, and cause of the gospel affirmation of "neither male nor female," it will use its fullest human vocabulary in speaking to human experience today.

The church's official recognition of the ministry of women will mean more than the ordination of those who already experience God's call and who are personally suitable and adequately prepared. It will mean more than recognition that in certain areas women ministers are already acceptable to the People of God. It will be a sacramental word, a gesture of loving acknowledgment to all women in the Christian community and to the world of its commitment to women as full citizens in its own realm and to the societal liberation of women in all spheres. It will speak its truth boldly and become a really credible sign of its concern for the whole of humankind under the sign of the gospel. The full acceptance of women will be a sign of recognition of the charismatic working of the Spirit in the church, a sign that its sacramental life is bound to that Spirit and not to canon law nor to the cultural conditions of the past.

The ordination of women need not mean admission to the clerical caste, as some fear,[68] or as the defensive jokes and cartoons—ridicule of the issue—suggest. Rather it would further the transformation of the priesthood: by admission of those who have traditionally only served, the sign will be clear. It would help to transform the ministry from a predominantly cultic role to a ministerial one, from a symbol of prestige to a symbol of service, releasing the imagination of half the church's population into fuller operation as the church moves into the future.[69] The priesthood would no longer be a male-dominated club with restricted membership, a bureaucratic hierarchy, but an open, collegial, spiritual service of unity. Nor would ordination do away with the variety of functions in the church. Only some ministries appropriately call for official appointment and sacramental ordination. But those women who have led a community in prayer on campuses, in homes for the aged, in hospitals, prisons, or neighborhoods, those who have enabled retreatants in their own discovery of God or the experience of reconciliation, recognize that the ability to celebrate the eucharistic meal, to baptize new life into the church, to give absolution, is the appropriate sacramental expression of the liberating action of Christ's grace in their ministries. For the Catholic tradition, in which sacramental experience is central,[70] the ordination of women would be a sign of the church's attentiveness to the concrete experience of its people, of its awareness of where God's grace is working in people's lives and where the authentic ministry of the word is occurring.

Emphasis on historical consciousness and on tradition raises the question of whether women seek ordination because of developments in the secular sphere or in the church. Clearly it is because of both—the church reflects its culture even as it meant to transcend culture as a prophetic voice. But there is a distinction between the women's movement in the church and in society. In the secular sphere, women justly demand equal rights and laws and programs to insure and protect those rights. In the church it *ought* to be different. All, women and men, are receivers and sharers. The grace of God in Christ and Spirit is a pure gift, unowed, incomprehensible benevolence. Intrinsic to the whole pattern of sacramental mediation of grace in the church is the awareness that grace cannot be hoarded, claimed, deserved. Nor is it rare or intermittent. It is given freely as it is received freely. The ordination of women in the church would be an appropriate sign in our time of the generosity and freedom of Christian grace.

Finally, there is the issue of what is "pastorally prudent." Are people ready for this? Would it be a stumbling block to faith in the community? Would it appear that the church has been wrong in the past if it were to now go against so enduring a practical tradition? And from the perspective of women, would it appear that women are merely, once again, being used, this time to fill the places of thousands of departed men? Certainly not all people are ready. For some (including some women) the very idea is distasteful, and this reaction reflects the depth of the cultural taboo—the gender valuation of women as inferior, the sense that women's reproductive processes are unclean, that women represent the temptation or evil of sex, or that women cannot bear the authority of leadership, cannot be theologically competent, or cannot be trusted with significant functions in the church. All of these ideas about women have been disproven, but they remain. The ordination of women to the diaconate and priesthood would be a profoundly educational sign of the human and theological truth of the matter. The ordination of women cannot be a stumbling block to faith because an authentic faith must recognize the full personhood of women, that they are not lesser human beings, auxiliaries, instruments, as the language of the church on the "use" of women in discussions of sexuality suggests. Women look for a new word, not a sign that they are suddenly useful because of the shortage of men, but a sign that the full personhood of women is affirmed and the ministries women perform are genuinely needed by the church.

Breaking this long tradition would mean an admission that the church was wrong in the past as it has been wrong on other matters, slavery for instance. It would mean an admission that the church in the past adapted itself uncritically to taken-for-granted social and political patterns in secular society. But the church is not, and never has been, a static entity; its tradition shows that it is a living church in process. And a significant part of the church's experience in modern times is a new awareness of its own historical process. This awareness makes it more responsible for its decisions, attitudes, and gestures as it conforms to the demands of the gospel in new times. A church responsible for its freedom and responsive to its own tradition and the contemporary situation cannot ignore the experience of more than half its membership and more than half the world to which it claims to be a sacrament of Christ. Will its environment remain "an unhealthy climate for women?"

The theological insight is already available for the church to recognize the ministry of women through sacramental ordination. The issue is not peripheral but reflects the church's whole posture toward people, women and men, and toward the central human questions of the future. The ordination of women will not solve all the problems of the church's mission; it is no panacea. It will simply be a very effective symbol, sign and cause, of the church's intention to engender a future in which it struggles to become the sacrament of the full personhood of all people in the grace of Christ.

3. Ordination for Women and Christian Thought: History, Theology, Ethics

As emphasized in the previous chapter, the question of the ordination of women is a central symbolic issue. In it a number of historical, theological, and ethical topics converge that are central in the discussion about the "place" of women in Christianity and in the church. This chapter examines some of the presuppositions that are entailed in the ordination question, particularly as these emerge in various practical discussions.

The women's movement, at the turn of the century and in our own time, has raised the question of women's "place" in all areas of culture and society. In its focus on sexism or discrimination against women and in its goal of equality and mutuality, the movement has indeed asked some essentially new questions and is seeking genuinely new answers. The novelty arises from the new situation in which women find themselves, emerging in large numbers for the first time in Western history from the status of an inferior class in the human community. For the first time, certain new questions about women's place in society are "seriously imaginable" and therefore seriously entertained.[1]

The insight that is fundamental to the women's movement and to the question it pursues is that the place of women has traditionally comprised a partial sphere, a domain or realm within the whole of a world that is male, and that this sphere or realm has been determined by men as the possessors of the whole. Thus the goal of equality or mutuality of participation logically includes the defining of women's place by women themselves. Over twenty years ago, theologian Karl Rahner recognized that women themselves would have to determine, from their own experience and as "the church of women," their place in both society and the church.[2] The contradictions inherent in the contemporary institutional structures of society and especially in the church are immediately apparent.

In its critique of societal structures and of the mythologies, intellectual legitimations, or cultural understandings operative behind them, the women's movement has called attention to the patterns of sexism in diverse areas. Few institutions have escaped scrutiny: marriage, child rearing, education, business, commerce, law, and science have all been analyzed and brought into question. Intellectually and academically, it has been shown how historians, philosophers, psychologists, sociologists, anthropologists have (consciously or unconsciously) defined women as the "other," the helpmate, auxiliary, and subordinate of man.[3] In this process, religion—its institutions of church and synagogue in the West, its rituals and practice, its mythologies and theologies—has been an obvious target of feminist criticism. This dimension of the women's movement has had unique impact on women and men in the churches and on the study of religion and theology as well, as it has exposed massive evidence of the exclusion of women and the distortion of women's personhood in the Christian tradition.

Among women in the churches are those feminists who seek a reform of institutional life and practice that is reflective of the mutuality and equality of women with men that is a fundamental premise of both Christianity and feminism. Among women scholars in the study of religion and theology are those who research the history of religious traditions to understand the "place" of women within their various symbolic systems, to find the stories of "forgotten" women, to analyze past and present theological conceptions of women, and to determine the significance of their findings for the experience of contemporary women. In this area of feminist religious scholarship, one finds a wide diversity ranging from, for example, more radical critique of the Christian tradition as intrinsically patriarchal and so irredeemable,[4] to those evangelical feminists who concentrate almost solely on the Bible, seeking to disentangle elements of patriarchy from the essential biblical message.[5] Between these extremes are those Roman Catholic and mainline Protestant feminists who engage in criticism of both Bible and Christian tradition at the same time as they attempt a revision or reformulation of theological understanding that is adequate to both the truth of the Christian message and to the contemporary experience of women.[6]

Church and religious scholarship have come together in the latter context. Two historians of the feminist movement write that, since 1962, "of all the religious communities the most radical (intellectual) analysis and militant actions about the 'woman question' have come from Catholics."[7] Protestant feminism, however, has a longer recent history, emerging as early as 1948 with the World Council of Churches but making its most dramatic impact in the 1969 formation of the Women's Caucus of the WCC. This group issued an important statement at that time describing the church as the best illustration of the situation of women in society. As "male-dominated" and "male-oriented" in theology and institutional forms, the statement claimed, the church is merely a reflection of the culture and makes no attempt to transcend its cultural situation, often maintaining its anachronistic stance long after other societal institutions have shifted.[8]

If the churches can be understood as the mirror of society, the issue of ordination can similarly be understood as a mirror or focal symbol through which to view the broader situation of women in the church. This is so even in relation to those churches that already allow for the ordination of women. For in most of these communions, widespread difficulties in the acceptance and placement of women in positions of ministry in local congregations reveal serious problems of attitude and prejudice among the general membership. The problem, however, is even more acute in those Protestant denominations that do not provide for the ordination of women and especially in the Orthodox and Roman Catholic churches, which have maintained firm positions against the admission of women to the pastoral office. It is in the context where the issue remains most controversial that it has received the most sustained intellectual analysis on the part of feminist scholars and where it can be examined most fruitfully.[9]

Three broad areas of discussion emerge when one surveys the feminist literature on the question of women's ordination: Christian history, theology, and ethics. Feminist writers have put the issue as one of mutuality versus patriarchy (or the rationalized subordination of women to men) and have claimed that patriarchy is in fact rooted in the ancient historical traditions pre-dating Judaism and Christianity but absorbed by them, traditions which have a continuing influence on theology and ethics in the church today.[10] The literature emphasizes those critical and questionable issues that demonstrate contradiction either within the historical, theological, or ethical traditions themselves or in relation to the contemporary experience of women.

CHRISTIAN HISTORY

Within the growing feminist literature on Christian history, one can discern the delineation of what some have described as "two traditions."[11] There is the earlier tradition, which includes Jesus' own innovation in relation to women in treating them as disciples and equals. Studies by both women and men have demonstrated that women were closely associated with Jesus in all phases of his ministry and the special theological emphasis of each of the Gospels in attributing to Jesus new and positive evaluations of women.[12] They have described the general Gospel picture of Jesus in his teaching and action as taking the part of women who suffered under the oppressive social customs of the period. This innovative tradition is further expressed in Paul's proclamation in Galations 3:27–28: "All baptized in Christ, you have all clothed yourselves in Christ, and there are no more distinctions between Jew and Greek, slave and free, male and female, but all of you are one in Jesus Christ." The implications of this Christian vision of equality found expression in the never-questioned tradition of Christian baptism for *all* persons who believed. And they hint at the possibility of earlier Jewish sources for Jesus' inclusiveness.[13]

Over against the revolutionary possibilities inherent in this Gospel tradition of innovative equality in earliest Christianity, feminist scholars (including some male scholars) delineate another, second tradition in which the early church appears to have accommodated itself to the dominant attitudes of its religious, sociopolitical, and cultural environments. This second tradition unreflectively absorbed ancient mythologies and taboos associating women with chaos, matter, and evil, especially in the figure of the temptress Eve, who led Adam to sin. While the complex history of the ancient symbolic identification of women with evil has not been completely untangled, association of women with matter, the flesh, the body, and sexuality *as polluting* is clear.[14] Together with the societal inferiority of woman as a class, expressed in the notion of her inferior nature in relation to men, these elements were powerful in the formation of the second tradition in early Christianity. They were at least partial causes in leading to the adoption, evidenced in other aspects of Paul's epistles and in the later strata of the New Testament, of passive and subservient roles for women within the churches. Injunctions to women about silence in the Christian assembly and subordination to male "headship," though clearly inconsistent with other New Testament data, were used to legitimate the subordinate position of women.[15]

This second tradition achieved dominance and was carried forward in the patristic period when women were frequently described as the symbols of evil, sexuality, matter, and sin, dualistically opposed to the good, spirit, mind, and virtue symbolized by the male. This anthropological dualism lies behind the fathers' lofty praise of women in their new Christian roles as virgins, capable of spiritual personhood, of becoming like men through the transcendence of their natural female humanity.[16] Thus there were two patristic models for women in the Christian scheme. In one, woman's salvation was attained through the submission of herself to man in marriage and child bearing, and in the other she overcame her female nature through the spiritual transcendence of virginity. Both models found an exemplar in Mary, the virgin mother of Jesus, and both involved roles of silence and subordination in which the stigma of being female could be overcome. The second tradition, affirming the natural inferiority of woman, her position as the child or property of the male—still exemplified today in marriage ceremonies in which the father gives the bride to her new husband—became the dominant Christian pattern.[17]

The two traditions can be discerned as well in the history of Christian ministry. From a variety of perspectives, scholars have pointed to evidence in the earliest traditions of women as apostles, prophets, deaconesses, disciples, witnesses, and servants in the ministry of the gospel.[18] They have demonstrated the existence of a vigorous female ministry in which women played an active and public role in the life of the early churches. This early tradition continued intermittently in the longer historical sequence in the women martyrs, saints, abbesses, deaconesses, and founders who constitute the line of "notable exceptions" in Christian history. This early tradition of active female ministry was gradually suppressed by the second tradition, which, in conformity with the prevailing cultural patterns, relegated women to the more private spheres of Christian life and allowed public ministry only to men. This second female tradition is related to the development of the more uniform, institutionalized, and fixed structures in the church's ministry (the system of overseer and presbyter) in the post-apostolic era, in contrast to the earlier Pauline congregations as "associations of free charismatic ministries."[19] This functional development demonstrates the changing historical character of the church's ministry (and eventually, priesthood) in relation to new cultural surroundings and can serve as a model for the necessary changes in the present situation. The point is, however, that the two contradictory traditions about the "place" of women in the church's ministry, parallel to the two traditions about women in the Christian scheme of salvation generally, are amply apparent within the larger Christian tradition itself.

This history raises important questions for contemporary theological, pastoral, and ethical reflection. Statements of the American bishops and of the Sacred Congregation for the Doctrine of the Faith on the question of the ordination of women[20] underline the central significance of "tradition" in determining the church's understanding of contemporary doctrine and practice. These documents also make clear the way in which theological and anthropological presuppositions determine the interpretation of Christian tradition. Hence it is important to note that the tradition is in conflict with itself and to realize that, although the Bible and tradition are sources of theological reflection, certain theological notions about women must be clarified before the tradition itself can be effectively understood as a guide for practical action today.

CHRISTIAN THEOLOGY

The question of the ordination of women touches on several important aspects of Christian theology. Such areas as theological anthropology, the doctrine of God, Christology, ecclesiology, the theology of the pastoral office and of ministry, the theology of revelation and of tradition, and the nature of theology itself enter into theological analysis of the question. A brief indication of some of the major issues may serve to provide an overview.

The first issue is *theological anthropology*, that is, the Christian understanding of the nature and destiny of the human person, as this understanding emerges in relation to the question of the ordination of women. It has been put succinctly, in a study of secular feminist writing by Mary Aquin O'Neill, as the question of one human nature or two.[21] Do women share the same human nature as men, or is their humanity an essentially different mode of human being? This fundamental question is raised when one confronts contemporary statements of the official church that invoke the "order of creation" and the "headship of the male" deriving from the Genesis 2–3 account of creation or the Pauline notion of "headship."[22] While the older assertion of the natural inferiority of women is seldom found in contemporary theological discourse or official statements, one does find the notion of the "complementarity" of the sexes, which in fact resembles it in a disguised form and which offers a new rationalization for the subordination of women. The idea of complementary roles and functions of women and men is understood to be founded in the revealed structures of creation presented in the Bible. Thus the goal of ecclesial and social life is held to call for a "harmonious complementarity," in the words of Paul VI, rather than a "levelling uniformity" between the sexes.[23]

Feminists reply that the notion of the order of creation derived from Genesis 2–3 is given in the context of the story of the Fall, of human sin. They are quick to point out that man as well as woman was responsible for sin in the biblical story (as Paul clearly indicates in Romans 5) and that women's subordination is presented as punishment for sin. It is precisely from such consequences of sin that the Christian message is meant to liberate the human community. And men need to be saved as much as women. The doctrine and practice of baptism for all, both women and men, held from earliest Christian times, demonstrates the Christian vision of the fundamental commonality and equality of human nature shared by women and men.[24]

The idea of the complementarity of the sexes, put in such a way that women's roles and functions in church and society are seen to be of an essentially different nature than men's, also appears in theological discussion and ecclesiastical statements that refer to a distinctive notion of "feminine psychology."[25] Here one often finds presuppositions and stereotypes that define women as particularly humble, sensitive, intuitive, gentle, receptive, passive. Implicitly or explicitly, these are understood in contrast to male aggressiveness, rationality, activity, strength, etc. The rather facile use of the idea of female psychology on the part of theologians and churchmen reveals assumptions about psychological differences that are hard to reconcile with the finds of psychologists.[26] On the one hand, it is sometimes maintained in arguments against the ordination of women that the human sciences are irrelevant to ecclesial discussion about the issue since the realities of faith are beyond their competence.[27] On the other hand, the use of certain assumptions about psychology, itself a human science, leads to a position that is very close to the Freudian view that "anatomy is destiny."

Feminists again are quick to indicate the un-Christian and irreligious ramifications of such a view. Beyond the empirical data of the psychological sciences, which are not clear on whether psychological differences between female and male human beings are innate or cultural, feminists argue that such a view is false to the Christian understanding of faith, hope, and love as the most important, and clearly spiritual, characteristics to which all persons are called, irrespective of their sex. It is from the personal or spiritual nature of human persons that characteristics, roles, and functions in church and society ought to be derived, not from biological or physical differences.[28]

This dimension of feminist theological discussion highlights the question of a theological anthropology based on either a unified or a dual human nature. In the unified view, sexual differences are understood as important but "accidental" to the one human nature that all human persons share. There are no preordained roles or functions for men and women beyond the biological, and either sex should be free to develop those qualities traditionally associated with the other. Though not without its difficulties,[29] this view is held by most feminist scholars in the church, for it offers clear grounds for equality and mutuality of participation between men and women in their roles and functions in society and church. The dual view, which holds that biological differences represent an essential difference in natures, severely restricts the roles and functions of women and men by segregating their appropriate activities, especially in the church, although logically such a position might be extended to societal roles as well. And the dual view is also held by the "woman-centered" views of the influential French feminists, who emphasize whatever is distinctively feminine as a counterpoint to the masculine structures of Western social and political life.[30]

Another theological issue brought to the fore by the question of men and women in the church is the *concept of God*. Most Christians derive their image of God according to an analogy with the human person as the highest form of spiritual existence known to experience. If one understands the priest to somehow represent God to the Christian community, and if the priesthood is entirely male, the priesthood would appear to reflect and reinforce a concept of God cast in entirely male terms. Again, there is contradiction for a tradition that theoretically understands God to transcend sexuality, a God whose characteristics, according to the Bible, include those traditionally ascribed to both sexes. God is a father, representing power, autonomy, authority, agency; but God is also a mother, whose nature is maternal, depicted in the record of revelation as tender love, forgiveness, and care.[31] Jesus, too, as the revelation of God in human form, embodies both sets of the traditional attributes of male and female, both autonomy and nurture.

This issue is closely related to the anthropological one touched on above. If God and Jesus the Christ are understood to represent ideal models for imitation by both male and female persons, then one must find both masculine and feminine characteristics in these models. Feminist theologians argue that such models would reveal the importance of the development of a "feminine" side in men and of a "masculine" side in women, rather than a one-sided emphasis for each sex. And the church, they insist, ought to represent such full human possibilities in its ministry as its most visible symbol.[32]

The question of *Christology* is obviously related as well. While emphasis has recently been placed on the maleness of Jesus and the importance of a male priesthood as representative of Jesus,[33] feminists counter that the significance of the incarnation is rather to be found (and traditionally has always been found) in the Word becoming flesh as *human*. Citing the patristic principle that "what was not assumed was not redeemed," they ask whether this new emphasis on Jesus' maleness would not mean that women in the Christian economy are not truly persons in the redeemed and redeeming community and perhaps should not be baptized.

Similarly, it is held, most clearly in the Orthodox but also in some Catholic statements, that while Jesus is the revelational model for men, Mary the mother of Jesus is the model for women. And Mary was not a priest. Her virtues have been portrayed as distinctively "feminine" (silence, receptivity, nurturance). Feminists maintain that the sounder and more biblical theological view holds Jesus as the model for all human persons, that the whole of humanity is changed in principle because of the incarnation and redemption, and that Christ is the central figure in Christianity. They point out that traditional discussions of why Mary was not a priest rest on assumed notions of women as an inferior class. Mary could not be ordained because she was a woman, and hence in a state of natural subjection.[34] Only in recent discussions of the status of women in the church is this christological assertion of the centrality of the humanness of Jesus disturbed by the notion of different models for men and women. And, in its emphasis on the importance of Jesus' sexuality, it raises the question of how a male savior can redeem women.

Equally complex is the discussion of *ecclesiology*, which involves notions of the theology of the *pastoral office, ministry*, and *ecumenism*. Different ecclesiologies are presupposed by those who argue for or against the ordination of women. Most of those who oppose ordination hold a "high church," hierarchical, sacramental view in which a two-fold priesthood is maintained. The priesthood of the laity is sharply distinct from the ordained priesthood. In this view, the ordained ministry represents God or Christ as masculine and active in relation to the community as feminine or receptive. Roman Catholic, Orthodox, and some Episcopalian communions hold this position, basing themselves on ecclesiological tradition. Those who favor the ordination of women (often, but not only, "the low churches") stress the more biblical, community aspect of the church, and the one priesthood of all believers through baptism. For them, ministry represents the entire community before God and thus symbolically includes both men and women.

While the view of the church as community and of ministry as community service stands in some contrast to the idea of church as hierarchical order and ministry as sacramental representation of the authority of God, ecumenical considerations enter into the discussion as churches of each persuasion become more open to one another. The documents of Vatican Council II, for example, contain both biblical and traditional perspectives. Roman Catholic ecclesiology today has recovered and incorporated biblical and communitarian aspects, while some of the Protestant churches have become more receptive to its sacramental views. And within the discussion in the sacramentally ordered churches, the question is asked today whether the presence of Christ mediated and "iconically" represented through bishop and priest is or can be independent of the presence of Christ mediated through the faith of the whole church. It is argued by some who favor the ordination of women that the priesthood directly represents the faith of the church and, only as a consequence, represents Christ. Such a position would require the representation of women in the ordained ministry because women are part of the church.[35]

Divergent views of the nature of ministry have further implications. Understanding ministry as a kind of sacrament of the church, frequently its most visible expression, those favoring the ordination of women call for a broad and inclusive notion in which pastoral service and the service of the Word are united with the sacramental, liturgical, and cultic aspects of priesthood. The wide range of ministries that women are already performing—teaching, counseling, preaching, retreat, prison, hospital, and campus work—need to be acknowledged and sacramentalized, these theorists argue, lest a split occur between pastoral service and sacrament in the sacramentally centered churches.[36] Those who oppose the ordination of women often have a more narrow and exclusive view of ministry in which the sacraments are understood as special cultic acts, words, and gestures quite distinct from the activity of everyday pastoral service and service of the Word. In this cultic view, especially criticized today by Latin American liberation theology, the priesthood is seen as a "gift from heaven" that does not arise from the needs of the human community but from the will and plan of God as a unique phenomenon.[37]

An interesting perspective opens up here when one considers current discussion of a vocational crisis, or shortage of nuns and priests, in the Catholic church. Vocation is thus understood to include only those in the clerical state or in religious orders. A broader, more inclusive view of ministry would affirm the many ministries being performed by Christians, lay and religious, male and female, as reflecting the manifold forms of ministry in the church. And it would indicate that there is no dearth of vocations. To resolve the "crisis," it is only necessary, feminists hold, to confirm some of these appropriate ministries of women with ordination to the pastoral office.

Finally, the question of women's ordination entails various understandings of the interrelated areas of *revelation, tradition,* and *theology* itself. Those who oppose ordination for women often presuppose a view of *revelation* that consists in a set of objective truths as propositions, given in the past once and for all. Such a position rests on the framework of understanding established for Roman Catholics at Vatican Council I. Those who favor women's ordination frequently hold a view that understands revelation as rooted in the past, but in an important sense, as continuing and ongoing throughout history. Rather than simply objective truths, revelation is, most fundamentally, the personal communication of God to human freedom and so makes new demands on the church at different times and in different ways. The view derives more clearly from the biblically oriented statements on revelation of Vatican Council II. Elisabeth Schüssler Fiorenza has called this a prototypical, as distinct from an archetypal view.[38]

Following from this polarity of views are differing concepts of *tradition,* so important in the Roman Catholic context, where the statement of the Congregation of Sacred Doctrine of 1976 holds that women may not be ordained because Jesus chose only male apostles and disciples.[39] Beyond the fact that this assertion itself is challenged by exegetes who point out that Jesus never ordained anyone, it also implies a view of tradition in which the church can do nothing that has not always been done since Jesus established the exact structures of church life and practice. Tradition in this view means the handing on of an essentially static and unchanging set of revealed truths: the function of the church is to repeat the past, not merely in the essential issues of doctrine and faith, but also in its customs and practices. Those who oppose this view argue that if the practice of Jesus were followed in all aspects, married men would have to be eligible for ordination—and only converted Jews could be ordained! More seriously, they point out that many, very long traditions have changed in the church, including attitudes toward Jews, toward usury, slavery, and the vernacular liturgy. These, of course, presuppose a different view of tradition as the handing on of the fundamental message of Jesus' life, death, and resurrection in ways that are ever responsive to changing historical contexts. Tradition is understood as an essentially dynamic process in the life of the church.[40] One might say that the more static view of tradition implies a "cosmocentric" universe with human persons conceived as objects, as unchanging natures on the unchanging stage of the world. The more dynamic view of tradition implies an "anthropocentric" universe with persons conceived as subjects essentially characterized by freedom and historicity.[41]

These views of revelation and tradition inform the differing understandings of the functions of *theology* in the church held by those who oppose or favor the ordination of women. The American bishops have asserted that unless a contrary theological development occurs, leading to a clarifying statement from the *magisterium*, the present exclusion of women from the priesthood must be maintained. It is clear that the teaching office of the church must be in a dialogical relationship with theology. But is the function of theology merely reflection on the *magisterium* and on the truths taught by the church in the past? If so, the task of theology would be mere repetition, the explanation, defense, and "proof" of this past truth of the church not only in its doctrine but in its practice.[42] In contrast, those who favor the ordination of women understand theology as going before the *magisterium* in loving but critical reflection and presenting it with the results of its reflection on faith as it is lived in the contemporary situation. Beyond reflection on the past of the church's faith (though it surely includes that), theology is the correlation of faith with other knowledge, with the natural, social, and human sciences, and with the common experience of humankind both in the present and with a view to the future. And, one must add, it should include serious reflection on the experience of the female half of the human community, which has long been excluded from theological discussion.[43]

This brief sketch of some of the theological issues entailed in the discussion of the ordination of women is enough to indicate the broad implications of different views on this question as it has become a central symbol of the situation of women in the church. Much work needs to be done in each of these areas and much has already been accomplished by feminist scholars in the church. This work, however, involves another dimension that must be included in this overview—the area of ethics.

CHRISTIAN ETHICS

The question of women in ethical discussion is usually placed in the wider context of social justice and within the discussion of minorities who are subject to discrimination because of their class or group status. Such discrimination is understood to be unjust in view of natural and Christian principles of equality and freedom. Even though women do not constitute a numerical minority or a class in the technical sense, it is appropriate to consider women in this way because of the long traditions that have understood women to comprise a naturally inferior or subjected group in society and because of women's experience of oppression in relation to societal institutions as based on their female status.

An ethical issue emerges in the discussion of the ordination of women when the principle of equality is invoked; it is argued that equality of rights among adult members of the church entails the imperative of including the participation of women in all areas of church life and decision making, especially in the ordained ministry. While those who favor the ordination of women insist that women have a right to such ordination, those who oppose it assert that no one has a right to ordination. Rather, ordination is a gift, a service in the church to which one is called by God. Feminists reply that while no individual has a right to ordination, it is unjust to exclude an entire class of Christians from the opportunity of having their vocations tested—as unjust as it would be if blacks or Asians were excluded.[44] Further, they present wide evidence of women who have experienced a call to the pastoral office.[45] Thus, feminists insist that present church structures are sexist, unjust, and must be reformed if justice is to be done and positive harm avoided. Those who oppose the ordination of women, which would involve the full participation of women in church life and decision making, affirm rather a principle of "separate but equal" or complementary functions and roles for women and men in the church. Hence the question returns to the issue of theological anthropology: Is there one human nature or are there two?

Three areas of feminist ethical concern can be sketched in the context of the moral imperative that many feminist scholars discern in the general question of women in the church. The first is a negative one, the *concept of sin.* Feminists point out that the Christian theology of sin as fundamentally pride, overriding self-esteem, or ambition is the result of a totally male-oriented set of reflections. And while this theology may adequately reflect male experience, the experience of women is precisely the opposite. The "sin" of women would more likely be characterized as a lack of pride, lack of self-esteem, lack of ambition or personal focus. The women's movement has encouraged women to develop these characteristics to offset the triviality, lack of discipline and serious responsibility that have constituted the stereotypes of the female personality.[46] Consequently when women who call for ordination are criticized for adopting male (sinful) styles, for being pushy and power hungry, such judgments are delivered from a totally male-centered ethical and theological understanding.

The positive side of the above issue is reflected in the ethical concern for the *concepts of human agency and responsibility* implied by feminist positions in the church. Arguing that cultural and social systems have often prevented women from developing strong self-concepts, women scholars have shown the moral and religious implications of the limited, self-sacrificing, and passive roles women have been conditioned to play. If the religious and moral dimensions of human persons are capable of development in some direct proportion to the achieved degree of human freedom and responsibility, then it is imperative that women be encouraged to take hold of their lives as responsible selves. While self-sacrifice is central to the Christian idea of love, there has to be a healthy and free self before genuine and responsible self-giving can occur. Thus the women's movement has put into the forefront of women's consciousness, including the consciousness of women in the church, the important moral significance of human agency in urging women to value their own lives as moral and religious agents, over and against more passive and resigned attitudes. Those who favor the ordination of women tend to be those in the church who recognize the need for new structures that aid *all* persons to exercise roles of responsibility and decision making.[47]

A final ethical issue is the question of societal values. This derives from the stereotypes about the special, more receptive "feminine" virtues that, feminists fear, relegate gentleness, love, honesty, sensitivity, etc., in a false way only to women and thus to the private realm. Such feminine virtues, if they exist, belong in the public sector as well, lest a false double standard be promoted.[48] In urging the ordination of women in the church, these women are quite clearheaded about the fact that women are no more virtuous than men. They merely indicate the danger of sexist structures that reinforce an unhealthy series of dualisms in church and society. If such dualisms are carried over into the life and practice of the church, they represent a denial of the ethical and Christian principle of equality and are thus unjust. A church that discriminates against women as a class through stereotyped notions of special virtues, roles, and functions needs to be purified if justice is to be done and if harm to both women and men and to society is to be prevented.

In the course of this chapter on some of the historical, theological, and ethical questions related to the ordination of women, it has become clear that the issue aptly symbolizes the wider question of women in the church. As women in society work to share equally in the responsibilities of public as well as private life, women in the church ask for equal participation in the fullness of the church's life and practice. Women today speak from a radically new cultural situation that has finally allowed them access to the education and professional possibilities heretofore denied. Out of this new experience, feminists in the church are asking genuinely new questions, questions never before "seriously imaginable." Since the questions are new, old answers—answers developed in a time when women were indeed an inferior class—will no longer serve. And yet these feminists are staunch defenders of the Christian tradition. The heart of that tradition as radical faith, hope, and love, made possible through the life, death, and resurrection of Jesus, is a message about human personhood in relation to God. Women seek the fullest expression of Christian personhood in the context of their own experience of a very traditional Christian vocation to service of the church.

II. THEORETICAL
PERSPECTIVES

4. The Scholarship of Gender: Women's Studies and Religious Studies

The women's movement in the churches affected and was affected by the wider impetus for change in the situation of women in society. A part of both these movements was the growth and development of women's studies as their academic, scholarly, or research side. Thus, the task of this chapter is an overview, historical and theoretical, of issues and accomplishments relating to women's studies, the question of gender, methods of feminist scholarship, and the place of women's studies within religious studies. The topics are complex and the literature is vast. The situation reverses the scene described by Virginia Woolf in *A Room of One's Own* in which she has gone, one misty London morning, to find out why women are poor.

Here had I come with a notebook and pencil proposing to spend a morning reading, supposing that at the end of the morning I should have transferred the truth to my notebook. But I should need to be a herd of elephants, I thought, and a wilderness of spiders, desperately referring to the animals that are reputed longest lived and most multitudinously eyed, to cope with all this. I should need claws of steel and beak of brass even to penetrate the husk. How shall I ever find the grains of truth embedded in all this paper, I asked myself, and in despair began running my eye up and down the long line of titles. Even the names of the books gave me food for thought. Sex and its nature might well attract doctors and biologists; but what was surprising and difficult of explanation was the fact that sex— women, that is to say, also attracts agreeable essayists, light-fingered novelists, young men who have taken the M.A. degree; men who have taken no degree; men who have no apparent qualification save that they are not women. Some of these books were, on the face of it, frivolous and facetious; but many, on the other hand, were serious and prophetic, moral and hortatory. Merely to read the titles suggested innumerable schoolmasters, innumerable clergymen mounting their platforms and pulpits and holding forth with a loquacity which far exceeded the hour usually allotted to such discourse on this subject. It was a most strange phenomenon; and apparently—here I consulted the letter M— one confined to the male sex. Women do not write books about men—a fact that I could not help welcoming with relief, for if I had first to read all that men have written about women then all that women have written about men, the aloe that flowers once in a hundred years would have flowered twice before I could put pen to paper. So, making a perfectly arbitrary choice of a dozen volumes or so, I sent my slips to lie in the wire tray, and waited in my stall, among the other seekers for the essential oil of truth.[1]

That was 1928; today, the volume of material about women is even greater. But most is by qualified women. Taking Woolf as a guide, one can search for the essential oil of truth by finding some illuminating examples across a few disciplines from a few scholars. Good examples can suggest perspectives, at least, on the issues.

Gerda Lerner comments somewhere that the emergence of feminist consciousness is both a blinding and an illuminating flash of insight for those who have had it. Patriarchy, androcentrism, and sexism have so pervaded history, culture, and ideas, the very language with which persons think, speak, and write, that nearly everything known is called into question. And this includes the heritage of learning that is prized in the university, scholarship. Less apocalyptically, consciousness of the issue of gender has not only opened new realms of research but has also, in subtle ways, changed the ways to look at the "same old problems."

WOMEN'S STUDIES

Women's studies in the United States emerged in the late sixties and early seventies as the academic arm of the movement for the liberation of women. Its history over the last decades reflects the creativity and the conflicts that have marked feminism itself: new discoveries, debate between academic and political concerns, struggles with racism, classism, homophobia, the question of autonomy or integration in the university system. One way of telling the story, with Florence Howe, is to locate the origins of women's studies in the perception of women faculty on many campuses that the battle to save the liberal arts from vocationalism in college education raised questions about the canon of great books that comprised the Western tradition. Feminist scholars who had been experimenting with single courses—women and history, women and literature, women and psychology—perceived that a return to the classic texts, say, to Aristotle, Augustine, and Erasmus simply would not suffice. The traditional male-centered curriculum with its "misogynist view of achieving men and domestic or invisible women would clash with or confuse the vision and aspiration of . . . a bit more than half the student body now attending college."[2] Moreover, a simple return to the fathers of the Western tradition would be false to the quest for *truth,* which is the mission of the liberal arts.

These women scholars realized that within the college curriculum, it is the liberal arts, especially philosophy, literature, history, religion, as well as biology, psychology, and sociology, that describe and define masculine and feminine human being. These studies offer images of the possible ways of life to young women and men. And they present an interpretation of the past in which women seldom appear. They offer many vocations and kinds of work for men and only a few for women. They educate the younger generation about their fathers and not their mothers; they "teach students not only how to think, but that men have been the only thinkers."[3]

The goals of women's studies programs were formulated early and have guided the development of programs over the last decade. Among these goals was the development of a body of research about women that would allow scholars to begin to envision the lost history and culture of women and eventually to change the mainstream curriculum that represents less than half of human history. The goal of a body of scholarship about women has been realized in important ways already. Significant advances have been made, for example, in women's history, in economic theory, theories of women's intellectual and moral development, study of sex differences and the socialization of children, and restoration of women artists, writers, intellectuals. One revealing example is women's history, where studies have proceeded both as a concern for women in themselves, deserving of their own history, and with a focus on women in relation to men, with a view toward achieving a truly universal human history.[4] The first approach represents the discovery of a new subject matter: what were women doing in the past? Women have always been involved in everything human. One aspect of women's history searches for answers to the question, looking for new evidence and asking new questions of old sources, finding appropriate contexts and categories that will shed light on the lost or hidden history of women. The second approach pursues the recovery of women's history as it involves relationship with, and relative status to, men in any historical period. The integration of the history of women into "history"—"men's history"—casts new light on that supposedly general history, on the significance of any period, and often challenges the historian's view of periodization itself.

So, one feminist historian argues, when looking at periods of great social change from the perspective of the liberation or repression of women, eras that had been understood to be progressive in important ways, such as classical Athens, the Renaissance, and the French Revolution, undergo surprising reevaluation.

For women, "progress" in Athens meant concubinage and confinement of citizen wives in the gynecaeum. In Renaissance Europe it meant the domestication of the bourgeois wife and escalation of witchcraft persecution which crossed class lines. And the Revolution expressly excluded women from its liberty, equality, and "fraternity." Suddenly we see these ages with a new, double vision . . . .[5]

Women historians have demonstrated "a fairly regular pattern of relative loss of status for women precisely in those periods of so-called progressive changes."[6] This analysis of European history is similar to that offered by Gerda Lerner, preeminent scholar in American women's history, in her work on women in the Jacksonian era. In this period, Lerner discovered an absolute lowering of status for women occurred in the preemption and professionalization of knowledge (especially medical knowledge) by men. Women were excluded from higher education and confined to domestic roles, factory work, nursing, and teaching. As teachers, they earned 30–50 percent of male wages. This era of expanding democratic freedoms produced both the "mill girl" and the "lady" in American society.[7]

Lerner's work on methodology combines the two foci—the study of women in their own history and in relationship to men—as she describes seven stages in the development of women's history. Starting from the observation that traditional history is men's history, she argues that the first point to establish is that women have a history. It is one that has been obscured by the patriarchal values that have formed Western culture and are unconsciously shared by most men and women. These values assume that biological sex difference implies God-given or "natural" separation of human activities by sex and a "natural" dominance of male over female. It is common sense that women are participants in human history, yet the record is pervaded by patriarchal values that have emphasized war and politics, not child rearing, as history.[8]

Lerner's second stage is analysis of the subordination of women, different because of women's intimate ties to men. Yet most men have been oppressed too. Thus women's subordination must be studied within the context of the oppression of males of their group. Women are not oppressed because of child-bearing and child-rearing roles, but because of social devaluation of these activities. Third and fourth are the search for new questions that will elicit women's experience in male-dominated history and the search for new sources. Lerner holds that the "dearth of sources" excuse is untenable, at least in the American field; the sources for demographic history—census, parish, birth, property, and tax records, wills, church and club minutes, family letters, diaries, etc.—are available. The fifth stage is challenge of traditional historical periodization. "The very potential for making decisions depends, for women, on lowering infant mortality and on having access to education."[9] Periods of progress or decline will be measured differently according to these criteria. Sixth is redefinition of historical categories in a woman-centered inquiry that looks at evidence through the values, concerns, and activities of women. Only after all six stages have been realized will it be possible to approach the last, the achievement of a truly universal history "based on close comparative study of different periods in which the historical experiences of men are compared with those of women."[10]

Lerner's stages in women's history parallel her own autobiography. Her interest in simply being a good historian, with women as her subject matter, changed as she discovered the inadequacy of traditional concepts, the irrelevance of standard questions. The search for a better conceptual framework, for appropriate comparisons of women with other groups, led to the use of new models, often borrowed from other disciplines. "At this stage," she writes, "women's history is no longer only a 'field'; rather it is a methodology, a stance, an angle of vision."[11] It is a stance in its demand that women be included in whatever topic is under discussion; an angle of vision as the historian perceives that women have lived in a world defined by men and yet have shaped and influenced that world. Thus new methodological questions emerge. Is there a different history of men and of women? Does gender determine a person's experience, activities, consciousness? "Women's history, finally," Lerner says, "is both a world view and a compensatory strategy for offsetting the male bias of traditional history." In its seriousness and range, it "aims for a new synthesis which will eventually make its continuation unnecessary."[12]

Women's history is not simply the manifestation of women's oppression and their struggle for rights. Rather, the historian searches to find out what women were doing, how they were doing it, and what their understanding was of their place in the world, since women were *active* participants in the past. At one point, Lerner distinguished her work as a scholar of women's history from her feminist position as a citizen. She became critical, however, of the "compensatory and contribution history framework," moved to the new social history, and finally to a woman-oriented history.

All efforts to treat women as a sub-group—minority, class, caste—are doomed to failure, since women are one half of humankind, evenly distributed in all strata of society. Their culturally determined and psychologically internalized marginality seems to be what makes their historical experience essentially different from that of men.[13]

What would the past be like if women were at the center of inquiry? What if men were understood as woman's "other"? Even to pose such questions shifts one's angle of vision. Lerner found that in seeking with others to uncover and interpret the female past, her identity as a woman scholar finally fused with her citizen-consciousness. She became a feminist scholar. The collaborative work of women's history (group projects, sharing of knowledge and resources, collective writing) turned collegiality into sisterhood.

Feminist historians need not be women. Carl Degler has centered his work on the history of women and the family in America. He argues that the equality of women and the institution of the family have long been at odds, that the historic family *depended* on women's subordination: women were expected to put the interests of others—their families—before their own.[14] Degler focuses on family structure and individualism in his analysis. As individualism extended to women in American history, it became part of women's self-perception and thus affected family life as well. Why was there a new women's movement forty years after suffrage was achieved in the United States? Because suffrage was no real solution to the situation of women in the patriarchal family, Degler believes.[15]

He holds that the new history of women has caused the most recent redefinition of history itself. Even before the women's movement, David Potter had pointed out that F. J. Turner's "frontier thesis" about American history was sexist; Turner applied to Americans what only applied to men—the individualistic, competitive egalitarianism of the new land. While men experienced a cramping of their freedom because of the end of the frontier and the emergence of a nation of cities, women discovered the opportunity to earn their own living, to be economically independent. The grim reality of the lives of women on the American frontier has recently become clear not only because new evidence is being studied but also because the historian is looking with new eyes—a woman's eyes.

Degler says that sex is to history as color is to black history; it is the source of differentiation, of different treatment by those in power. In marriage it is the primary basis for subordination. Thus sexuality itself becomes subject matter for historical inquiry. And it is important here to distinguish its *cultural* from its biological character. Degler agrees with Lerner that women are *sui generis;* women cannot be dealt with under other categories, as a minority group, for instance, since they are not separate from the rest of society but intermarry with the master group. He also warns about avoiding anachronism— "disenthralling our thinking" in historical judgments—as he argues that domesticity in the nineteenth century was a way station toward autonomy for women rather than a prison.

If the new history of women redefines history itself, what about the transformation of the curriculum? For Degler the aim is to have women included in the study of the nation, not simply as a separate course or special question, but in a composite history that is not one-sided. As a curricular change on the way to that composite history, Degler describes Stanford's "feminist studies" major. The name does not mean that it advocates feminism but that it moves beyond "women's studies," which deal with those areas where women have figured, to areas where they have not and to ask what difference it makes that women were or were not included. In suggesting this framework, Degler implies the use of gender as a universal interpretive category. Just as, since Marx, no study of an historical situation is complete without economic analysis, the suggestion is that no historical study is complete without gender analysis.[16]

History is just one example of the many disciplines in which women's studies are growing. There is new research and theory building in a number of areas of study. In some, the effect is "to 'enlarge the sample' of what scholars study."[17] Thus, in economics, the unpaid labor of women in the home and community needs to be included in definitions of gross national product and a nation's economic productivity. In psychology, Lawrence Kohlberg's theory of moral development, based on an all-male sample, has been challenged by the work of Carol Gilligan in her study of female moral reasoning.[18] In this case, enlarging the sample meant the construction of a new theory about a different pattern of moral development among women.

In other areas, existing theory is reinterpreted from the standpoint of women's contribution to the social order. In anthropology, for example, the central significance attributed to the male hunter is questioned.

Big game hunting becomes a more logical development when it is viewed as growing out of a complex of changes which included sharing the products of gathering among mothers and children, deepening social bonds over time, increase in brain size and the beginning of cultural intervention for purposes such as baby-carrying, food-carrying, and food preparation. Such hunting not only needed the prior development of some skills in social organization and communication; it probably had to await the development of the "home base."[19]

In the humanities women scholars question what is to be considered "art." Is it only that which is produced by institutionally trained individuals and appears finally in public view, or can the practical and beautiful work of women's quilts with their abstract designs be included? In literature, women critics retrieve the published books and unpublished diaries of women as important texts for analysis of women's writing. A new body of scholarship has emerged, both practical criticism and theory, as scholars search for the "difference" in the plots, characters, styles, and genres of female texts.[20] Feminist criticism now includes several aspects: critical readings of the texts of the male canon of literature, interpretation of female characters and the texts of women writers, and a highly debated move toward a comparative framework.[21] While some worry that the new focus on women writers fails to make distinctions of excellence, others believe it important to document the full range of literature in any period and then develop new definitions of quality.

In philosophy, women's scholarship has centered on feminism as a political philosophy in relation to theories of justice, equality, and freedom; on questions of androgyny, sexism in ordinary language, equal opportunity and preferential hiring, marriage, rape, abortion.[22] There is debate about whether equality means that men and women must be alike in personality. Jean Bethke Elshtain argues that a "unisex" view of androgyny confuses equality in rights and opportunities with uniformity or identity. Equal respect and equal treatment, demanded by justice, allow for significant differences between the sexes. Another version of androgyny simply means "freedom from stereotypes and pressures to develop in sex- specific ways," thus allowing for a greater pluralism of personalities rather than constriction within two human gender types. A third position holds for a continuation of differences between the sexes: such differences are not permanent and essential nor are they merely accidental. The claim is that there are "normic archetypes," patterns "to which individuals choose to conform."[23]

Some women philosophers have questioned the abstract and analytic nature of philosophy itself as a product of culture rather than a disciplinary or logical necessity. Others have suggested that feminist consciousness makes a significant contribution to philosophical style:

> Women do not think in terms of dismantling other people in the process of philosophical discourse: . . . . They are more conversational, more interested in collective thinking, more interested in building support than antagonism. They will talk about work in progress. Few feminists are satisfied with *one* model of thinking. We are also interested in using the tools of philosophy to clarify issues of genuine concern rather than to address problems of interest only to a small group of professional philosophers.[24]

That feminist scholarship and women's studies are more conversational and collective than the traditional academic pattern is frequently suggested. The seven guest editors of a *Yale French Studies* feminist number discussed their collaborative project under the rubric "collectivity as method." They described their collaboration as "a new tradition emerging in feminist studies—that of reading collectively, of speaking in a plural voice, of contributing individual work to a group project." They acknowledged that their activities challenge the system of "credit" in which scholarship is solitary and ideas are owned, that they were warned that collective thinking can be reductive. Their male colleagues were both surprised by their nonhierarchical way of operating and skeptical about its efficiency and validity. Nevertheless, these women said that mutual support enabled them to work more productively, that reading and writing together was intellectually rigorous and led to more daring exploration of differences. They admitted to challenging "the inherently competitive characterization of critical discourse as individual property: rather than allowing ourselves to be pitted against each other, we choose to combine effort, responsibility, and recognition."[25]

Their experience is revealing in another way. Concerned not to romanticize their collaboration, they recognized that they were also "caught in the conflict that feminists in academia perpetually face:

that of continuing a male-dominated tradition of scholarship while questioning its assumptions," the split between the "inherited discipline" and "feminist practice."[26] Literary critic Elaine Showalter has written about this split:

We are both the daughters of the male tradition, of our teachers, our professors, our dissertation advisors and our publishers—a tradition which asks us to be rational, marginal, and grateful; and sisters in a new movement which engenders another kind of awareness and commitment, which demands that we renounce the pseudo-success of token womanhood and the ironic masks of academic debate.[27]

While not uniquely feminist, a style of collaboration as friends and co-workers is a real alternative to a patriarchal model of scholarship and is an ideal of feminist scholarship. Carolyn Heilbrun writes that feminist literary criticism avoids the most dehumanizing quality of androcentrism: "the individualistic ambition which fears those similarly engaged." Although the ideal community is not yet achieved, feminist scholars have a sense of collective purpose in their struggle between using the discourse of their training and gestures toward what Elizabeth Abel calls "unthinkable alternatives." Heilbrun remarks that the perfect mode of female discourse is found in Alice (in Wonderland) who represents "the female use of male logic against itself."[28]

Similar issues are broached when feminist logic questions the natural sciences. Not only women but minority, working class, and poor men have not been involved in the making of science and the formulation of its questions. Women scientists challenge the content of science, its social context, and its value system "in which an individual scientist—normally a man—directs a team of scientists in hierarchical and authoritarian fashion and receives personal credit for what is essentially a collective effort." Biologist Ruth Hubbard suggests that the current interest in recombinant DNA is a result of the social organization of scientific inquiry: "....a less individualistic society, one that cared less about the traits, accomplishments and successes of individuals, might also care less" about how genes are passed "from parents to their very own, individual offspring." She observes that Descartes' notion of the organism as a machine leads scientists to try to answer the question of life by "taking living organisms apart into smaller and smaller units—to reduce them to chemistry and physics—even though the attributes of 'life' or 'living' are lost in the process." Hubbard believes that women are more inclined to "see the organic world as much more than the sum of its parts," and so "to imagine a future with women integrated into science is to imagine a culture transformed."[29]

Other areas might be sketched—psychology, political science, sociology, law, popular culture, education[30]—but enough has been indicated of the scope of women's studies. The body of scholarship is emerging, though the list of its tasks remains long. What about the transformation of the curriculum? In its first five or six years, there was a kind of creative anarchy in the development of women's studies, but by 1976 it was becoming institutionalized, with modest budgets, paid coordinators, minors, and then majors at the undergraduate level. In addition to twenty-eight centers across the nation for research on women in 1981, hundreds of campuses have formal programs, drawing faculty from traditional departments into its interdisciplinary networks. Some colleges, like Smith, have no formal programs but offer more "courses on women" than schools that do.[31] In recent years, there has been new concern with "mainstreaming" the curriculum lest women's studies courses become ghettoized. "Add women and stir" means there may be one lecture in a course of forty, one week on suffrage in the standard United States history course, one or two women writers in a literature course. Really to integrate the curriculum, women scholars argue, is a reform *all* faculty need to work on. And it is impossible to move from the male-centered curriculum without passing through some form of women's studies; one has to teach a whole course on women, become immersed in the scholarship, before this research can be integrated. But the resources are available: a core of persons on almost every campus who are concerned with the new scholarship, a body of knowledge, and a conceptual framework that deals with the feminist perspective as it animates women's studies.

A feminist perspective is necessary to teach women's studies. And a feminist perspective is simply the painful understanding that the world is divided into male and female, and that those categories, like those of race, are not to be changed or exchanged. Unlike students who might become teachers, or children who often become parents, males and females do not in a sexist society change places any more than blacks and whites.[32]

While unable to replicate female experience, men can study and understand it, be alert to the differences, and learn to value it; women too have difficulty in learning to value female authority. The political side of the feminist perspective is more complex. One could argue that all teaching is political, and if half the human race is excluded, that is a political issue. There is a world-political issue in the research needed on women for decisions of public policy today, especially in developing nations. The question is hardly a luxury in India, for example, where there is a declining percentage of adult women, despite the higher rate of female births. In Italy, women's studies are a part of trade union activity. Study of women is not simply an academic question. But it is *also* an academic question of the right of women to a place in the curriculum, to images of achievement. There is politics involved in taking the growing body of knowledge about women seriously, in overcoming or continuing the devaluation, trivialization, and indifference that attaches to the question. The university's mission to search for the truth is deeply implicated in the question of women.

Is women's studies a new knowledge or a new discipline? In the excitement and anger that fired its beginnings, the question was not asked. There were discoveries to be made, new materials brought to light, misapprehensions to be corrected:

As the enterprise proceeded on energetically, there was a growing curiosity about the intellectual significance of this new work . . . . It looked occasionally as if the discoveries were so different in kind from other, conventional work as to point toward a new way of studying people and things altogether.[33]

Women's studies are generally inter- or multidisciplinary. A scholar finds herself reading widely in other fields, and the borrowed concept is frequently found in the literature, for example, as literary critics debate the idea of a "woman's culture," drawing on history and anthropology,[34] or as students of religion raise the question of gender. The issue of knowledge or discipline is linked, as well, to the practical one of integrating women's studies courses in the university in a period of economic cutbacks. Programs are more feasible than new departments because they can use faculty from established disciplines, yet they run the risk of failing to attract students and faculty outside a small group of enthusiasts. Though some maintain that women's studies should become an autonomous discipline, most believe that they serve a transitional purpose, with an aim toward integration in the general curriculum. As that aim is pursued, the concept of gender, borrowed from the social sciences, has taken on new importance.

THE CONCEPT OF GENDER

In ordinary language, gender is used in two ways: as a polite synonym for sex and in a transferred sense as a grammatical classification more or less related to sexual differentiation. More technically, however, sex and gender are distinct. Sex refers to a set of biological facts while gender refers to the social, cultural, psychological, or religious meanings that are attributed to sex. Judith Van Herik writes that sex is irreducible, nonoptional, while gender is perceived, prescribed, in a sense optional. Sex is a biological given and gender is a social acquisition.[35] Recent studies of women in anthropology have focused not simply on women as a group of individuals but on gender as "an aspect of social identity."[36] The distinction underscores the way in which an implied, assumed, or explicit *meaning* of sexual differentiation comes into play whenever the study of women (or of men) is undertaken.

The new importance of the concept of gender emerged in two ways with the development of feminist criticism and women's studies. The first was the discovery of androcentrism, the male-centered character of scholarly disciplines in their Western context: the androcentrism of the scholar or researcher, of the disciplines in their historic frameworks of understanding, and of the subject researched—male-centered societies and groups of individuals in those societies.

In androcentric thinking, "the male norm and the human norm are collapsed and become identical . . . . To study males is to study humanity," and when women do become the focus of attention "they are studied as a class of objects, as other, as a problem somehow external to the heart of the matter—the male world."[37] Thus gender, as the interpretation of sex differences and as a theoretical perspective on equality or inequality, balance or imbalance in the valuation of the sexes, becomes significant.[38]

Second, when women's studies began its effort to right the imbalance of traditional scholarship, gender emerged as a category for exploration of the meaning of sex differences and so of the experience of women (and men) in different historical and cultural contexts. For women were/are always there. What is different in different situations is the *meaning* attributed to their sex. Where some of the disciplines have considered sex simply as a biological factor—a given that constrains society in only minimally changeable ways—current research on sex roles shows that "gender must be viewed from the perspectives of economics, politics, religion, philosophy, art—in brief, that gender is a total social fact that takes on its meaning from the wider cultural system of which it is a part."[39] While one can set out to study women simply as subjects in history, psychology, or religion, one is led to gender—the *meaning* of women and of men in any cultural and historical situation. The subjects of study may conform to or deviate from the cultural, religious, or psychological norm, but their identity and their experience will be understood only in relation to the gender patterns prevalent in their social worlds.

Psychogist Robert Stoller defines gender as the "psychological and/or cultural attribute of maleness and femaleness which need not necessarily accompany biological sex."[40] He believes that gender identity, once established in the first two years of childhood, cannot be changed unless there has been ambivalence from the beginning. Van Herik adds:

The concept of gender is a way of naming this situation in which we are prisoners of our conceptions and of specifying those conceptions, which are interpretations of the meaning of sexual distinction. "Gender" refers to the differences made (whether to a child, a psychologist, a parent, a society, a theory of human capacities, or a religion) by the fact that there are two sexes and the differences made by which sex someone is . . . ."[41]

Anthropologist Judith Shapiro argues for the need to study gender rather than women because of the problem of "markedness." This concept, borrowed from linguistics and semiology, describes the asymmetry between a pair of categories that designate equal opposites within some larger class, for instance, men and women within the human race. At the same time, since man is the more general term, a hierarchy is indicated. The more general term is "unmarked," the lesser term is "marked." The best known example of this skewed relationship between supposedly equal opposites is Inge Broverman's text of clinicians' views of adult maturity. She found that "behaviors and characteristics judged healthy for an adult, sex unspecified, which are presumed to reflect an ideal standard of health . . . resemble behaviors judged healthy for men, but differ from behaviors judged healthy for women."[42] Shapiro argues that the emergence of women's studies has shown how apparently "unmarked" courses are, in fact, men's studies. The curricular solution to this problem cannot merely be an additive one but calls for fundamental rethinking of the relations between the sexes. An exclusive concern with women's studies may be a useful short-term strategy but self-defeating in the long run because it continues the marked status of women as problematic, a special case. It does not view men as an equal problem. The category of gender, on the other hand, means that studies of men as well as of women are needed for a complete picture of any society. Gender is thus an analytic category for dealing with a universal social reality. Like rank, class, kinship, it should be included in the study of any culture.

The cultural notion of gender, as distinct from biological sex, is as conventional and arbitrary as grammatical gender; it is not derivative from natural facts but varies from one culture to another. In anthropology, it can be analyzed as part of the interpretation of cultural and religious symbol systems, where the studies of Victor Turner, Mary Douglas, Clifford Geertz, and others have shown that the "meaning of male and female is neither self-evident nor everywhere the same." Or gender can be studied in relation to social hierarchy, as in the anthropological work of Sherry Ortner, Michelle Z. Rosaldo, Nancy Chodorow, Harriet Whitehead, and Peggy Reeves Sanday. Feminist anthropologists take two positions on the issue of social hierarchy. One is to affirm the universality of male dominance and account for it without recourse to biological determinism. The other is to deny the universality of the pattern by producing examples of societies where more equal systems obtain.[43] A further issue in studying the social hierarchies of societies other than one's own is the relationship between social science (or, by extension, religious studies) and social criticism. Their union may be acceptable when feminist scholars study their own social and moral universes but may become missionizing in relation to other cultures. Shapiro asks: Is there a "theoretical double standard: a critique of society for us and functionalism for the natives?"[44] For her, the way beyond this difficulty is the use of gender as a comparative framework for dealing with social hierarchy. To question merely the "status of women" marks women as a special problem. Gender, however, is a more general rubric under which a social order may be analyzed. Is it equal or hierarchical? And how is it related to other patterns of social differentiation—classes, ranks— between the sexes and within the same sex?

As a wider grid for analyzing the social meaning of the relations of the sexes, gender is also relevant to the sociology of knowledge. If knowledge is power, the question of who controls not only the material means of production but the means of symbolic production is central. Do men and women represent subcultures? Does one obtain different pictures of the same society through female and male eyes? Recent studies suggest that cultures of male dominance may be men's cultures, not shared by women who have their own views about life, their own cultures. Thus, one must investigate women's culture as well as men's, determine the conditions that provide for a women's culture, discover if it is separate or overlapping with men's and whether it is a support or a challenge to the society's dominant views.[45]

Anthropologist Kay Warren reports on the split between the "official" symbol system of the Andean village that she studied and the lived experience of the women in the village. While the religious symbolism of the people set forth a pattern of complementary genders and division of labor, the on-the-ground experience of women registered inequality and subordination.[46] Historian Carl Degler distinguishes the "image" of women found in men's sermons from the reality of women's behavior and activities,[47] the gap between the nineteenth century's "cult of true womanhood" and the experience of working class and immigrant women. In religious studies, biblical critic Elisabeth Schüssler Fiorenza argues that New Testament passages that enjoin women's submission do not simply reflect taken-for-granted religious behavior in the early Christian communities but witness to historical struggles in which two different social and symbolic forms were competing—the egalitarianism of the early Jesus movement and the patriarchal codes that eventually triumphed in Christianity. Such passages are prescriptive not descriptive.[48]

Anthropologist Edwin Ardener claims that it is generally men who control symbolic production in a society and who are the central creators of its dominant worldview. Women's views are "muted." Ardener links this social factor to bias in ethnography: men talk to men.[49] For Shapiro, the issue is tied to that of subjectivism and thus to hermeneutical, phenomenological, and political questions. The sex bias of the researcher must be distinguished from the sex bias of the community researched; the sex (and interests) of someone expressing an idea must be distinguished from its authorship. At the same time, it cannot be assumed that only women can study women nor that women can only study women. If that were the case ("it takes one to know one"), many of the disciplines, including anthropology, religious studies, and history would topple.[50]

Thus sex, or better, gender has emerged as a necessary category in several of the disciplines. Much of the initial excitement in women's studies, according to Joan Kelly-Gadol, was due to the discovery that what had been understood to be natural was really "man-made, both as social order and as description of that order as natural and physically determined." Such descriptions are ideologies and go back to the story of Eve and centuries of Eve's interpretation in doctrine and sermon. But Kelly-Gadol points out that "the social sciences have been functioning in the same way, as myth reinforcing patriarchy."

There is assertion, for example, of the natural superiority of women as child rearers and socializers by male scholars, even when there is little empirical research on male-infant or father-infant relations and their effects. There are so-called scientific positions that the monogamous family and male dominance are characteristic of all primates, when the evidence shows that neither is universal and that when they do appear they seem to be environmental adaptations. There are historians who do not have special knowledge of the "natural" relations between the sexes but nevertheless seem to know what that order ought to be: they *know* that there were no great women artists because women's concerns were love and the family. The historical *problem* posed by women and art was raised only when feminist art historians inquired into "the institutional supports, rather than the native gifts, that sustain artistic activity." For one historian, fact becomes argument in his study of Athenian society; the denial of education to girls is defended because of the central importance of the family in providing legitimate heirs. As for the *hetaerae* in Athens, this historian writes, they are "adventuresses who had said No to the serious business of life. Of course they amused men—'But, my dear fellow, one doesn't *marry* a woman like that'." This historical work on the Greeks, obviously addressed only to men, was written in 1951 and reprinted in 1962.[51]

Thus the sexual order, or gender, as shaped by the institutions of family and state is not only worthy of historical inquiry but central to it.

The activity, power, and cultural evaluation of women simply cannot be assessed except in relational terms; by comparison and contrast with the activity, power, and cultural evaluation of men, and in relation to the institutions and social developments that shape the sexual order.[52]

Comparative investigation into gender as a social meaning and institutional framework of both women and men would include analysis of class, property relations, changes in the modes of production, and the relations between the domestic and public orders. Drawing on Marxist and anthropological theory, Kelly-Gadol suggests that while "patriarchy is at home at home," the historic forms of the family are rooted in societies' differing modes of production. The combination of property and work "shapes both family and public domains and determines how they approach or recede from each other." When the lines between family and society are blurred, sexual inequalities and the double standard are diminished. This occurred before the rise of the state for the feudal noblewoman and is occurring today as private household functions—child care, production of food and clothing, nursing—are socially organized. The family is shaped by the structure of social relations and by social interests, not just private ones.

The most novel and exciting task of the study of the social relations of the sexes is still before us: to appreciate how we are all, women and men, initially humanized, turned into social creatures by the work of that domestic order to which women have been primarily attached. Its character and the structure of its relations order our consciousness, and it is through this consciousness that we first view and construe our world.[53]

Gender may provide the relational analytic category for studying the meaning of the relations between the sexes and the symbolic framework in which that meaning is developed in practical and political life. But it is not unproblematic as *the* answer in what has been called the third stage of women's studies: after deconstruction of error and reconstruction of reality from a feminist perspective, the construction of general theories. The search for a unifying framework is important for the integrity of women's studies in the academy. Gender, or "di-morphics," was the phrase used by Kenneth Boulding when he suggested that "women's studies constituted the beginning of the new science ... which in a hundred years might be able to explain the implications of the human gender system." But gender is also seen by some thinkers as yet another way of "institutionalizing gender differences that feminists hope to overcome."[54]

This position is intensified in the French feminist discussion with its analysis of "phallogocentrism," described as the "current tradition that constitutes a signifying system organized around gender." In this context, gender refers to a

binary concept of relation that assumes such dichotomies as male presence/female absence, male word principle (*verbe*)/female verbal object, male center/female margin. I regard gender as the "logical" dichotomizing principle of phallogocentrism. This organizing principle regulates a set of systems that maintain the male-identified subject at the center of words. These signifying systems occur in all the arts and sciences . . . .[55]

For Monique Wittig, gender is too closely related to sex and to heterosexuality to deal adequately with the problem of "markedness" or the " 'unmarked status of the masculine that led Simone de Beauvoir \. . . to identify it as both 'neutral' and 'positive,' while the 'marked' status of the feminine led her to identify it as 'negative.' " The unmarked is "desirable, expected, familiar" while the marked is "undesirable, unexpected, unfamiliar"; the unmarked is shorter, easier to say. That words like "poetess" or "woman doctor" or "male secretary" appear and that the quantitative overrepresentation of male figures in textbooks has been frequently observed leads to Wittig's position "that lesbian metaphor must overwrite phallogocentric metaphor." The binary gender system is broken or displaced by lesbian writing, an "illicit" poetic method that "escapes . . . the dichotomizing organizational mode of sex-gender itself."[56] Julia Kristeva sees the women's struggle as no longer concerned with equality but with "difference and specificity," "the specificity of the female" and "of each individual woman," the relation between specific sexual differences and the symbolic social contract.[57] "Kristeva quietly and consistently rejects any thought that *desexualizes* the structures framing us and our thought."[58] French feminism generally is a woman-centered form of feminist thought, unlike American forms that are oriented toward equality.

So there is continuing debate about gender as another form of dichotomous thinking and suggestion of more woman-centered paradigms, just as there is debate about the autonomy of women's studies or their integration into established disciplines or the rejection of disciplinarity itself as a fragmented, male mode of analysis. But it is clear that, on the American scene at least, "the social creation of gender is a basic assumption of women's studies" and so remains a central category if not the basis for a general theory.[59] To question gender, rather than women, provides a comparative framework of analysis that allows for understanding the relational experience of women and men in different situations, the meaning of human lives as socially formed. The implications of gender stretch from the personal and familiar worlds to the social, political, and public realms and to the meaning of the whole, which is the province of religion.

WOMEN'S STUDIES AND RELIGIOUS STUDIES

Like their colleagues in other fields, women scholars in religion, in the late sixties and early seventies, brought the issues of the women's movement to bear on their academic work. It was obvious that many texts, traditions, symbols, and practices in Judaism and Christianity reflected negative valuation of women and severely restricted women's roles in religious institutions, ritual, and practice. Interest in the question of women in non-Western traditions grew as well. Aware of the power of religion in forming human lives, in establishing the fundamental worldviews and ethical frameworks that shape individuals and groups, of its significance both as a stabilizing, conservative social force and as a critical power for social change, these scholars set about a threefold agenda.

CRITIQUE OF TRADITIONS

The first task was critique of traditions, both religious and scholarly. Women scholars analyzed the sexism and androcentrism in the history of religions, religious psychology, ethical theory, biblical scholarship, in the history and theology of Judaism and Christianity, and in the texts and traditions that formed the canon of religious studies. Anthologies of readings were collected on the religious history of the West, focusing on the views of women in the classical writers and texts, views that reflected what Rosemary Ruether later described as a three-layered ideology: views of women as property or objects, as dangerously sexual and carnal, and romanticized as morally and spiritually superior.[60]

With regard to scholarship Rita Gross argued, for example, that "the conventional program and methodology of history of religions . . . reflects an . . . androcentric worldview and that the average historian of religions is intensely and unconsciously androcentric in outlook." She defined androcentrism as the identification of the male

norm with the human norm, the assumption "that the generic masculine habit of thought, language, and research is adequate" with its
discussion of women as "an object exterior to mankind, needing to be
explained and fitted into one's worldview . . . ."

They are there in the world, but they are discussed as an "other" of the human subject attempting to understand his world . . . , as the problem to be
solved, not as a co-subject in a mutual attempt to understand human, sexual
differentiation and all its manifestations.[61]

In an important paper, Valerie Saiving (who also wrote the first
modern critique of the androcentrism of Christian theology) took as
her point of departure Mary Daly's claim that the questions of and
data about women are erased in androcentric scholarship, together
with Ardener's view that in anthropology "the inarticulateness of
women is only apparent, a creation of the model operative in the
mind of the ethnographer." Saiving analyzed a classic text on religious initiation; only nine pages treat female rites because the ethno-
graphical data about women is so external and poor. The author's
interpretation of female rites, however, is careful in pointing to their
religious character and to a female sacrality "which cannot be trans-
lated into masculine terms."[62] He shows that although women share
in sacrality in their own rites, they are symbols of the profane in the
male rites. This may be derived from the ethnographic accounts or
from the men's own perception of women in their rituals. Certainly
the author is sensitive to the differences between women's and men's
models of the world. Yet when he describes the *human* meaning of
initiation, the metacultural aspects of male initiation are transposed
as *the* meaning of initiation rites and symbols as such. The earlier
interpretation of female rituals is not included. Women are excluded
from the realm of spirit and culture in their association with the natural: the rituals reveal that "one becomes truly a man in proportion
as one ceases to be a natural man."[63]

Saiving argues for the need to obtain new ethnographic data, to
reexamine old reports for significance that the ethnographer himself
missed, to look at documents deriving from women with new eyes.
She writes:

Not until we have . . . unearthed and studied a dense body of new data can we begin to speak with any confidence about the specific character of women's experience of and reflections on the sacred. Meanwhile it would be advisable for scholars in religion to speak more carefully about their subject—for example by substituting the word "male" for the generic "man" or "human" . . . .[64]

She further suggests that if the text's interpretations of female and male sacrality are correct, they exhibit a total incompatibility with one another: women's religious experience is bound to the sanctity of life, the mystery of childbirth, and universal fecundity, while male experience is connected with "the desire to break the bonds that keep him tied to earth, and to free himself from his limitations."[65] For Saiving, women's sense of the sacred has been denigrated, ignored, then extirpated in Western history with its deathly model of domination. She speculates that the sense of the sacred in precivilization may have been, for both women and men, "awareness of the holiness of life and desire for full participation in the sacrality of the cosmos" and that a fundamental shift of consciousness took place with the beginnings of civilization.[66]

Another example is Elisabeth Schüssler Fiorenza's work in New Testament studies. She writes that "biblical texts have to be read in their communal, social, religious contexts . . . as faith response to historical situation." No systematization of, for example, New Testament moral teaching is possible. Both "hermeneutical reflection" and "critical evaluation" are necessary since appeals to the Bible have been used to justify *both* the oppression of slaves and women *and* the rejection of slavery and patriarchy.[67] Schüssler Fiorenza criticizes the household codes of the late New Testament as "patterns of patriarchal submission" that share an Aristotelian understanding of household duties (*oikonomia*) and political ethics (*politeia*), a relationship of rulers to ruled based on "nature." She argues that the early Christian mission "conflicted with the existing order of the patriarchal household because it converted individuals," wives, and slaves, even when the head of the household remained pagan.[68] Pagan accusations that Christianity was disruptive of households were accurate because the house church was a community of equals, including women and slaves, a new family that was in conflict with both the patriarchal familial and political order.

The prescriptive *Haustafel* trajectory attempted to soften this threat by asserting the congruence of the Christian ethics with that of patriarchal house and state . . . . However its paraenetic and prescriptive character indicates that such a patriarchalization was not yet accomplished even in the beginning of the second century.[69]

Behind the prescriptions of the household codes was the pattern of equal discipleship of the earliest Christian communities. The household codes' affirmation of natural differences between women and men and between slaves and freeborn meant a humanizing of Aristotle's ethics of inequality but a major loss for women in the Christian context. As patriarchy became institutionalized, "Christian faith and praxis no longer provided a structural-political alternative to the dominant patriarchal culture."[70]

Schüssler Fiorenza urges critical evaluation of these two Christian frameworks from a feminist point of view. She argues that justifications of patriarchy as necessary for the church's survival or as deriving from Jesus' call to service are ideological. A feminist evaluative hermeneutics judges the pluralism of biblical paradigms from the perspective of women and releases a "dangerous memory" of the past suffering of women and other subordinate groups. That memory must be kept alive as well as memory of the other, egalitarian Christian ethos, often labelled by scholars as heresy, as "enthusiasm, gnostic spiritualism, ascetic emigration, or antinomian behavior." A critical feminist hermeneutics questions the political, social, and ecclesiastical interests that inform such scholarly judgments and sees biblical revelation not as timeless truth or archetype but a prototype, a "formative root model" that can be placed in dialogue with contemporary feminist theory, for example, about the family.[71] She cites philosopher Susan Moller Okin:

It is not the fact that women are the primary reproductive agents of society, in itself, that has led to their oppression, but rather that reproduction has taken place within a patriarchal power structure, has been considered a private rather than a social concern and has been perceived as dictating women's entire lives and as defining their very nature.[72]

Once again we are led to the concept of gender, the social meaning and valuation that structures sexuality. To the family, Schüssler Fiorenza adds the socializing forces of the churches in American society: while Christianity failed to develop structures that might have prevented the split between the private sphere of interpersonal love and the public sphere of competitive self-interest, the early Christian ethos of equal discipleship could provide a transformative religious model for the restructuring of home and society today.

RECOVERY OF LOST HISTORY

The second task of women's scholarship is the recovery of the lost history of women in religion, aspects of which are suggested in the previous example. It is already clear that in Christianity there is "an alternative history and tradition that supports the inclusion and personhood of women,"[73] that women exercised leadership in almost all the traditions and historical periods: as apostles in the earliest Christian communities, as scholars and foundresses in patristic and medieval times, as socially activist organizers in Catholic Reformation circles, as religious and social reformers in nineteenth-century America.[74] Scholars are studying the activities of Protestant, Catholic, and Jewish women throughout American history where, "both for religion and for women,"

America has been a new theatre. Religious revivals have strengthened female identity, called forth female charisma, and encouraged social reforms through which women have found places in modern society . . . . The Judaeo-Christian heritage, however, while imparting common hopes for freedom, has blocked women's way through ancient teaching about women's place and male-female relationships. Ever millenialists, we seem to see the day approaching when femaleness will be no more than a biological distinction, when . . . men and women will have forged new concepts of religious authority and the majority will be silent no longer.[75]

The question of women in the world religions is also studied in ways that include both analysis of positions of women in the traditions and recovery of their authentic religious lives.[76] The anthology of Rita Gross and Nancy Auer Falk, studying women's religious lives in non-western contexts, charts the experience of women as leaders, and describes women's rituals, women's religious experience in male-dominated systems, and some "success stories" in which a measure of social equality obtains, where "gender is irrelevant to attaining the tradition's highest goal."[77] That a good deal of the work in this anthology is done by anthropologists indicates the paucity of material on women that is available in the textual traditions usually studied by historians of religion.

Some continue the debate over the question of a lost or hidden matriarchy, characterized by the worship of the Great Mother. While Bachofen's thesis of an original matriarchy would seem to be laid to rest, Goddess worship has reemerged in a new context today— feminist Wicca—a witchcraft spirituality that claims connection with ancient and medieval traditions. Rosemary Ruether, however, has criticized this historical claim, insisting that worship of the Great Mother emerged in a patriarchal context concerned with kings, not with the liberation of slaves and women.[78] Another thesis has been put forward by Judith Ochshorn, who studies the relationships among gender, power, and religious participation in the religions of the ancient Near East. She holds that gender is relatively unimportant in polytheistic cultures, while it becomes determinative in the monotheistic religions of the Bible. However, her approach to Mesopotamian and Greek texts has also been questioned and her treatment of the New Testament is literalistic and unsophisticated. But despite "her failure to perceive the pervasive effects of patriarchy, whether in a polytheistic or monotheistic setting," her work is important "because she ties the larger, theoretical question to a detailed, painstaking study of many ancient documents, thus enabling us to see more clearly the patriarchal web that obfuscates theological language and disadvantages women."[79]

AN INCLUSIVE WESTERN THEOLOGY

This web of theological language is the focus of the third task in women's studies in religion—the attempt to frame a more inclusive construction of Western theology that is sensitive to the experience of women. As is well known, some feminists criticize the biblical and theological tradition in a way that finds Judaism with its male God and Christianity with its male savior, and their male-dominated structures, irredeemably biased against women. Mary Daly has argued powerfully for a women's religion, beyond the death of God the father, that builds on the framework of Christian symbols— radically reversing them in favor of women.[80] Carol Christ seeks a distinctively female spirituality by analyzing literary texts of women. In their stories of spiritual quest, women "have preserved certain values that have been devalued by the dominant male culture," values that may be critically reclaimed by women today.[81] She advocates Goddess worship for women, using Clifford Geertz's definition of religion— "a system of symbols which act to produce powerful, pervasive, and long-lasting moods and motivations"—to assert the psychological and political necessity of female religious symbols to affirm women and female sexual identity today.

Religions centered on the worship of a male God create "moods" and "motivations" that keep women in a state of psychological dependence on men and male authority, while at the same time legitimating the *political* and *social* authority of fathers and sons in the institutions of society.[82]

Christ traces aspects of Goddess symbolism important for the religious experience of contemporary women: affirmation of female power, the female body, the female will, and women's bonds and heritage. She suggests that the reemergence of the Goddess is natural in the new culture that women are struggling to create from their own experience. Naomi Goldenberg has also written in favor of Goddess worship and witchcraft as a new religion for women. Using a feminist version of Jungian themes, she suggests dream analysis as a source of spiritual revelation.[83]

This kind of feminist spirituality, as a religion based solely on the experience of women, is a significant movement, especially in its courageous affirmations of female value and dignity. Yet is has been criticized for its supposed dependence on Jung and Geertz, neither of whom would agree that religious symbols can be generated at will; they are, rather, granted, *received*. Caroline Walker Bynum questions the assumption that women need female religious images in view of her research on medieval mysticism: "If women are more particularly attracted by images of women, why is it that monks refer more frequently to the virgin Mary, while women concentrate especially on the infant or adolescent Christ?"[84] Paula Fredrikson Landes observes that "what these women actually offer, in Geertz's terms, is not religion but ideology."[85] Both Landes and Ruether note that this spirituality, which characterizes male religion as hierarchical and female religion as egalitarian, reverses domination in religious symbols, is separatist in orientation, assigns goodness to females and evil to males, and perpetuates the nature/culture dichotomy in female/male symbolism.[86] Landes notes that while these perspectives "emphasize the nurturant maternal nature of women as a central aspect of the feminine experience," the heroines of the novels that serve as their "canon" of religious texts "all in some way turn their backs to their own children." She judges a "recycled earth goddess," a "posthumous deity" too empty and too late for the spiritual search of contemporary feminists.[87]

Schüssler Fiorenza's point is important, that those who simply abandon the Jewish and Christian traditions fail to perceive the powerful hold of biblical religion on Western culture and on many women, all of whom need to be included in the feminist vision of liberation. Ruether adds that these are the religious traditions that have formed Western language and culture; they provide modes of critical judgment and moral guidelines that contemporary women cannot ignore. Ruether uses the prophetic and messianic traditions of the Bible as the source for an inclusive theology that takes account of the interstructuring of racism, classism, and sexism in the development of traditional Christian theology and practice. She also relates feminist theology to ecological issues in arguing for mutually supportive rather than hierarchical or dominating models of relationship. Biblical scholar Phyllis Trible uses literary criticism to show the "countervoices" in the Bible that dispute and judge its central patriarchal themes, to show that "de-patriarchalizing" is required by the Bible itself as it offers the basis for new theological construction. Margaret Farley rethinks the meaning of Christian love as equal regard and equal opportunity, Christian justice in relation to the individual and the common good, and notions of self-sacrifice and servanthood as "active receptivity" in calling for new patterns of relationship within the Christian community.[88]

Such efforts at theological revision take seriously both the radical feminist critique of Judaism and Christianity and the experience of many thoughtful women who remain within the synagogues and churches. Both historically and in the present, the Jewish and Christian symbols have been oppressive *and* liberating for women. Recognizing the religious, cultural, and linguistic contexts of Judaism and Christianity as formative both of the androcentric tradition *and* as the source of its criticism by women, some feminist theologians argue for the critical transformation of received religious symbols rather than their abandonment. This is the position that the following chapter articulates: a critical retrieval of the central Christian symbols understood in the context of the wider discussion in contemporary Christian theology. It is a position that recognizes, with Elisabeth Schüssler Fiorenza and Rosemary Radford Ruether, the power and truth of Christianity for so many women. It also recognizes the many transformations the Christian symbols have sustained throughout the Christian centuries. In the next chapter, I suggest ways of understanding such transformations and offer some reasons to hope that the women's movement of our time, in addition to constituting a challenge, is a transformative grace for Christianity today.

METHODOLOGICAL CONCLUSIONS

The emergence of feminist consciousness is having important effects on scholarship in many areas of the "field-encompassing field" of religious studies. New awareness of gender as a social construction, not as some natural given, and the research and theory building it has impelled, have placed in question much of the scholarly consensus in history, anthropology, sociology, psychology, philosophy, and theology. Women's studies—as academic programs and as multidisciplinary fields of research—represent a series of new questions, explorations and discoveries that seriously reorient the humanistic, social scientific, and theological aspects of religious studies.

The concept of gender as the social, political, cultural, and religious frame of understanding that defines "masculinity" and "femininity" provides an important critical tool in moving the study of women beyond protest to evaluation of the new evidence about women through nuanced comparison with the status of men in the contexts of historical period, locale, and social class.[89] Analysis of religious symbolism, ritual, roles, practices, moral beliefs, and behavior from the perspective of gender reveals not only the oppression and devaluation of women as a sex but also the creative ways in which women were/are active in their lives and cultures, agents in their own histories, shapers of another culture, history, religion.

To regard women as the majority of the human race in fields where men have long studied the religious experience, expression, and understanding of other men (and men's understanding of and reports about women) means that much of past scholarship is placed on a new map of religious reality. Less than half the story has been told. To begin to tell the other part is to acknowledge that women have always been involved (even when excluded or ignored) in everything human, in everything religious. As the distinct subject matter of women's studies is the experience of women, that of women's studies in religion is the religious experience, expression, and understanding of women. But the concept of gender reminds us that the experience of women has been and always is in relationship to men in the whole of human society. Thus women's studies affects the study of men (now seen as part of the whole), the study of the human in its wholeness, and religious studies generally. That wider whole will not be fully understood, given the androcentric history of the disciplines, without women's studies as a subject matter in its own right and as a necessary transition to the transformation of scholarship and the university curriculum.

How is the experience of women discovered? The methods of such study are varied, beginning with traditional disciplinary approaches that may be modified to correspond to the data available or newly discoverable. The major questions in any period or area of study are: what was/is happening to women, what were/are women doing and thinking, what was/is the relative status of women and men with regard to symbolization, valuation, creativity, participation, opportunity, power, institutional and informal support and constraint? What images of the female and the male are employed in any religious context, and how are these used? What are their practical effects? How is sexuality viewed? What issues of family and society, the public and private, class and race, need to be taken into account?

In addition to a pluralism of methods and questions, there is a feminist perspective or angle of vision that distinguishes women's studies as it has developed in recent decades from studies that are (apparently) disinterested or that argue to preserve some traditional views of women. While there are "hot" and "cool" (more explicit or implicit) feminist approaches, they are similar in their recognition of the subordination of women in much of human (and religious) history, the androcentrism of much past scholarship, and their concern to right this false imbalance. This unifying perspective in women's studies includes a feminist awareness that is at once critical of many past and present formulations and self-critical about the difficulty of presenting more adequate ones, of not becoming another ideology. While feminist consciousness sharpens critical perspective it does not guarantee important and insightful scholarship; it is necessary but not sufficient. Good scholarship in women's studies is good scholarship. And good scholarship in women's studies calls into question what any scholar's standards should be.

Women's studies belongs, as a corrective at least and as a major reorientation at most, in all aspects of religious studies. In some cases, as perhaps in the study of religions of the distant past, there may be no data other than the observations of men about women. Yet such absence of data is significant, indicating both the diminished status of women and the necessarily fragmented picture that is available about certain past traditions. In other instances, different sorts of material are available that are not thought significant until the question of women is explicitly raised. In more theoretical, contemporary fields (ethics, philosophy of religion, theology, psychology of religion, sociology of religion, etc.) women's studies has an important and necessary "place" until it is taken for granted that any adequate scholarly reflection on religion must explicitly include that distinctive variable that is the female majority of the whole human experience. Such reflection will inevitably alter perceptions of female and male, the masculine and feminine, and perceptions of gender in religious studies as a whole.

5. The Possibility of a Christian Feminist Theology

The question explored in this chapter is posed within the sisterhood of all women who share the concerns of religious feminism. It is reflected in the sizeable literature in the West that represents the women's movement in the synagogue, the Christian Church, and the feminist spirituality movement, and that has already developed into a tradition that is ecumenical, pluralist, and academically serious. Religious feminists are united in the conviction that both feminism and religion are profoundly significant for the lives of women and for contemporary life generally. That shared concern includes the perspectives of Jews, Christians, and those who claim no bond with either tradition. It includes feminists who work for the reform of traditions—Jewish, Roman Catholic, mainline or evangelical Protestants—and those who declare Judaism and Christianity irredeemably biased against women and find their religious homes in the new forms of feminist spirituality.

Feminist scholarship within the Christian context, for all its variety, is unified in its critical perception of sexism as a massive distortion in the historical and theological tradition that systematically denigrates women, overtly or covertly affirms women's inferiority and subordination to men, and excludes women from full actualization and participation in the church and society. It is unified in its aim of freeing women from restrictive ideologies and institutional structures that hinder self-actualization and self-transcendence. And it is unified in its attention to the interpreted experience of women as a source of religious and theological reflection, especially as those analyses—whether secular or religious—reflect the collective experience of women, in whatever groups of race, age, class, nationality. Thus it is an interdisciplinary, ecumenical, and cooperative task.

The differences within feminist religious scholarship as it relates to Christian theology are accounted for by different perceptions of the depth and pervasiveness of sexism within Christianity. As noted in the previous chapter, Carol Christ argues that the essential challenge is posed by Mary Daly's claim that the gender and the intrinsic character and attributes of the Christian God are patriarchal.[1] Christ divides feminist scholarship into "reformist" and "revolutionary" approaches, and notes that few reformists working with the tradition have responded to this criticism of Christianity's core symbolism. Feminist "revolutionaries" use the experience of women not only as a corrective but as a starting point and norm. Free of the authorities of Judaism or Christianity, they attempt to create new symbols and traditions on the basis of their own perceptions of ultimate reality. While it remains to be seen whether the writings of the revolutionaries—mainly concerned with new symbols and new forms of spirituality—will develop into more traditional forms of theology, the reformists face the deeper challenge of a "radical feminist transformation of Christianity":

A serious Christian response to Daly's criticism of the core symbolism of Christianity either will have to show that the core symbolism of Father and Son do not have the effect of reinforcing and legitimating male power and female submission, or it will have to transform Christian imagery at its very core.[2]

In recent years, a number of publications have advocated what Christ calls the revolutionary approach. Among them, Mary Daly's *Gyn/Ecology* and *Pure Lust* are among the most powerful and provocative explorations of feminist analysis and spiritual transformation. Others deal with witchcraft, Goddess worship, women's spiritual experience in literature, in dream analysis, and in natural bodily processes.[3] The growth of Goddess worship and witchcraft, or feminist Wicca, has elicited criticism from Rosemary Ruether, who points out that the cult of the Great Mother, claimed by feminist Goddess devotees, emerged historically from a patriarchal culture and "has to do with putting kings on thrones of the world, not with liberating women or slaves."[4] Similarly, witchcraft was never perceived in medieval times as involving a female deity nor were witches organized into cultic groups, as some proponents of feminist Wicca claim. All historical religious traditions are biased, Ruether argues, and thus it is difficult to see how these "new" feminist religions are more radical than the transformations sought by Christian feminists who work with the critical or liberating traditions of the Bible. We have seen that Ruether criticizes the revolutionary groups for separatism and reversal of domination, perpetuation of the nature/culture split in female/male symbolism, assignment of goodness to females and evil to males, and failure to work toward synthesis and transformation. She adds that those who are alienated from Judaism and Christianity and the culture formed by them are nevertheless part of that culture.

If they try to negate that culture completely, they find themselves without a genuine tradition with which to work, and they neglect those basic guidelines which the culture itself has developed through long experience in order to avoid the pathological dead ends of human psychology.[5]

While sharply criticizing Judaism and Christianity, these religious feminists, Ruether argues, remain unself-critical: "instead of creating a more holistic alternative such feminist spiritualities succumb to the suppressed animus of patriarchal religious culture."[6]

Nevertheless, the alienation and the criticism of this feminism is profound and must be taken seriously. Daly's critique of Christianity, as the radical example, centers on God understood as "father," the supreme patriarch in heaven who rules *his* people on earth and thus legitimates the male-dominated order of society. Eve as the originator of evil symbolizes, Daly suggests, the original sin of patriarchy, a reification of sexual difference in which evil is projected onto woman as the original "other." The figure of Christ represents idolatry of the male person of Jesus—"Christolatry"—and projects models of victim, scapegoat, and self-sacrifice, especially presented to women in Christian history. The male symbols of God and savior, or the "ultimate symbol" of "the all male Trinity," the "procession of a divine son from a divine father," are not adequate symbols for women.[7] These symbols strongly suggest that Christianity is a religion of fathers and sons.

In laying out the framework of her feminist critique of the major symbols of Christianity, Daly charges male theology with a cerebral "methodolatry" that renders the questions of women "nonquestions" and data about women "nondata." In contrast, she makes such nonquestions and nondata central in rejecting Christian symbols for their devastating effects on women; she argues that feminist experience itself is the source of liberating spiritual experience for women in a world *without* models. She adopts a method that entails moments of "castration" and "exorcism" on its way to "liberation," and employs a powerful countersymbolics in her deconstructive and constructive efforts.[8]

Daly's attack is on the broad symbolism of Christianity and the way it has legitimated the subordination of women and reinforced women's internalized inferiority. Theologians have long maintained that God transcends sexuality (although God is "he" for most) and that the humanity of Christ, not his maleness, is central in the Christian scheme (although for many, maleness was and is essential for Christian priesthood). But these theological distinctions have no impact on the ways symbols actually function to support religious and cultural ideologies that are crippling to women. To check this claim one need only review the explicit statements about women in Tertullian, Clement, Jerome, Augustine, Aquinas, Luther, Calvin, Knox, Barth, Bonhoeffer, Teilhard de Chardin, modern and contemporary pronouncements of the Vatican, and, of course, the Bible. Daly warns against the most common evasion of the issue—trivialization—and her imaginative and powerful constructive efforts drive home the necessity of reformulation. A thorough revision of Christian theology is needed to redress so fundamental a distortion.

And yet, although some feminists leave Christianity as destructive and exclusionary, many thoughtful women remain in the churches. Christian feminists who take the radical critique seriously continue to struggle with the symbols and their transformation. Both historically and in the present, the Christian symbols of God, Jesus, sin and salvation, the church, the Holy Spirit have been life-giving and liberating for women.[9] Recognizing that Christians live in the religious and cultural context of traditions that have formed them and in part freed them, held by faith, Christian feminists attempt to cope with Christianity from within. The problem is not solved simply by adding mother or parent images to God as father (although to image God as female, to think of God as "she" may be important). For parental images of God are problematic in relation to the experience of women and the problem of selfhood.[10] Rather, the task is to search for resources within the biblical, theological, and intellectual traditions that enable Christian feminist theology to be understood as an *intrinsic* theological task unlike other partial theologies (of play, work, even so-called theologies of women), that is, applications of Christian themes to contemporary issues. For the task implies not only a Christian critique of sexist or patriarchal culture but a feminist critique of Christianity.

RESOURCES FOR FEMINIST THEOLOGY

In the search for resources that enable Christian feminist theologians, male and female, to work fruitfully within the tradition and to take radical feminist criticism seriously, several critical requirements present themselves. The first is the need to ground the possibility of understanding past theological tradition both critically and constructively, of seeing it anew from the perspective of contemporary questions. Women are in the cultural and religious traditions formed by Judaism and Christianity. These traditions provide the very language with which they formulate their criticism and the symbols and countersymbols with which they imagine the new.

Recent discussion of hermeneutics and critical theory provides an important resource in this context. H. .G. Gadamer's work on the universality of the hermeneutic standpoint offers an important perspective for Christian feminist theology as it attempts to understand the tradition adequately and to forge new interpretations.[11] Gadamer has shown how *all* real understanding (truth as event) is in fact *new* understanding as it occurs in the dialogue with tradition. Thus tradition is conceived as a living address and responsive source for questioning and reinterpretation, and it is only within this ongoing conversation that tradition itself is understood. Gadamer argues further that all understanding intrinsically bears its own moment of "application"—the unity of cognitive, normative, and reproductive interpretation. The inherent connection of issues of practical action with all genuine interpretation of tradition thus overcomes any "merely cerebral" view of authentic theological work. A text *must* be practically and intellectually related to the interpreter's situation if it is itself to be adequately understood. Finally, Gadamer describes effective historical consciousness, awareness of the history of effects of texts, themes, or traditions as these have been interpreted and reinterpreted, and as the context in which the interpreter stands. It is this self-awareness that feminist theology attempts to achieve in its discussion not only of biblical and historical texts, but also of the ways these texts have been interpreted through centuries of preaching and teaching, their continuing effects on practical life for women and self-understanding of women. Christian feminist theologians recognize, I believe, that it is impossible to work outside the effective history of tradition that offers us the subject matter, the very questions with which they struggle.

While accepting much of Gadamer's formulation, the critical social theorist Jürgen Habermas has argued against certain conservative, elitist tendencies in Gadamer's reverence for the authority of past tradition and his insistence on its universal linguisticality. Besides language or texts, Habermas maintains, there is also a history of work and of power (or force or domination). And language itself can be ideologically distorted. Thus hermeneutics or interpretation of texts must be joined by a critical theory that analyzes the societal context, the life praxis in which all texts are embedded. Using psychoanalysis as a cognitive analogue on the individual level for critique of systematically distorted communication in the interest of transformation, Habermas points to the necessity of critical reflection on social structures of authority and domination with an explicit interest in emancipation. In addition to hermeneutical "translation" of traditions, critical theory provides "ethical and productive distance" from those very traditions in which we live. Habermas argues against the illusory self-understanding of value-free scholarship or the pursuit of "pure" knowledge—the illusion of objectivism—by showing the particular interests necessarily presupposed by all human cognitive achievements, whether in the empirical, the historical-hermeneutic, or the critical social sciences.

Orientation toward technical control, toward mutual understanding in the conduct of life, and toward emancipation from seemingly "natural" constraint establish the specific viewpoint from which we apprehend reality as such in any way whatsoever. By becoming aware of the impossibility of getting beyond these transcendental limits, a part of nature acquires, through us, autonomy in nature.[12]

Thus it is a matter of "coming to terms" with the interests that in fact underlie the pursuit of knowledge. The connection of knowledge and interests ultimately means that "the truth of statements is linked to the intention of the good and true life."[13] The Christian feminist critique of ideology, developed in the study of the theological tradition in its historical, social, and ecclesiastical contexts, is not merely negation of the past. As theology, both systematic and practical, it explicitly claims to be rooted in an eschatological and emancipatory interest in the future.

Paul Ricoeur joins the hermeneutical and critical perspectives by pointing to the necessity of both past and future orientations: "There are no others paths . . . for carrying out our interest in emancipation than by incarnating it within cultural acquisitions. Freedom only posits itself by transvaluating what has already been evaluated.[14] The use of hermeneutical and critical theory in feminist theology clearly offers grounds for the double possibility of exposing the distortions of the past and of seeing something more, a future possibility beyond the distortion, in the light of new questions, questions raised by the feminist critique in both its cultural and religious dimensions.

A second requirement for a feminist theology that takes seriously both the radical contemporary critique and the authority of historical Christianity is a theory of religious symbols that grounds both negative and positive moments in its interpretive horizon. Tillich's discussion is helpful in showing how symbols open dimensions of transcendent reality inaccessible to technical or instrumental reason.[15] He argues that symbols are borne out of the collective unconscious, within particular situations. Symbols participate in the reality they signify, but participation in the depth dimension is *not* identity: the transcendent or unconditioned always transcends every symbol of the transcendent. Thus religious symbols remain under the "law of ambiguity"—reflecting the tendency of religion to substitute symbols for the divine itself, a tendency toward idolatry and the demonic. In every religious symbol there is tension between the unconditioned in which the symbol participates and the immanent, the appearance, the bearer of the holy in a particular cultural situation. The truth of religious symbols is independent of empirical criticism; they die when the situation in which they were created has passed or on inner symbolic grounds, through a religious criticism of religion. "If Christianity claims to have a truth superior to any other truth in its symbolism, then it is the symbol of the cross," Tillich says, in a denial of the idolatrous tendency of all symbols.[16] Theology can neither affirm nor negate symbols; it can only interpret them. In criticizing the functions of the symbols of God and Christ, feminist theology exposes the idolatry that occurs when preliminary or conditional concerns are elevated to unconditional significance; something finite (maleness, sexuality) is lifted to the level of the infinite.

This law of ambiguity of symbols is intensified by Ricoeur, who points out that symbols are profoundly double or multivalent in their meaning. Their richness is constituted precisely by the "close alliance" of regressive and progressive elements.[17] The conjunction of "archeology" and "teleology," disguise and revelation, means that interpretation includes two essential moments: an unmasking of regressive meanings or demystification, and a restoration of meaning. An adequate feminist interpretation is dialectical: it is suspicious as it unmasks the illusory or ideological aspects of symbols that denigrate the humanity of women, and it is restorative as it attempts to retrieve the genuinely transcendent meaning of symbols as affirming the authentic selfhood and self-transcendence of women. Ricoeur argues that the two moments of negation and affirmation are not extrinsic to one another; "they constitute the over-determination of symbols," their "surplus of meaning," and each requires the other.[18]

When the mixed texture or double intentionality of all religious symbols, the law of ambiguity, is taken seriously, the third requirement for feminist theology emerges. An adequate theological method must exhibit a double critique. On one side, the pluralism of feminist cultural and religious interpretations must be related to the Christian symbols in their over-determined meaning, and their hidden, regressive, or ideological dimensions exposed. On the other hand, the restored or purified meaning of the symbols, in their transformative possibilities, must be brought to bear on the culture, and on religion itself.[19] This double critique takes serious account of the experience of women and at the same time holds itself bound to the progressive and anticipatory power of the gospel and its symbols for women and for contemporary life as a whole. The interpreted experience of women in society— economic, cultural, religious—is used to criticize those dimensions of the Christian tradition, the doctrine of God, Christology, ecclesiology, etc., that serve to legitimate the exclusion, denigration, and subordination of women both in theology and in the practical life of the churches. And the newly interpreted understanding of the gospel and of Christian symbols as authentically liberating for women is used to criticize a sexist culture in which women are systematically exploited. Christian feminist theologians are convinced that the symbols both of the religious tradition and of culture say "something more" than is apparent on the surface.[20]

CURRENT DEVELOPMENTS

As feminist theology has developed, the critical correlation of the Christian tradition with the contemporary cultural situation has consistently broadened to include wider dimensions of women's experience. In facing arguments that the women's question is peripheral, middle class, or trivial in relation to the global problems of war and peace, poverty and affluence, race, hunger, and violence, feminist analysis has demonstrated the interrelationship of sexism, racism, classism, and has shown, for example, that "the majority of the poor are women, and children dependent on women"; that "internationally women's occupations are characterized by low pay and low status"; that black women in the United States face a double jeopardy; that women are more likely to suffer physical and psychological violence; that "personal sin is intimately related to structural sin."[21]

The major work of Christian feminist theologians thus far has been negation, unmasking cultural and religious ideology that denies women's full humanity. While important studies of the forgotten history of women have indeed appeared, the first task has been analysis of the distorted traditions about women in the Bible, the church fathers, medieval, reformation, and modern theology. These criticisms are now well known and need not be repeated. The result of these studies, however, together with secular feminist research, is that feminist theologians have at hand interdisciplinary analyses, preeminently that of Rosemary Radford Ruether, that describe several layers in the ideology of sexism and the complex issues that must be taken into account.[22]

On the basis of her historical studies she describes a first layer of ideology in which woman is the servant, object, or tool of a male power, and shares inferiority with other reduced groups, lower classes, subjugated races. A second describes women as evil or fearful, representing bodilessness, sexuality, and carnality. A third layer is the romantic split or reversal in which women are idealized as more moral or spiritual than men, privatized, along with religion, art, and culture, and again *used* as mediators of a lost female side of the male, as havens in a materialistic, immoral, public, male world. The romantic idealization of women is frequently found in contemporary theological or ecclesiastical statements that, no longer overt about women's inferiority or dangerous sexuality, now speak of "complementarity," a romantic term that bears the suspicion of yet another rationalization for subordination. In addition, Ruether urges the need to work on several levels, lest the cooptation of feminism by racism, classism, and romanticism in the nineteenth century be repeated. There is need for individual and subjective consciousness raising and the exorcism of debased self-images; social analysis of structures and the envisioning of a reconstructed society; self-criticism about class and racial contexts lest women be divided against each other; and ecological concern, in which nature and the earth are understood analogously in feminist or nonhierarchical, mutually supportive ways rather than in dominating or conquest models.

While feminists are rightly warned not to propose premature solutions to the radical criticism of Christian symbols,[23] there have been some efforts, especially in biblical scholarship, that have already shown the possibility of interpretations that are both Christian and feminist, that negate and affirm, unmask and restore. These studies demonstrate sophisticated appropriation of resources within the intellectual and theological tradition. The work of Phyllis Trible, for example, employs a complex hermeneutical method to show that "scripture in itself yields multiple interpretations of itself" in its continuing interaction with the world: with the black experience, Marxism, psychology, ecology, and in this case, feminism.[24] She writes:

As the Bible interprets itself to complement or contradict, to confirm or challenge, so likewise we construe these traditions for our time, recognizing an affinity between then and now. In other words, hermeneutics encompasses explication, understanding, and application from past to present.[25]

Trible reads the biblical texts from a feminist perspective, using rhetorical criticism as a clue to the fusion of aesthetic and religious visions. She takes the biblical metaphor of "the image of God male and female" (Genesis 1:27) as a topical clue for her study of God and the rhetoric of sexuality to show how "this basic metaphor contrasts with the imbalance of . . . partial metaphors"— God as father, husband, king, warrior, God as pregnant woman, mother, midwife, mistress.[26] Acknowledging that "the Bible overwhelmingly favors male metaphors for deity," she explores its female imagery for God and uncovers traditions that, within the context of the goodness of creation, show the equality of female and male in creation and disobedience, in erotic joy, in mundane crisis. She concludes that female imagery "is not a minor theme" but "with persistence and power it saturates scripture"; some texts about male and female yield "the grace of sexuality, not the sin of sexism." Recognizing the permanent patriarchal stamp of Scripture—accepting the radical feminist critique—Trible shows the Bible at the same time to be a "potential witness against *all* our interpretations." Her work exposes the dominant interest of past exegesis and interpretation, while it uncovers neglected strands that "reveal countervoices in a patriarchal document,"[27] voices that offer possibility for the future.

In New Testament studies, Elisabeth Schüssler Fiorenza similarly demonstrates the possibility of scholarship that is both Christian and radically feminist. She joins historical-critical methods, hermeneutic theory and feminist analysis in her discussion. Not only are there patriarchal texts and traditions in the Bible, and texts that centuries of exegesis, preaching, and theology have misinterpreted. In addition, she questions androcentric (male-centered) *traditioning:* "whether the original narrator or author in an androcentric way has told history that was not androcentric at all."[28] She points out that

the New Testament does not transmit a single androcentric statement or sexist story of Jesus, although he lived and preached in a patriarchal culture. . . . In the fellowship of Jesus, women apparently did not play a marginal role, even though only a few references to women disciples survived the androcentric tradition and redaction process of the gospels.[29]

Those references lead Schüssler Fiorenza to uncover the importance of women as apostolic witnesses of Jesus' ministry, death, and resurrection *and* the tendency of the New Testament authors to "play down the women's role as witnesses and apostles of the Easter event."[30] She analyzes traces of women's history in the New Testament to demonstrate the presence of a vigorous female ministry and participation in early Christianity. When the evidence about women is presented, there is a mass of data to show that Galations 3:28 was not an abstract ideal, but a political reality in the early church.[31]

Schüssler Fiorenza further challenges the interpretive models used by scholars whose understanding of reality is androcentric. She goes beyond the thematic approach of "women and the Bible" or "female imagery for God" to argue for an interpretative model of early Christianity that accounts for the data about women disciples, apostles, prophets, teachers, missionaries, patrons, founders, and leaders of congregations *and* the importance of women and the divine female principle in the Gnostic communities, the complaint, for example, of Tertullian in the second century that women dared "to teach, to debate, to exorcise, to promise cures, probably even to baptize." She suggests that the early Christian writings are not objective, factual history but pastorally engaged writings that, despite the androcentric traditioning process, reveal another story.[32]

Schüssler Fiorenza shows that the orthodoxy/heresy framework of interpretation has already given way to a theory of ecclesial patriarchalization occurring over centuries through the New Testament and patristic eras, understandable sociologically, but sometimes argued by historians as *necessary* for the early church's survival. In this way, patriarchy is used to legitimate the historical subordination of women. In contrast to this position, she offers an egalitarian model of early Christianity as a conflict movement, based on the discovery that Christianity was not originally patriarchal or integrated into patriarchal society.[33] That the Jesus movement and the early Christian missionary movement were countercultural, radically egalitarian and inclusive, accounts for the evidence about women (and other marginal people) in the Jesus traditions and about women (and the abolition of social distinctions of race, religion, sex, and class) in the early missionary traditions.

Only an egalitarian model for the reconstruction of early Christian history can do justice to both the egalitarian traditions of women's leadership in the church as well as to the gradual process of adaptation and theological justification of the dominant patriarchal Greco-Roman culture and society.[34]

Schüssler Fiorenza works from an interest in the past that attempts to free its emancipatory impulses and traditions for the future and with an implicit notion of the ambiguity of religious symbols and texts when she suggests that "a biblical interpretation which is concerned with the *meaning* of the bible in a post-patriarchal culture" would have to hold that "biblical revelation and truth about women are found . . . in those texts which transcend and criticize their patriarchal culture," that is, texts which display an authentic religious horizon, and that "such texts should be used to evaluate and to judge the patriarchal texts of the Bible."[35]

From these examples in historical and biblical studies, the profoundly ambiguous character of the Christian tradition and its symbolism when read from a contemporary feminist perspective is apparent. At the same time, the challenge raised by Mary Daly and Carol Christ—of the essentially patriarchal and so irreformable character of Christianity's core symbolism—is itself brought into question. Ruether's critique of the ideologies of sexism is itself based on basic Jewish and Christian symbols of love: equality, mutuality, reciprocity, service, in the context of the prophetic traditions of the Bible. Trible and Schüssler Fiorenza, in different ways, use the "countervoices" of the Bible as theoretical and practical witness against traditional sexist interpretations. Each finds in the tradition itself not merely "something more" to affirm but a more that bears within itself the moment of negation. These biblical and historical studies suggest that theology too, when interpreted from a feminist perspective, will yield a similar dialectic.

THEOLOGICAL CONSIDERATIONS

Feminist theology is just beginning to address central theological symbols of Christianity from a systematic perspective.[36] The implications of feminist critical theory for the doctrines of the human person, sin and grace, ministry, have been the immediate issue.[37] The most important and difficult symbols, however, because of their centrality in the tradition and the issue of maleness, are the doctrines of God and Jesus Christ. The work of Trible, Schüssler Fiorenza, and Ruether, however, undercuts the claim that these symbols are *intrinsically* patriarchal, that they *necessarily* legitimate the subordination of women. In Trible's study:

The repetition of the word *God* establishes similarity between the Creator and the human creatures, while the addition of the word *the-image-of* connotes their difference. Here the lack of any formal parallelism between the two components suggests a semantic disparity. Thus, this latter metaphor saves the former from idolatry by witnessing to the transcendent Creator who is neither female nor male nor a combination of the two. Only in the context of this Otherness, can we truly perceive the image of God male *and* female.[38]

Schüssler Fiorenza writes:

The fatherhood of God radically prohibits any ecclesial patriarchal self-understanding. The lordship of Christ categorically rules out any relationship of dominance within the Christian community. According to the gospel tradition Jesus radically rejected all relationships of dependence and domination.[39]

And in a similar vein, Ruether:

Traditional theological images of God as father have been the sanctification of sexism and hierarchicalism precisely by defining this relationship of God as father to humanity in a domination-subordination model and by allowing ruling-class males to identify themselves with this divine fatherhood in such a way as to establish themselves in the same kind of hierarchical relationship to women and lower classes. Jesus, however, refers to God as father in such a way as to overthrow this . . . relationship of the rulers over the ruled.[40]

Stressing themes of the otherness of God in the Bible, or icono-clasm and egalitarianism, or women's service in the ministry of Jesus and in early Christianity, however important, does not suffice. These historical themes must be brought to explicit theological, ethical, and practical reflection today. For as Daly and others point out, Jesus was a male; the dominant biblical images of God are male. And in-herently male symbols are no help to alienated women *because* they have functioned so effectively in history to legitimate the subordina-tion of women. This point may not be trivialized. Feminist reflection on the doctrines of God and of Christ that shows that God is not male and that Jesus' maleness is a purely contingent fact must further at-tend to the effective history of these doctrines, their practical and po-litical uses. Only if the effects of these symbols and doctrines are transformed now and in the future can it be claimed that the symbols and doctrines are not intrinsically patriarchal, that they can be made available to women. A pragmatic criterion of the future emerges that holds that the truth of theological formulation lies in its effects.[41] Given the effects of the past, any adequate contemporary formula-tion of the doctrine of God or of Christology must unmask past ideo-logical uses of the symbols and attend to their transformative, ethical, and futural horizons of interpretation. The contemporary hermen-eutic situation includes both past and future in its "applicative" mo-ment. And given the universality of the hermeneutic viewpoint, this applies to any responsible theology, not just "liberation" theology.

Theology reflects on the symbols of God and Christ given us by the Bible and centuries of tradition. Each symbol is partial, embed-ded in a cluster of other symbols and a network of myths out of which its meaning arises. It is the symbol, in Ricoeur's aphorism, that gives rise to thought and bears within itself both regressive and anticipa-tory possibilities. Thus the symbols for God, whether mother or fa-ther, king or servant, warrior God or God of slaves, intrinsically demand their own negation. The fatherhood of God bears its own critique and its transcendence of human fatherhood, especially in the Christian narrative perspective of Jesus' radical relativization of all family ties and affirmation of God's closeness in a new spiritual family.[42] All the symbols yield finally to awareness that none of the pictures depicts God; none of the symbols grasps the transcendent. They can only be interpreted anew, in succeeding historical situations, "constantly needing," in Schleiermacher's phrase, "to be refashioned for these present times."

The interpretive framework of our time must include critique of the social effects and ideological uses of symbols and doctrines of God as well as ethical and transformative application in the present situation. While feminist theology points out the false uses of an idolatrous male God and its damaging effects on women, on other oppressed groups, and on nature, its further task is to search out a doctrine of God that is related to the intellectual, practical, and ethical concerns of the present situation of women and that suggests transformative or emancipative possibilities for the future. At present it may reassert the "not-yet," eschatological dimension of the Bible or the powerful tradition of negative theology, the ultimately hidden God, the mystery and final incomprehensibility of God. Beyond these negations, however, it continues to affirm God's intimacy to persons and to the human community in its present experience.[43]

Contemporary interpretations of the doctrine of God have in fact developed concepts derived from the Bible and tradition in dialogue with contemporary experience that, while maintaining the transcendence of God, newly affirm God as involved in the ordinary experience of women and men in this world. There is a widespread theological affirmation that the God of Christian faith, while remaining God, is intimately involved in the joy and the pain, the hope and struggle of human existence and comes to be known, in fact, precisely there. These interpretations reveal common themes: the mystery of human experience and its transcendent source or horizon; temporality, the future, and the historical process; human autonomy, freedom, and responsibility; ultimate human dependence and limit, fundamental trust, the reasonableness of belief in God in one's individual life. These themes are open to critical feminist appropriation insofar as they have moved beyond parent/child models of the divine/ human relationship: they are conceptions of God as future, as the enabling source of human freedom and autonomy, as the ground of trust in the experience of the self and its possibilities of actualization and self-transcendence.[44] Similarly, political and liberation theologies, with their criticisms of a privatized, individualistic understanding God and of human persons, and their attention to the history of the suffering of oppressed groups, have developed these themes in relation to the collective struggles of humankind for liberation in a social and political apprehension of God's reality and character in corporate human existence.[45]

It is precisely here, I believe, in the collective interests of human liberation, that Christian feminist theology is self-critical as well as critical of the tradition, is willing to revitalize—not trivialize or negate—its claims in relation to social and political issues and to fully human religious issues of finitude, suffering, death, hope, transformation— the question of God. This feminism relates itself to wider concerns: other liberation movements, social reconstruction, distributive justice, ecology, peace, and masculinity (not men) as a system of hierarchies and dominating, exploitative, manipulative powers.[46] This Christian feminist theology sees feminism itself—the woman— as the focal symbol, the original "other" in a culture and society that generates a series of oppressive relationships. It is a peculiarly powerful symbol, at once public or collective and closely personal. Transformation of the male/female relational system and the analogous series of exploitative relationships parallels new interpretation of the doctrine of God in relation to the self, human freedom, autonomy, the future, and to collective struggles for justice.[47]

In Christology, feminist criticism has attended to the uses of the maleness of Jesus as a symbol that legitimates dominating systems in family, church, and society (for example, the notion of headship) and to messages of self-sacrifice, sacrificial love, and *imitatio Christi* that have been detrimental to the essential self-affirmation of women. It is clear why Christian feminism has focused so far on the ministry and message of Jesus in his acceptance of women and his prophetic reversals of societal and familial orders. Jesus' maleness is understood theologically as purely contingent in the light of the patristic dictum about the incarnation: "what was not assumed is not redeemed." In a profound sense, Jesus' sex does not make any difference for feminists whose cause is, finally, to emancipate sexuality from its distorted societal and religious valorization, to overcome and transform traditional dualisms into a broader pluralism that accounts for the variety of human qualities, talents, and choices, to move beyond anatomy as destiny in human valuation. But such an affirmation may not be made too soon; it is a projection of a future possibility if and when the maleness of Jesus ceases to be used theologically, ethically, and ecclesiastically against women. Jesus as the Christ is affirmed by feminist women only after a series of negations of traditional interpretations and uses of this symbol.

At the same time, recent developments in Christology offer possibility for critical feminist appropriation in their emphasis on the truly human Jesus and the story of his conflict with the dominant powers as the revelation of God. A searching Christology (Rahner), the Logos as creative transformation (Cobb), human suffering, oppression, and liberation in the cross of Jesus (Moltmann), the active discipleship of Jesus in the cause of justice (Sobrino), the rhetoric of inclusion of all human concerns (van Beeck), the prophetic iconoclastic Christ (Ruether), are Christological interpretations that transcend traditional biases toward women; images of lordly power, domination, and triumphalism have been left behind.[48] Emphasis on the future *humanum* as the liberating "wholeness that we seek" is especially clear in the hermeneutical Christology of Edward Schillebeeckx, who argues that it is necessary "to have a constant movement to and fro between the biblical interpretation of Jesus and the interpretation of our present-day experiences," that the story of Jesus is revelatory only if it effectively discloses that sought for *humanum* in contemporary terms.[49]

What place has Jesus of Nazareth in this whole history of human suffering in quest of meaning, liberation and salvation? . . . Jesus' universal significance cannot be affirmed unmediated or by some abstractly objectivizing argument, apart from continuing, concrete effects of Jesus' history. . . . What speaks to us in Jesus is his being human, and thereby opening up to us the deepest possibilities for our own life, and *in this* God is expressed. The divine revelation in Jesus directs us to [the human] mystery.[50]

The present-day experience of Christian women finds, in the New Testament and traditional doctrines of Christ, symbols of the divine and of the human to negate and something more to affirm, both memory and anticipation. The negative critique of past and present uses of Christ to legitimate the subordination of women (and other groups in Christian history) emerges from the positive, new, even surprising contemporary and futural apprehension of the revelation of God in Jesus: the unconditional assurance that humanity's cause is God's cause, in Schillebeeckx's words, that the God of "pure positivity" wills human beings to live, that God gives a future to the hopeless *in us*. Hence, Christian feminists do not project an alien cause on the figure of Jesus. It is rather through a religious critique of symbols, "on inner symbolic grounds," that feminism can identify with Christ and the world of possibility he projects.

Women's religious protest and affirmation can indeed be understood as a grace for our times. In its protest about the clear and real issue of women, it raises to view the scandal of the past and that scandal's confident, often idolatrous, assertions about God and Christ and human persons. In its courageous iconoclasm and its symbolic association with the other "others" of history and the present, Christian feminist thought exposes and denies the splits and dichotomies, manipulation and exploitation—the sin of our times from a particular and practical perspective. In its new apprehension of God and of Christ it affirms a vision of human wholeness, integrity, and relational community, a genuinely new Christian consciousness that extends inclusion, mutuality, reciprocity, and service beyond its own causes. In so doing, Christian feminism transcends itself and presses the tradition to transcend itself, to become the hope, the future that is promised.

III. FEMINISM AND THEOLOGY

6. Theological Anthropology and the Experience of Women

In this chapter, the theoretical concerns mentioned in chapters 4 and 5 are brought to bear on one of the deepest issues in feminist theology—the question of what it means to be human in a Christian theological framework of understanding. I argue that the "nature" of being human is in human hands and that human being is changing because of the reflection of women on their own experience.

Contemporary theology is widely characterized by its concern with human experience in all its variety. Theologians such as Tillich and Rahner have argued for the need to correlate the kerygma with the "situation" in theology, the need today to search for "the connections by correspondence" between revelation and experience.[1] David Tracy has reformulated Tillich's method as "the critical correlation of the meaning and the truth of the interpreted Christian fact (. . . the texts, symbols, witnesses, and tradition of the past and present) and the meaning and truth of the interpreted contemporary situation."[2] This concern with the pluralism of experience of the human situation is apparent in the focus of political and liberation theologies on the experience of the poor under oppressive social and economic systems, and in the radical grounding of theological discussion in the specific contexts of the particular experiences that characterize the Latin American or the black communities.

Christian feminist theology, too, has explored the implications of the gospel and the Christian tradition in relation to the experience of women as a subordinate class in both church and society. Feminist theologians have criticized theological perspectives and institutional structures that place women in secondary status and have been concerned to reformulate Christian theology and to restructure the church's institutional life in a manner consonant with both their own new experience and with the gospel, particularly in its message of equality: "there are no more distinctions between Jew and Greek, slave and free, male and female, but all of you are one in Christ Jesus" (Galatians 3:28).

One part of this critical and revisionist work of feminist theology has focused on the meaningfulness of traditional theological categories in relation to the experience of women, sometimes suggesting the harmfulness of certain masculine theological perspectives and sometimes offering alternative approaches. This chapter explores aspects of this recent discussion as it touches on fundamental issues of Christian theological anthropology and thus affects the church's theology, preaching, patterns of pastoral care, and its liturgical and institutional life generally.

THE EXPERIENCE OF WOMEN

Where does the theologian locate the experience of women as a source for theological reflection? Here the significance of Tracy's notion of the *interpreted* meaning of the contemporary situation becomes clear. The theologian studies interpretations of various sorts: reflections on personal and collective experience, cultural creations, social scientific studies, and other religious and theological interpretations of women's experience. In the large body of feminist literature, secular and religious, which has accumulated in recent decades, there is broad agreement about the situation of women as subordinate in the context of patriarchy and sexism, both in the private and the societal dimensions of human life. Feminists are united in efforts to analyze the fundamental injustice in this situation and in discussion of strategies for overcoming it.

In this search for the meaning and truth of the contemporary experience of women, however, a particular problem arises. It is difficult to universalize this experience, for women are as uniquely individual as men. Because of the variety of female experience, especially in different cultures and classes, one must be wary of absolutizing any particular set of experiences or any single interpretation as *the* experience of women.

Thus, Judith Plaskow indicates that her description of the experience of women refers to white, middle-class, Western women as disclosed in contemporary novels about women and women's fundamental problem of autonomy or self-actualization.[3] The temptation or "sin" of such women, she argues, is that of not acquiring a strong sense of self, of failing to assume responsibility, to make reasoned and free decisions, to take hold of their lives. She concludes that theological formulations that view sin primarily as prideful self-assertion and grace as self-sacrificial love fail to speak to the experience of women who have sacrificed too much of their selves. It is clear that while this discussion has powerful meaning for some women, it may not be appropriate to women in other cultural situations or to some women within the white, Western middle class. Like the pluralism that characterizes theology generally today, there is pluralism in the experience of women and so in feminist theology as well. Women theologians are not of a single mind with regard to all issues or strategies. This pluralism, moreover, is partly due to radically different interpretations of the experience of women in our culture.

An enduringly valuable analysis of some of these diverse interpretations is provided by Aquin O'Neill in an article from the midseventies that describes contemporary secular feminism in its three "faces."[4] In a survey of the then current literature, she discerned three fundamental interpretations of the experience of women with regard to the sources of sexism and its remedies. The first group explains the cause of women's subordination simply as male supremacy; men are the agents of oppression. In this view, male domination is the oldest and primary form of exploitation, and all other oppressions are its extensions. The strategy proposed by this form of feminism, both in cool analytical terms and in rhetorical challenge, is radical separatism, celibacy. Men must be forced to change. None of the blame can be placed on women themselves. The second face of feminism is quite opposite. In this view, women are to blame for their current situation of inferiority and powerlessness. They are unwilling to grow up, to assume responsibility for themselves and to make the decisions demanded of them by rapid social change. Victims of their own self-hatred, women are accused of a failure of nerve in which they have not dared to claim their own freedom. This form of feminism does not question the character of the greater liberty that men enjoy, but urges women to assume it for themselves. The third face of contemporary feminism is critically directed toward social structures and reigning cultural mythologies about women. Elizabeth Janeway, for example, argues that two myths about women undergird the age-old division of "man's world, woman's place"— myths of female weakness and female power. "The first, which is older . . . holds the second at bay" and constitutes a strong pressure for keeping women in a defined, secondary position in society.[5] This traditional notion of a single, defined "place," however, runs counter to the whole trend of Western civilization (and, one might add, Christian views) that stress the freedom, responsibility, and transcendence of the human person. Women long to be treated as complete persons, and the way for this to come about is through concerted critique of myths about women and change of societal structures. Such change would mean that men as well as women would have wider choices in a less rigidly gender-based social system. These feminists propose specific changes in social policy to free women and men, and society itself, from patriarchy and sexism.

Another set of fundamental differences within feminist thought concerns the cultural and religious valuation of female sexual power and the traditional relation of women to natural processes and to nature itself in contrast with the valuation of the male and the masculine relationship to culture. Much feminist analysis recognizes some form of dualism as the basis or consequence of this difference in valuation and as the source of the asymmetry in interpretation of the masculine/feminine distinction in Western urbanized society.[6] Rosemary Radford Ruether, for example, argues persuasively that, while in tribal and pre-urban cultures the close relation of the entire community to nature and natural process is commonly celebrated in myth and symbol by both women and men, a sharp split occurs between nature and culture in the transition to urban and then to industrial society.[7] Males celebrate freedom and transcendence of nature in cultural creativity, while the realm of nature and natural bodily processes becomes the domain of women. However, feminist theorists take several positions on the issue of dualism.

Some accept the dualism, celebrate the uniqueness of female spiritual experience, and insist that there is a transformative power in women's close relationship to nature and natural process. This power may derive from women's own bodily and spiritual makeup or may simply be the result of centuries of historical and cultural conditioning. While these writers recognize that women's roles of childbearing and nurture of the young often have been oppressive, they believe that a legacy of oppression can be turned into a source of vision and power. Carol Christ's method of literary analysis is a striking example of this form of feminism. She explores the unique dimensions of women's spiritual quests, using Erich Neumann's psychological theory about female knowing as primarily a mode of participation and identification, whereas the male mode is differentiation. In religious terms, "participation and union of a nonpersonal core of the self with the whole" would be the most typical, though not the only, form of female religious experience, as contrasted to "confrontation or encounter" as the primary form of male religious insight.[8] This position is viewed with some nervousness by other feminists who are conscious of the danger of stereotypical thinking that such a celebration of male/female difference can encourage.

A second position on this question accepts the male/female differentiation and views the transcendent, cultural pole as more highly valued than the immanent, natural side. Women are therefore urged to assume their place on the transcendent side of the duality. Though not a widespread view, it is the position taken by Shulamith Firestone in her controversial manifesto *The Dialectic of Sex.*[9] She envisions a future when technology will free women from their bodily ties to reproduction and thus to nature. Artificial reproduction would mean not only the liberation of women but also a situation in which there would be no significant distinction between male and female; women would in fact become like men. The experience of women, in this view, is so alienated that women seeking equality would give up completely their natural and biological positions as bearers and nurturers of the young in order to participate equally in male liberty. Firestone dedicates her book to Simone de Beauvoir who, though she does not accept the male/female dualism, nevertheless accepts a transcendence/immanence polarity, a body/mind dualism that is inherently conflictual.

For de Beauvoir, the male/female dualism is a mythology to be overcome. The experience of women in oppressive immanence, "the eternal feminine," is richly documented in her feminist classic *The Second Sex*.[10] She describes the experience of women as one of longing for participation in transcendence and liberty. Arguing that there are no eternal essences of male and female, she envisions a world where women are welcomed into full "brotherhood" with men. Since de Beauvoir's groundbreaking work, feminist analysis has more commonly taken a position that also recognizes the dualism of male/female, culture/nature as culturally imposed and created ideologies that are destructive of human wholeness. Dualism issues in stereotypes that are as harmful for men as for women. Women's experience is one of deep dissatisfaction with relegation simply to the private realm of immanence, of home and family, though its values are not ones they wish to forego. Rather, women look for participation in the public world as well, and for the incorporation of traditional, so-called feminine values into that world. This feminism urges that women (and men) must assume their place in the fullness of both dimensions of human experience. Ruether argues that rejection of the traditional identification of women with nature would be to "buy into that very polarization of which we have been the primary victims."[11] And Plaskow criticizes the dualism of culture and nature as it finds expression in theological views that stress the conflict between transcendence and creatureliness rather than their harmony. She claims that "immersion in and transcendence of nature" are "two scarcely separable moments of experience."[12]

While the first approach to the nature/culture dualism focuses on it as the source of the unequal situation of women and develops strategies for overcoming it, the second is concerned with women's experience of identification with nature and its consequent significance for their experience. In both approaches, however, it is evident that "experience" is an elastic term. It includes the past, both personal and historical, the present, however variously interpreted, and the anticipated future: a variety of hopes, longings, desires are clearly a major part of women's experience. Further, neither approach signifies airtight categories. Feminist theorists stress one or the other way of viewing the experience of women depending on the problem being addressed. But all are one in asserting the historical and contemporary oppression of women as a class, whatever variations in experience arise from the particular conditions of women's universal subordination.

THE NATURE OF WOMEN

It is not surprising that similar versions of the experience of women appear in recent Catholic discussions of theological anthropology in which distinct positions on human nature or the nature of women emerge again. It was O'Neill who first suggested that three basic "visions of humanity" arise from the chorus of voices that comprise contemporary feminism. In her first type she sees a new expression of the traditional view that the division of female and male involves a polarity in which each sex embodies different possibilities of being human, possibilities from which the other sex is excluded. Derivations are made, in this view, from the biological to the psychological, social, and spiritual planes in determining the characteristics of male and female. The emphasis here is on difference and complementarity. This position, she points out, is fraught with problems, the chief of which is that defining male and female polarities (activity/passivity, reason/intuition, emotion/will, etc.) denies the wholeness of human experience and the hopes of women themselves. In this vision of humanity, the activities of each sex are rigidly limited, as is the scope of human freedom, judgment, and responsibility over nature. It is a version of "anatomy is destiny" that ignores the impact of cultural conditioning and expectations. "Neither sex can embody the fullness of humanity, nor can a person of one sex serve as a model for the other."[13] In O'Neill's second vision of humanity, the goal of human life is androgynous existence. In this view, sexual differences are seen as purely biological, affecting only the reproductive roles of human beings. Men and women are free to adopt styles of being that include the best of traditional masculine and feminine characteristics—both strength and sensitivity, rationality and gentleness—in the search for the fullness of humanity. In this view, emphasis is placed on the similarities rather than the differences between men and women. While it is an attractive vision, it has problems as well, for it ignores the importance of human embodiment so emphasized, for example, in recent phenomenology. And it presents the specter of a single human ideal, which may be destructive of the variety and difference in human beings. O'Neill's third type envisions a unisex goal for humanity. And though one could imagine that sex being female, in fact the proponents of this vision call for assimilation of the female to the male model of humanity. Firestone's arguments for freeing women from the oppression of bodily tyranny seem to indicate a stage of female alienation where male characteristics are so highly valued that all real differences between the sexes should be obliterated. Nevertheless, the unisex goal may have a rhetorical power that serves to jolt society into awareness of the seriousness of the marginalized position of women and thus encourage less radical steps toward genuine equality.

O'Neill concludes by pointing to the challenge of feminism to Christian theological anthropology: what vision of humanity, what goal for human life is proposed in Christian revelation? Is it the same for both men and women? Would it be sinful to cultivate certain ways of being human? How does salvation in Christ relate to the traditional dominance of men in Western society? And what does such salvation offer to women? Two theological studies have attempted some answers to these questions.

The issue of the "nature of women" is considered in the 1978 *Research Report* of the Catholic Theological Society of American (CTSA), which studied official theological argumentation about the question of the ordination of women.[14] In one of its sections, the *Report* notes the difference in anthropological presuppositions in such arguments. Using a simplified typology, it suggests that arguments against the ordination of women imply a two-nature or dual anthropology in which a complementary duality between the sexes is seen as inherent in nature (the "order of creation") and therefore part of the divine plan. This duality "is the ordering principle for complementary roles, functions and activities of women and men." On the other hand, arguments in favor of the ordination of women generally presuppose a one-nature or single anthropology in which "there are no preordained roles or functions, beyond the biological, for either men or women since the appropriate activities of the individual are extrapolated from spiritual and personal characteristics."[15] As the *Report* indicates, fundamental theological differences are entailed in each view.

While there are no longer assertions of the inferiority of women in Christian ecclesiastical or theological discourse, many official Catholic documents affirm a dual anthropology, the complementarity or "different but equal" status of men and women as inherent in nature, in the created order, and therefore as part of the divine plan. This is the basis from which the complementary roles and functions of the sexes are determined. Beyond the biologically determined psychological and sociological characteristics and the limited scope of human freedom already noted, the *Report* states that this view finds a central analogy between "nature" and the economy of salvation. This is often expressed in the marriage symbolism of the relation of Christ to the church (activity-passivity) as a relation of husband to wife (male to female). The dual anthropology emphasizes the unchanging structures of nature and views revelation, tradition, theology and ethics as past-oriented: what is, has been given in nature by God and must not be changed. New knowledge of the human person, derived from the biological and human sciences, is irrelevant to theological discussion since the goal of theology is to preserve the past order as natural, as the order of creation, and therefore as revealed by God.

The single anthropology is radically opposite. Besides its negation of rigidly defined roles for men or women beyond the biological, the *Report* observes that this anthropology puts emphasis on history and the data of experience rather than on "nature," and so affirms the importance of the human sciences for theological reflection. Greater scope is given to human freedom and responsibility, since past social patterns are more likely to be construed as human products rather than as God-given permanent structures. The emphasis on history, whose changing patterns are seen as the responsibility of human agency, entails views of revelation, tradition, theology, and ethics as sourced in present experience as well as the past.

In evaluating the two models, the CTSA *Report* notes that while the single anthropology may be criticized for its neglect of the significance of human bodiliness and sexuality and of the results of centuries of social and cultural conditioning on the "nature" of women, it is nevertheless the sounder basis for theological discussion. Thus contemporary biology, as it indicates the active and not merely passive role of women in sexual relations and procreation, for example, cautions against the use of biological dualism as male activity and female passivity in theological argument. Contemporary psychology discredits unproven assumptions about "feminine psychology" and distinctive feminine characteristics or virtues. Historical studies demonstrate the variety of leadership roles that women have assumed in the past, showing that stereotyped notions of women's nature, place, or role are not universal or unchanging.[16] Sociology and anthropology analyze the position of women in patriarchal cultures, so as to caution against arguments that the nature of women can be determined from particular past societal patterns.

Moreover, the authors of this *Report* point to the Second Vatican Council's affirmation of the importance of history, of revelation as historical, personal, and ongoing as well as past, and of the increased centrality of human responsibility in relation to the structures of church and society, all signaled in the phrase, "the signs of the times." The importance of these themes argues against the assumption of a dual anthropology or of a one-sided emphasis on established structures as natural, the order of creation, the divine choice. Noting recent Vatican statements recognizing the women's movement as a necessary and positive effort for the achievement of equality for women in society, the *Report* concludes that "the assumption of a dual anthropology, derived from cultural and religious situations which assumed the inferiority and subordination of women as a class, is unsound."[17] It urges the need for the church's self-criticism with regard to institutional and ideological forms that perpetuate and legitimize unequal views of women and asserts that a dual anthropology means an uncritical acceptance of patriarchal structures as "normal" and so willed by God rather than as historically conditioned human products. The feminist critique of cultural and religious stereotypes about women as passive, emotional, and dependent must confront theological arguments that invoke "feminine psychology," the "headship of the male," and the "complementarity of the sexes"—all of which can be understood as rationalizations for the subordination of women.

When the CTSA met the following year for discussion of "The Meaning of the Human," the question of theological anthropology and the feminist critique was picked up once again by Mary Buckley. Using a form of the critical correlational method, she analyzed the experience of women, especially as reflected in the social sciences, in the light of biblical revelation and Christian faith.

In Buckley's view, a third vision of humankind is struggling into existence today, a "transformative, person-centered model." She sees both the dual and single anthropologies as inadequate because they reflect society as it was and as it is. Further, these models place the impetus for change simply on individual efforts. Her third, transformative model is both personal and public: it transforms the old gender stereotypes at the same time that it aims to transform the social and cultural structures that are their inseparable context in human life. She argues that this transformative model receives its impetus from changes that have begun to take place in society and from the Christian faith as it calls all persons to likeness to the God of Jesus in "love, compassion, mercy, peace, service, care and community."[18] Both men and women are called to this likeness, not the half-person-hood of complementarity that often conceals a hidden domination, but to an equality that breaks the confines of sex and race and class.

But how, in fact, is this model different from the single anthropology of the CTSA *Report* with its expressed aim of an androgynous goal for all humanity in which "either sex can and should develop those qualities traditionally associated with the other" and in which "greater scope is given to human agency and responsibility in changing . . . the structures of human life?" It is different, according to Buckley, because of its more explicit acknowledgement that anthropological models are not merely formal, individualistic concepts but rather are embedded in particular social contexts. Thus the dual anthropology corresponds to a hierarchic-elitist model of society. It is a model present in clearest form since the rise of the state and the development of political ruling classes, although it was broken in principle by the English, American, and French revolutions. On the other hand, the one-nature model corresponds to the "one-dimensional" society, a product of the modern period, and is associated with the revolutions' ideals of freedom, equality, brotherhood, and democracy. Despite the inspiring ideals of this vision, experience has proved that "under the cloak of democracy, the real ruling groups have been hidden."[19] In America, for example, blacks, Indians, newly arrived immigrants—and women—must struggle to have a voice; the upper elite is really the paradigm for all people, and thus women and minorities must conform to the single (male, white, Protestant) norm.

Buckley adds that, in order for this transformative vision of a new society to come to pass, a critical task must be performed that probes deeply into the distorted social systems in which we live. This is an arduous task that calls for courage, knowledge, independence, initiative, and responsibility, the ability to challenge and to struggle—qualities traditionally associated with male humanity. Hence, she argues, both "feminine" and "masculine" qualities are needed by both women and men. And in religious terms, repentance and conversion are needed not only by individuals but also at the institutional levels of church and society. The transformative vision may appear utopian, but such is the liberating vision of the reign of God in which the personal and the public are joined.

THEOLOGICAL REFLECTION

This experience of women, in its plural contemporary expressions, surely demands the attention of the church in its theology, preaching, and pastoral care, its liturgical and institutional life. Here, some initial theological appraisal of that experience is suggested through a dual critique. What does the experience of women have to say to the church? And what does the church's gospel message offer to the experience of women? Finally, a perspective will be sketched on the relation of experience to the question of human nature.

There are important dimensions of truth in each expression of the feminist experience we have described. The first "face" of feminism, which expresses anger toward men and appears to entail a reverse sexism, can be a necessary stage in the experience of Christian women. Feminists have long recognized the significance of women's anger as a first step toward greater self-determination. The church can sensitively deal with the anger women sometimes feel, their need for a period or place of separation in which to discover, affirm, and strengthen their own powers. Such separation, in which women find support and challenge from one another, may be a temporary or ongoing but partial dimension of an authentically Christian experience, particularly in the shedding of false forms of innocence and in the assumption of adult responsibility. There is a legitimate anger on the part of women toward those structures (more often than individuals) or traditions that have demanded and expected less than full personhood of them. Nevertheless, the ultimate goal of any Christian perspective demands a wider, indeed universal, vision of the community and solidarity of all persons. In the light of gospel values, then, a "separatist" position cannot be a final one for Christians: the ultimate goal is an inclusive mutuality: "all one in Jesus Christ."[20]

A similar Christian critique relates to the second "face" of feminism, which claims that women themselves are to blame for failing to assume responsibility for their lives. Placing blame, either on men or women, can only be a provisional moment in the process of coming to full adulthood. And while blame, either of oneself or another, may be an important step, too much blame is finally destructive. The church can reflect on Jesus's word about loving the neighbor as the self: the message of love, not hatred of self, is an important Christian word for women to hear. A moment of self-blame can be significant to the extent that women are content to hide behind myths of dependency, fail to decide about their own lives, drift into decision according to familial or societal expectation. The feminist critique, however, plays back upon Christian interpretations that keep women in a "place" that prevents their equal and responsible participation and upon a church that fails to challenge women to full adult freedom and responsibility.

The face of feminism that focuses on social structures and the underlying myths that support them is one that the whole church needs to reflect on seriously. While such myths and structures are not the entire truth about the human person from a Christian perspective, they do condition the scope of human freedom. While affirming individual freedom, the church can aid women in coming to full personhood by applying its gospel principles in critical scrutiny of the culture in which women's self-understanding and range of choices are formed. The message of human dignity and equality before God differs radically from cultural and religious myths about women as moral paragons or temptresses, superwomen or helpless housewives. Such myths deserve not only feminist but Christian criticism as well. Images in the media, for example, are powerful symbols that work on the imagination to shape notions of value, meaning, success. What image of authentic human life does the church present to women, and to the whole Christian community, about women? Is the perspective of its preaching on the situation of women (whether single, married, divorced, working inside or outside the home, professional) one that aids the authentic discovery of self and God in contemporary culture? If the church fails to speak to the experience of women, perhaps feminist criticism ought to be a regular part of sermon preparation. The church's critique of the culture that produces *Cosmopolitan, Playboy* and *Penthouse* must at the same time heed the feminist critique of its own institutional forms and traditional myths about women if it is to speak to the heart of the matter for women today.

Feminists who celebrate women's special relation to nature have an important insight, born of centuries of historical experience, to offer to an over-mechanized culture faced with ecological and nuclear crises and to a church whose institutional life often appears bureaucratically structured, rigid, sexist. If such women leave Christianity to find their spiritual homes in the new feminist religions, what response does the church offer? While it may offer critique of the separatist tendencies of some feminist spirituality, its word will not be seriously heard until it integrates women and their experience more fully into its own structures, practical life, and worship in genuine solidarity.

So too with the opposite feminist experience that places absolute value on the transcendent, cultural pole of the traditional male/female division. If the church is to address contemporary women's desire to participate in the full range of cultural, societal, and public life with a meaningful Christian perspective, it will have to see that its own institutional life offers opportunity for that full participation as well. Then its gospel critique of this position—the values of home and family; the inherent limitations of all human choice; sin, finitude, suffering, and lack of human fulfillment as abiding human problems and not simply the result of patriarchy—will be a wisdom that can be welcomed by contemporary women.

The more common feminist experience that values both sides of the traditional dualism relates most closely to gospel norms. For the nature/culture polarity can readily be transposed to biblical and theological ideas of the limitations of human creaturehood or finitude and the transcendence of human freedom and spirit. Both are dimensions of human personhood, experience, and action. While the church focuses its critique on social and political forms that fail to reverence both poles (natural life *and* human agency or responsibility), the feminist critique must be heard in the church as well, with its insistence that neither pole is more fully embodied in either sex. Nature and culture are the responsibility of both men and women as human beings. The integration of this biblical and theological anthropology would be truly revolutionary in both church and society, changing the dual, gender-based character of the separation between private and public life. The gospel vision of the integrity of human creatureliness and transcendence has something important to teach the culture and women. But the feminist experience has something to teach the church as well.

What is the relation of the plurality of women's experience to the question of human nature? Karl Rahner's theological anthropology is helpful at this point. Rahner argued that the idea of nature as a static essence is false. He criticized that concept in traditional theology as one based on an uncritical, external observation of merely factual continuities in individual and society. These continuities are always in need of scrutiny lest they becomes rationalizations of given, but historically relative, social institutions. Rahner points, rather, to the importance of the creativity of human freedom, decision, and praxis as these play back into the elaboration of a never-finished concept of human nature. In Rahner's view, the unchangeable aspects of human beings are consciousness (or knowledge) and freedom in a worldly, historical context, the very conditions of possibility within which persons shape themselves before God in time and history. It is within this fundamental framework that the Christian message of sin and grace should be placed in a theological anthropology.[21]

Thus Rahner emphasizes the importance of human self-creation, and of human freedom and decision-making in the determination of what human being is and will become. It is the choice of persons themselves. Therefore, he argues, Christian women themselves will have to determine their future position in society and in the church largely out of their own experience, and this precisely within the contemporary pluralistic situation. Rahner referred to "the church of women" as central in this new determination of human nature.

While it may be true that human nature as constituted by the distinction of the sexes may endure throughout as a metaphysical reality, still the actual mode in which this one nature is objectively realized in the concrete is stamped and conditioned by the specific circumstances of history which correspond to the plurality of types and situations justifiably existing in the church.[22]

While Rahner recognized that societal situations may severely limit human freedom in its self-determination, it is the political and liberation theologians who above all have stressed even further the depth and persuasiveness of societal conditioning on freedom and responsibility as these provide the very basis and precondition for human and religious response to God.

These themes are helpful in appraising the variety of views of human nature or the nature of women, especially as they emphasize past, present, or future perspectives. While the dual anthropology conforms at least partially to the past experience of women, the single anthropology corresponds in part to women's present experience and aspiration. The transformative model indicates especially the future hopes of women for both the individual and social dimensions of human life. The single anthropology and the transformative model also indicate the element of radical human freedom in determining what human nature will become: humankind will choose whatever future human beings will be. The dual anthropology, though adequate to the historical past, clearly proves inadequate to the experience and aspiration of women and many men today and to the gospel message of equality. The single anthropology is more adequate, but fails if it capitulates to an individualistic, or single male or female model; all the virtues of the gospel are needed by all persons and must inform public, ecclesial, and societal structures as well. The transformative model is more adequate to a fully social vision of the future as it preserves awareness of the historical conditioning of the past and recognizes the struggle for equality and authentic transformation on the part of feminist women and men in the present.

Women's recent reflection on their own experience in all its variety and women's efforts to develop corresponding models of humanity is an important development in theological anthropology. Far from a merely speculative enterprise, it is a necessary exploration of past and present experience that has now become focused on the question of the future: what will humankind become? For if human persons have the power to determine, in part at least, what the human future will be, then indeed the experience of women must be heeded. How will the perspectives of the gospel, with its messages of sin and of liberation in Christ, be integrated into that future for both women and men? The church needs to pay critical attention to the changes in human nature that are occurring in the experience of women and in the "church of women" or "womenchurch" today.[23]

7. Feminist Reflections on God

Christian women who have appropriated the feminist critique of Christianity encounter both their deepest struggle and their most profound security in the fundamental doctrine or symbol of God. On the one hand, women struggle with almost exclusively male imagery for God as king, lord, master, and especially father in the language of Christian tradition and the church's practical liturgical life. The dominance of the metaphor of God as father, for example, has been described by one critic as an idol that functions to legitimize patriarchalism as a total worldview and practical ordering of reality.[1] On the other hand, women recognize in the symbol of God, in the Christian tradition and in their own experience, the ultimate source of all that is, the name of the hidden one who remains mystery, who transcends and relativizes all our human images and concepts of God.[2] According to the tradition itself, God surpasses any human attempt at naming. In Karl Rahner's metaphor, God is like the infinite sea surrounding the tiny island of our finite human existence and knowledge.[3]

Thus feminist criticism of a dominant God language that literally interprets our human metaphors, especially that of father, and reduces the reality of God in a single male measure, is a powerful grace for theology and for the church in our time. It challenges a pervasive idolatry that has crept into Christian thought and practice and at the same time provides new awareness, for women and for the whole church, of God as the fully transcendent mystery who encompasses *all* of creation, *all* of our lives in universal presence. This chapter reviews some of the important aspects of the feminist critique of language about God and suggests some of its positive implications for a renewed and empowering Christian understanding of the reality of God. It does so within the broader context of recent theological discussion that, like feminist theology, has already begun to resymbolize and reformulate the Christian understanding of God.

THE FEMINIST CRITIQUE

Feminist criticism has focused on the exclusive use of masculine language for God and especially on the literal interpretation of the father metaphor because of the negative uses, the historical and practical effects of this language for the lives of women and the human community generally. The question is bluntly put: Is God male? Despite the long theological tradition that maintains that God transcends sexuality, that there is no sex in God, both popular and theological language suggest that God is "somehow masculine," that God is "he."[4] Because of the historical contexts in which Christian images and symbols for God emerged, contexts that ascribed all eminence, superiority, dignity, and value to male human beings as distinct from the inferiority of the female, it was almost always considered appropriate to designate the personal God of Christianity as "he." The persistent use of masculine pronouns for God in theology and liturgy, the nervous reaction, even sense of blasphemy, felt by many Christians today if one dares to refer to God as "she," have led some feminists to claim that the Christian God *is* male, and that Christianity is intrinsically patriarchal, a religion of fathers and sons that is inherently demeaning for women.[5]

The feminist critique of Christian language for God as the literal interpretation of God as male or as "somehow masculine" centers especially on God as father as that metaphor derives from and legitimizes human patriarchal structures.[6] *Patriarchy* means the rule of fathers. As the dominant political, social, and familial structure in Western Christian history, patriarchy has served to stabilize a Christian church and social order that is both hierarchical and androcentric. *Hierarchy* designates a sacred or holy pattern of ruling relationships that are ordered according to status, as over and under, higher and lower. Thus they are actually or potentially dominating relations in which one person or group rules over another. Patriarchal patterns imply, first, the literal rule of fathers: men over women, husband over wife and children. Women and children are the property of husbands and fathers; women are "given" and "taken" in marriage; women and children bear the names, the identity, of husbands and fathers. In the patriarchal structures of antiquity, fathers possessed absolute rights over their children, could abandon infants, especially girls, if they were undesired. Feminist thought argues further that such patterns have issued, in the Christian West, in a whole series of unequal power relations; God as father rules over the world, holy fathers rule over the church, clergy fathers over laity, males over females, husbands over wives and children, men over the created world. Feminist criticism holds that these patriarchal and hierarchical patterns are actualized personally and politically from the most intimate of human relationships in the family, through parochial and wider church structures, to the broadest international context in which superpowers vie with one another for dominance over each other and over smaller and less powerful nations. They are patterns of dominating control, characterized by paternalism, imperialism, colonialism, and elitism. Built on the basis of the unequal father/ child or male/female relationship between God and the world or God and humankind, they are patterns of dominative inequality— dominance/submission, oppressor/oppressed—inculcated throughout the whole of human relationships and our relationship to nature.[7] And they are rooted in the oldest, perhaps originating, pattern of male domination and control of women. And as hierarchical, they claim to be holy, divinely ordered.

Androcentrism is intrinsic to patriarchal hierarchy and means male-centeredness. It indicates a worldview in which men possess all dignity, virtue, and power in contrast to women who are seen as inferior, defective, less than fully human, the alien or "other" in relation to the male human norm. Insofar as Christianity has given to the symbolism of father and son a central, determinative role in shaping its theology and practice, it is androcentric. Throughout Christian history, as theology has interpreted God as "he," as male, there has been a corresponding dominance of men in roles of leadership and authority (popes, reformers, theologians, ministers, priests) within the church. In androcentric theologies women are seen as inferior: passive, defective, complementary, auxiliary, privatized, weak, helpless, dangerous, childlike, seductive, unclean, polluting, or angelic and superior, but not fully and equally human. These theologies (or mythologies) are criticized in feminist perspectives as ideologies that elevate the interests of one group (men) to universal status and mask their real effects: the subordination and denigration of women. If Christianity is, in fact, literally and essentially a religion of fathers and sons, then the radical feminist critique is accurate; Christianity is intrinsically patriarchal and androcentric. Women who respect themselves, their mothers, sisters, and daughters as fully human, must simply depart.[8] It is harmful for women.

Feminist scholarship in anthropology and religious studies further suggests that the patriarchal image of a male God issues in "gender asymmetry" and both the religious and cultural devaluation of women. "Gender" is the highly variable cultural aspiration, attached to but distinct from biological sex, that attributes appropriate roles, behavior, and characteristics to men and women. While sex is named by the terms "male" and "female" or "man" and "woman," gender is named by the adjectives "masculine" and "feminine." And while gender appears to be "natural" in any particular culture, its variability across cultures indicates that it is a human construction, a cultural creation that nevertheless takes on powerful "objectivity" as it is deeply internalized by individuals and groups.[9]

In patriarchal societies, women have been associated with nature, as distinct from masculine culture, and with the home and private realm, as distinct from the masculine public realm. Women are ascribed secondary roles as helper and complement in relation to masculine authority, leadership, headship. And psychological and personal characteristics like passivity and emotionality are ascribed to women in contrast to masculine agency and rationality. In the systematic dualisms that emerge from this gender asymmetry, everything associated with the female—nature, the material world, the body, sexuality—is devalued while the masculine, associated with culture, mind, and spirit, is elevated as the higher value. In patriarchal culture, the religious devaluation of the feminine "other" of the masculine norm further associates women and the feminine with pollution, evil, temptation, sin: witness the history of "Eve" in the Christian context and the question of women's ability to be the image of God.[10]

In the cultural and religious world of patriarchy, powerfully legitimized by a male God, men often exhibit conscious or unconscious fear, aversion, hostility, and aggression toward women, especially women who, in their bodies, dress, or activities, trespass the boundaries of assigned context, behavior, roles, or characteristics. Some theorists suggest that the roots of this misogynism lie in male uncertainty about biological fatherhood, unconscious envy of women's child-bearing potential (and their certainty of motherhood), and/or male desire to transcend the terrors of mortality ("having been born of woman"). Thus, for example, men in patriarchal religion take over women's roles of birth and feeding in giving higher, spiritual, eternal birth (or rebirth, "birth done better") and the spiritual food of immortality, while they explicitly exclude women from these religious roles. Other theorists suggest the notion of projection: men project on women, as their intimate "other," their own negative self-perceptions. Women are thus identified with the finitude, mortality, evil, and sin of the human condition in the male attempt to disown negative human qualities.[11].

Hence, feminist criticism challenges the fundamental *reasons* for the exclusion of women from real equality in the church when it challenges the effective history, the uses and hidden functions, of an exclusively male symbolism for God in Christianity. For not only does such symbolism produce and support hierarchical and dominating family, social, and political structures, it also perpetuates, even as it masks, ancient mythologies that scapegoat and denigrate women. These patterns continue to hold women in secondary, subordinate roles in church and society while their implicit messages of inferiority are internalized by women and are continually reproduced in succeeding generations of mothers and their daughters and sons.[12]

The idol of a male divinity in heaven issues in a divinizing of male authority, responsibility, power, and holiness on earth, despite pious avowals of religious leaders about women's equality. For the symbolism is so deeply embedded in Christian theology, church structure, and liturgical practice that the Christian imagination unconsciously absorbs its destructive and exclusionary messages from childhood on. And the consequences are helpful to no one. Boys grow up believing that they really do—or should—represent God on earth in roles of authority, knowledge, dignity, and power. If they succeed, they reinforce structures of male superiority, both socially and privately. And if they are unable to actualize these superior roles, they consider themselves failures and succumb to aggression or depression. Girls internalize images of themselves as inferior, wrong, incomplete, guilty, unsure, incapable. The negative self-images perdure, even in the wake of the contemporary women's movement with its new messages. Carol Christ writes:

> Religious symbol systems focused around exclusively male images of divinity create the impression that female power can never be fully legitimate or wholly beneficent. This message need never be explicitly stated . . . for its effect to be felt. A woman completely ignorant of the myths of female evil in biblical religion nonetheless acknowledges the anomaly of female power when she prays exclusively to a male god. She may see herself as like God (created in the image of God) only by denying her own sexual identity and affirming God's transcendence of sexual identity. But she can never have the experience that is freely available to every man and boy in her culture, of having her full sexual identity affirmed as being in the image and likeness of God. . . . Her "mood" is one of trust in male power as salvific and distrust of female power in herself and other women as inferior or dangerous.[13]

In Carol Christ's perceptive analysis, an exclusively male symbolism for God effectively functions to deny women the possibility of religious affirmation of their own power, their bodies and sexuality, their will, and their positive connections with other women in history and in the present. And as women have begun in recent years to examine their inherited understandings of God, Christ's analysis is confirmed. Women report that the official language for God, received in their churches, has given them a powerful, white, male God who is a protector, benefactor, judge, a stern but loving father who requires unquestioning obedience. It is an image of God as authoritarian, as a judge "over against" the self, humankind, the world. It is an image of

God as power, in the sense of control, domination, even coercion. Women report that this image of God has instilled in them a sense of their status as children, a sense of powerlessness, dependence, distrust of their own authority, experience, and knowledge. And while such perceptions may be religiously helpful correctives to men in patriarchal culture, they are no help to women in their quest for adult autonomy, interdependence, freedom, responsibility, bodily and sexual integrity, and self-respect—characteristics necessary for an adult and fully Christian life. For some women, this God is a terror. For others, he is irrelevant and boring. While many women try to focus on the loving aspect of the father God, Christian feminists maintain that this male image of God is simply idolatrous and inadequate to the reality of God suggested in the full range of biblical and Christian tradition and in their own experience, where around and behind the church's official image of God as "he," they have discovered the reality of "the God beyond," the real God.[14]

As we have noted in previous chapters, Christian feminism disputes both the exclusive use and the literal interpretation of masculine images for God. For *no* image or symbol is an adequate "picture" of God. Every symbol requires interpretation that insists on the unlikeness of the human image to God even as it suggests some dim likeness. All human knowledge of God is analogical, and as the tradition maintains, analogies are more unlike than like in their comparison of aspects of human reality or of creation to God. This unlikeness is forgotten when a literal interpretation forgets what Sallie McFague has called the "whispered and-it-is-not" of every religious metaphor as a disclosive but partial and limited mode of religious knowledge.[15] Literal or simplistic interpretation of religious symbols has been criticized not only by feminist thought but by contemporary theological hermeneutics as well. Paul Tillich, as we saw earlier, points to the demonic and idolatrous character of interpretation that mistakes the real participation of the symbols in the depth or transcendent dimension of reality for *identity*.[16] Paul Ricoeur argues that every symbol bears both regressive (or disguised) and progressive (or revelatory) meaning within itself: all symbols must be interpreted in ways that both demystify and restore.[17] And Karl Rahner writes:

"The true radicalism in the doctrine of God can only be the continual destruction of an idol, an idol in the place of God, the idol of a theory about God." He maintained that in the Christian perspective, any knowledge or way of understanding God which absolutizes a particular mode of approach must "come under the hammer of its own principle of 'destruction'. . . ."[18]

Feminist theology here joins a wider theological tradition of critique and reformulation that has resulted in an emerging new paradigm of Christian understanding.[19] Specifically feminist perspectives, however, represent a dramatic intensification of this revisionist tradition from the particularity of the historical and contemporary religious experience, not of one oppressed race or class or minority, but of women as the majority of the human race. In its pluralism of voices, Christian feminism denies that symbols can be interpreted literally to mean that God is really a father or that God is masculine, even as it might agree that fatherhood can be interpreted nonpatriarchally, especially in the context of new cultural practices. For no symbol is oppressive in itself but becomes so in the way it is used, in its effects on the lives of people. The overwhelming weight of the demeaning and destructive historical uses and effects of the father symbol suggest that this primary symbol of God may be irretrievable for many women today. At least, it must be relativized by the use of many other images for God. These would include female symbols as the sharpest challenges to the idolatry of maleness in God and the clearest affirmation of women as the image of God. It is surely as appropriate to call God "mother" as "father" in the attribution of parenthood to God.[20] And to call God "she" would reorient and defamiliarize the Christian imagination, expand Christian understanding of God in provocative ways, not least in suggesting the goodness of female sexuality and the equal authority of the experience of women.

As we have seen, some feminist theologians argue for the importance of Goddess or Great Mother symbolism as the center of women's religious devotion, as necessary for the full religious affirmation and transcendent referent of women's power, bodies, will, and collective bonds with one another.[21] This perspective suggests that, whether innately or because of historical experience, women are heirs to a different knowledge, vision, a different approach to reality and to God. It is this knowledge that has been erased, repressed, suppressed, excluded, subjugated by masculine knowledge, culture, religion, and institutions.[22] It is a knowledge that has erupted at some places and times in history and that has burst forth anew in feminist consciousness in the present. It is a knowledge that threatens traditional, normative male institutions and patterns of knowledge so severely that it is caricatured and trivialized, or angrily rejected or ignored by men in male-dominated institutions. Or if the "different reality" of the feminine is accepted, as for example in the religious symbols of Mary and the church, it is accepted, even glorified, but always as subordinate to exclusively male language for God and male institutional control. It is co-opted and so still suppressed in its real power. The worry of churchmen about women's control of their own sexuality in the birth control and abortion controversies suggests that deeper issues of control of women and of female knowledge are at stake. Thus, while recognizing the dangers and pitfalls of the romantic myth of the "eternal feminine," this feminist approach is willing to risk its dangers because of the possibilities of, in Carol Gilligan's phrase, "a different moral voice" and vision desperately needed in our world to counteract its aggressive and dominating knowledge and institutions.[23] Both the feminist spirituality movement in America and French feminist thought thus focus on the specific *difference* represented by women rather than the sameness and equality stressed by many American feminist theorists.

Other feminist theologians believe that it is necessary to move beyond male, female, and parental images entirely or to include but relativize them by the use of many other images and symbols drawn from the Bible and Christian tradition, from adult human relationships, and from the nonpersonal realm of nature and the cosmos. Exclusively female images of God or Goddess worship can suggest a reversal of patterns of domination rather than genuine transformation: surely mother symbolism can quickly become as oppressive—suffocating, sentimental, possessive—as an authoritarian father symbolism. A self-critical Christian feminism is aware of the dangers of a single image, especially a parent/child image. The use of many images more clearly affirms the fully transcendent and incomprehensible reality of God while natural and cosmic images work to subvert not only sexism but the related homocentrism of the Christian attitudes that have supported technological exploitation of earth, land, sea, and air.[24] Rosemary Radford Ruether holds that "we have no adequate name for the true God/ess, the 'I am who I will become.' Intimations of His/Her name will appear as we emerge from false naming of God/ess modeled on patriarchal alienation."[25] God/ess is Ruether's name for the mystery and matrix of all that is, an unpronounceable word that challenges, with its suggestion of female divinity, the traditional Christian image of God. Nevertheless, the unpronounceability of the name, and its diminutive form, have prevented its wide acceptance.

Other new names for God and for the divine/human relation have been offered by feminist theologians. At one point in her feminist journey, Mary Daly described God as the "Verb," to indicate the dynamic intuition of Being that is the experience of God.[26] Carter Heyward suggests that God be conceived as "the power of relation" connecting human beings among themselves and with God.[27] And more concretely, Sallie McFague offers the image of God as "friend," a human metaphor that is startling in its suggestion of some genuine equality between human beings and God, in contrast to the hierarchical image of parent and child. McFague points to a number of biblical uses of the imagery of friendship, especially Jesus' sayings about laying down one's life for one's friend (John 15:13) and his reference to the Son of man as the friend of tax collectors and sinners (Matthew 11:19). In her study, Jesus is the parable of God's friendship with us, a friendship revealed in the parables of the lost sheep, the prodigal son, the good Samaritan, and the "enacted parable" of Jesus' table fellowship with sinners. The Gospels describe Jesus as critical of familial ties in relation to the new bonds of the realm of God that he preached, while his presence transformed the lives of his friends. The ideal of friendship, both on the personal level and on that of friendship toward the stranger, "the alien both as individual and as nation or culture," suggests a model "for the future of our increasingly small and beleaguered planet, where, if people do not become friends, they will not survive."[28]

CONTEMPORARY REFORMULATIONS

Christian feminist theology has rightly insisted on the urgent necessity of re-imaging and re-conceptualizing the symbol or doctrine of God if the gospel themes of inclusivity, mutuality, equality, and freedom are to be realized in society and in the church today. And it finds many resources in contemporary theology that support its critique of male God language and its effects. It is not alone in its quarrel with popular or theological perspectives that "objectify" God, that render the reality of God as one object beside other objects of human knowledge, man writ large over against humankind and the world. Feminist criticism is thus part of a broad and respected theological tradition of protest against a literal interpretation of a few biblical images that too easily domesticate the ultimacy, incomprehensibility, infinity, and essential hiddenness of God at the same time as that interpretation fails to adequately express biblical themes of God's paradoxical presence and intimacy to *all* creation and *all* human experience. Feminist theology is part of a broad tradition of theological reformulation that includes process theology in its several contemporary versions, Tillich's conjoining of Protestant neoorthodox and liberal themes, and post-Vatican II Catholic thought, exemplified in Rahner's transcendental Thomism and Schillebeeckx's hermeneutical theology.

Christian feminists can appropriate contemporary theological language for God as the ground and dynamic power of Being, the infinite and incomprehensible horizon of Holy Mystery, the absolutely related Thou, language that serves to underscore the final transcendence and absolute immanence of God beyond all human understanding. Women can appropriate these theological concepts as they affirm that God can be known, as the term of human questioning at least and with paradoxical clarity, in the event of Jesus Christ and thus can be inadequately but truthfully named in human images, symbols, and concepts. Nevertheless, feminist theology's particular critique of male images for God and of God's attributes bears its specific contribution to the wider contemporary theological discussion. In particular, it focuses on the meaning of power and authority in our human understanding of the reality of God. Many traditional theological and popular concepts of God are rooted in naive and crude perceptions of God as the epitome and ultimate personification of masculine stereotypes of power as domination.[29] The theological tradition and (more often) popular Christian usage have spoken, perhaps too simply, of God's omnipotence, omniscience, aseity (absolute independence), immutability, impassivity. Though not alone in its criticism of these traditional notions, feminist thought challenges them in a dramatic way. If such concepts of God are derived from the patriarchal male image as an androcentric, and so distorted, aspect of the whole human and Christian experience, important correctives and reorientations emerge when the other half, indeed the majority of human experience, is taken into account in the analogical symbolization of God as the transcendent referent and horizon of the whole of human experience.

Feminist theology turns to the experience of women in its quest today for fuller understanding of God. This experience includes, but is not limited to, the experience of motherhood, with its relational themes of birth and gestation, nurturance, and compassion. In probing this experience as a source for symbolizing parenthood in God, theology is opened to rich perceptions of authority as life-giving, power as enablement of the autonomy of others, as gentle persuasion, as patient love and encouragement, themes consonant with the biblical descriptions of God.[30] But women also know the aloneness and the loneliness that accompany contemporary life, the loss of familiar categories that accompanies new personal awareness, the anxiety and pain that are entailed in their new options and the hard decisions they require. Women know what Mary Daly has called "the experience of nothingness" in the discovery of their loved Christian tradition's distorted views of themselves as less than the image of God. In exploring these experiences as a possible source for understanding God, theology is led to reflect on the hiddenness and mystery that is God, the silence and apparent absence of God in the experience of suffering and evil, an experience exemplified for us in the ever-shocking story of Jesus's crucifixion and death.[31] And in the specific experience of rejection by the church, women can turn to the central Christian mystery of their participation in the suffering of Christ as it is seen as God's mysterious yet redemptive way with the world.

In Christian perspective, however, suffering and death are not the final word. Women's experience today confirms the reality of resurrection as well, in the joy of new personal awareness, of self-discovery and self-affirmation, in women's friendship and traditions, especially in their own Christian heritage. God is then known as the inexhaustible source of the unique mystery of human personhood, as the one who wills life and not death, as the God of Jesus who is on the side of the poor, the lonely, the outcast, the women. While women can make no claim to a unique knowledge of God, they can trust that their experience and understanding of God provide an important and necessary corrective to an imagery and understanding derived from an over-masculinized church and culture. And in the Christian context, the experience and insights of women allow for a genuinely critical retrieval of traditional and contemporary ways of understanding God.

In searching for insight, Christian feminist theology finds its central focus in the event of Jesus Christ, in his teaching, and in the "parable" of his message and ministry, his life, death, and resurrection, as this event shatters our ordinary and conventional ways of interpreting both God and the world. Feminist biblical and historical studies have made it clear that Christianity did not invent or create patriarchy and that Christianity was not itself originally patriarchal. Patriarchy is far older and more widespread than Christianity, and it is found in many other religions.[32] The accommodation of an originally egalitarian Jesus movement and early Christian mission to a patriarchal framework can be discerned only in the later strata of the New Testament and subsequent Christian history. As Elisabeth Schüssler Fiorenza has shown, patriarchalization was a gradual process that was accomplished only over the course of several centuries and in the context of a real struggle about the question of women in the church.[33] Another New Testament critic, Madeleine Boucher, has challenged the frequent claim of both biblical scholars and theologians that the image or metaphor of God as father was unique and central in the teaching of Jesus. She demonstrates that this metaphor is one among the many in the Gospels, especially the synoptics, and "is not more or less revelatory, authoritative, and normative than any other element of Jesus' teaching."[34] Further, several scholars have shown that the whole context of Jesus' message and ministry indicates an anti- or nonpatriarchal attitude on his part.[35] Jesus posed a threat to both the religious and political orders, according to one analysis, because he proclaimed and embodied a new and socially disruptive understanding of God, a nonpatriarchal, inclusive understanding of salvation.[36] If Jesus' death is interpreted first in human and historical terms as the response of the religious and political orders of his time to his new understanding of God and the divine/human relationship (an interpretation suggested today by political and liberation theologies)[37] and only secondarily (in a carefully nuanced way) as God's "will" or "plan," then it can further be suggested that Jesus' proclamation of God in his preaching was disruptive of the human religious and political orders precisely because it was so radically inclusive. In its inclusivity, this new understanding of God disrupts conventional ideas of divine power and divine (or historical) order as surely as it does exclusionary human distinctions of class, race, and sex. Just as Jesus' parables were and are shocking to religious and political sensibilities, the parable of his life, death, and resurrection can still shock our everyday worldviews and expectations in what it suggests about some of our traditional concepts of God.

As feminist theology suggests new images of God as mother, sister, and friend, its goal is to find language that can freshly evoke, for our time with its particular struggles, the inclusive, compassionate, and passionate love of God for all creation that is proclaimed in the message and the life, death, and resurrection of Jesus. It is a search for a more adequate understanding of God that addresses the experience of women who have been marginalized in the church, excluded from full recognition and participation for centuries. Such concrete images of God issue in new models or concepts that have been recently suggested by a variety of voices in the theological community, concepts that are nonhierarchical and that fit the experience of women today. These new concepts must still be interpreted in strictly metaphorical and analogical ways. But in their evocation of the disclosive truth of the Christian message about God, their broad incorporation into the church's preaching and teaching might well reorient the Christian imagination today and in the future.

The liberating God is a concept familiar from the Latin American and black theologians and movements for emancipation. Like the women's movement, these movements include both secular and religious components and their theologians insist that the religious or Christian meaning of liberation encompasses the *whole* of human life, including the secular. Rooted in the biblical themes of the exodus from slavery to freedom and of the liberating action of God in human history for those held in bondage, the concept of the liberating God is particularly evocative for all who search for new freedom today, including Christian women.[38] On one level, the image of God as liberator is an image modeled after important human liberator figures in history. On another level, the idea of a liberating God moves into the realm of concept as it affirms a specific attribute of God and the specific character of God's power. In the Latin American context, Christian freedom is interpreted as the possibility of becoming persons, subjects, responsible agents in history.[39] And the action of the liberating God is seen as that which empowers human persons to become genuine subjects in the context of human solidarity and collaborative human action in relation to God. To speak of God as liberating is to evoke the God who does not will human suffering but justice, the God who is on the side of the poor, and who favors and graces the oppressed, the marginal, the outcasts of society, those who hunger and thirst for justice.[40]

Knowledge of God's active empowerment of people who are powerless drives out fear, gives human communities—and the Christian community of women—new faith, courage, and ability to take risks in speaking and acting for the cause of those who have little or no power because of their class, race, or sex. The understanding of God as liberator is liberating in itself in its suggestion that in the cause of justice one is not acting alone, but with others and with the Other with whom all things are possible. The suggestion of the power of God as liberating precisely in the human power of the oppressed makes it clear that God's power, in some mysterious way, waits upon and works through human power, works through human freedom, agency, and responsibility. To speak of God as liberating is, of course, to speak metaphorically and analogously. But it gives primacy of place to a biblical reading of human life and history in relation to God, rather than a metaphysical, rationalist, or simply naturalistic point of view.

If the retrieval of the biblical idea of the liberating God is perhaps the most important new concept of God in our time, its closer analysis, which shows that God's power is resident in human power, leads to a very traditional Christian theme in the idea of *the incarnational God*. While the theological tradition focused its attention on the meaning of Jesus as the incarnation of God, the contemporary feminist context suggests some further ramifications of this theological affirmation. For women, the central theme of incarnation suggests that in Christian perspective, there can be no fundamental split, no ultimate dualism in the world. The richly symbolic idea of God's incarnation in Christ, which means the enfleshment or embodiment of God and the consequent sacramentality of all creation, especially human creation, indicates that God and creation or the world are not in competition but are irrevocably united, joined, made one in God's self-gift to humankind and so to the world. The symbol of God's embodiment also suggests that there is no fundamental matter/spirit, body/mind, female/male dichotomy in which one member of each pair is inferior to the other. Nor is there, in incarnational understanding, a hierarchical dualism between humankind and the world of nature. The relationship of the divine and human and of God and creation in the incarnation is rather a relationship of irrevocable union, reverence, and compassionate love.

Yet, within the irrevocable union of incarnation and the sacramentality it entails, there is diversity: divine and human, grace and nature, spirit and matter. How does one think of the transcendence, the power of God if that transcendence and power are only and always mediated through Christ, through the sacraments of the human, the natural, the material? The notion of the self-limitation of God[41] has been proposed to indicate the superabundance of God's compassionate love for that which is other than God in creation, incarnation, and grace. God is self-limited in a way that allows creatures, especially humans, their own autonomy. As one follows the clue of incarnation, the important principle in Karl Rahner's thought about the inversion of the proportion between autonomy and dependence takes on clear meaning: the more autonomy creatures possess, the more dependent they are (precisely through union) on God.[42] We usually think in human terms that autonomy means independence. In the Christian incarnational scheme, the opposite is true. God is the self-limiting creator of human autonomy. God wills human freedom in creation and grace and so is the God who desires the equality of friendship with humankind.

The image of God as friend has sometimes met with the objection that the metaphor is not appropriate because there is no real equality between God and human beings. On a philosophical or metaphysical level this is true: God infinitely transcends the reach of the human. But in Christian, New Testament terms, in the parables of Jesus and the parable of the Christ event, the compassionate love of God is revealed in the image of friendship: "I call you friends" (John 15:15). The image is disturbing precisely because it shows us the love of God as desiring and giving humankind the equality of friendship.[43] A biblical interpretation of God from the perspective of the experience of women shows that this favored metaphor is firmly grounded in the incarnational tradition as a disclosure of the character of God who desires relationship, even the relationship of equality that is friendship.

The relational God is a concept that has long been proposed by process theology as more adequate to the biblical record of revelation than the classical concept of a distant God that is rooted in Greek philosophy. Following Whitehead's doctrine of internal relations, process theologians argue for the notion of the intrinsic relationship between God and the world in their metaphysical concept of the dipolar God.[44] They represent a "neoclassical" theism in contrast to the classical philosophical thought of, for example, Thomas Aquinas, who maintained that God is not related to the world "really" but only through a "relation of reason." While the classical position more clearly upholds the metaphysical distinction between Creator and creation, between the infinite and the finite, in order to preserve the absolute freedom of God, the neoclassical view more clearly expresses the biblical message, especially the New Testament data about God's grace as the unexpected intimacy that God gives to those who are no longer servants but friends.

Carter Heyward's evocative conception of God as the dynamic power of relationship, a power that extends from the relation between two friends to relations among races, sexes, classes, and nations, offers a feminist integration of relational categories that underscores a reinterpretation of God's power as the power of relation given to humankind. While not developed in process categories, Heyward's important intuition about the centrality of relational understanding in the "redemption of God" for women and for our time can be grounded in both incarnational and process terms. It also opens new perspectives on the thorny problem of God's power.[45]

The traditional concepts of God's omnipotence and omniscience have long been under fire in modern philosophy and theology, especially in the context of the problems of theodicy—the "justification" of a beneficent and all-powerful God who apparently does not or cannot intervene in the face of overwhelming evil in the world. The question has become intensified in our time in response to the Holocaust: the question is asked whether theology is possible "after Auschwitz."[46] The meaning of the biblical understanding of God as acting in history is deeply problematic today, as is the miraculous nature of God's interventions in salvation history. How can the omnipotence of God be understood in a way that is faithful to the Bible and Christian tradition and to contemporary experience of evil as well?

This question has been extensively debated in philosophical theology.[47] The contribution that feminist reflection offers to that discussion and to contemporary Christian understanding of God concerns the resymbolization of the concept of power. Feminist understanding of power in relational terms, as empowerment of the other, corresponds to process theology's distinction between two kinds of power, coercive power and persuasive power. Process thought maintains that God's power works in the world only through persuasion, not coercion.[48] Feminist images of God as mother, sister, and friend suggest that God's self-limitation is such that in a relational and incarnational framework God's power is *in humans* as embodied human agents. God's liberating action occurs through human power and action that imitates the persuasive, nonviolent power of God, a power that, as human experience teaches and the symbol of the cross reveals, all too often fails in sinful human history. While women's experience underscores the compassion and so the gentle power of God, a power in the world that is apparently helpless without human cooperation, it also heightens awareness of human freedom and responsibility. For Christians, deep and total dependence on God means a corresponding gift of agency, autonomy, and responsibility in history.

The compassionate God of the experience of women means *a suffering God*. In process terms, Whitehead spoke of God as "the great companion—the fellow sufferer who understands."[49] While such a notion can be interpreted in sentimental and romanticized ways, it is a deeply biblical understanding that has been powerfully retrieved today by political and liberation theologies. The idea of suffering in God can seem strange because of our traditional notions of God's removal from the world of suffering, pain, passion, and conflict. Yet the traditional attributes of God's impassivity and immutability are derived from Greek philosophy, from Aristotle's "unmoved mover," for example, and not from the Bible. Taking their cue from "the gentle Galilean," process thinkers maintain that God's dipolar nature means that in one aspect, God's primordial nature does involve absolute transcendence of the world but that it is a transcendence that is absolutely related because God's consequent nature is strictly and internally related to the world. Hence, God participates in the sufferings of the world and of humankind.

In another, more explicitly biblical context, Jürgen Moltmann has powerfully argued that a theological reading of the history of Jesus, especially the story of the crucifixion, reveals the grief of God in the death of Jesus, the suffering of God in the suffering of the world.[50]

Moltmann's understanding of "the crucified God" has been adopted by some Latin American liberation theology because it fits with the experience of suffering that is so prominent there.[51] To attribute suffering to God, using the biblical sources of revelation rather than Greek philosophy, indeed reverses human categories as one thinks of God as participating in the suffering, death, and grief of the world. Of course one does not know fully what it means to say that God suffers in the suffering of the world. Applied to God, the term is, again, strictly metaphorical and analogical. But its disclosive truth is revealed in the symbol of the cross, a central Christian symbol and an important one for Christian women who experience the pain of exclusion and denigration in their own religious heritage. Sandra Schneiders has said that in a special way today "women participate in the mystery of the salvation of the world which God works out through the suffering of the just at the hands of the unjust. . . . Like Jesus, they do not suffer at the hands of a neutral power but ultimately at the hand of the church they love."[52] And finally, the symbol of the cross is not the end point for Christian thought: the Resurrection, and the hope for the future that it entails, is from God and in God as well.

The God who is future is the God of resurrection faith. If the terms liberation, incarnation, and relation can suggest new ways in which the immanence of God can be freshly expressed in the experience of women today, our final categories designate ways in which God's transcendence is newly affirmed. The future of God is an important theme in the whole of the Bible with its categories of hope, promise, the new, the not-yet, the realm that is to come. And the experience of Christian women looks to a future in which the church will express in its life and practice the equality and full personhood of women as Christians. To envision God as future, as ahead, rather than above and over against the human and natural world, is a reorientation that helps women to see the feminist dilemma in the church as a temporary one.

Women confront a centuries-old, and seemingly intransigent, tradition of exclusion. But, as feminist scholarship has demonstrated, the tradition of women's struggle and of women's agency and leader-

ship is equally old. Elisabeth Schüssler Fiorenza argues for understanding the initial vision of the earliest Jesus movement and the early Christian mission as a prototype for the future.[53] Other
theologians have recently retrieved the eschatology of the Hebrew
Bible and the New Testament to show the (forgotten) centrality of
the idea of God as future: for Moltmann, the God of promise who is
future sustains the hope that is at the heart of the Bible.[54] Wolfhart
Pannenberg, further, takes seriously the atheist criticism that human
freedom is denied in the concept of "an almighty and omniscient being thought of as existing at the beginning of all temporal processes."
He claims that "freedom is the ability to go beyond what already exists." In his view, traditional Christian theism innocently thought of
God on the analogy of what already exists and linked this analogy
with the biblical God's omnipotent action in history. Such a being
would render freedom impossible and would not be God since human freedom would remain outside its determining grasp. For Pannenberg, true biblical omnipotence is irreconcilable with the idea of
God as existent being. Rather, God is to be understood as the origin
of human freedom, the future that determines human experience as
it is oriented forward in either hope or fear. Since "freedom consists
of possibilities not yet realized," the correspondence between freedom and future means that God is already implicit as the origin of
freedom, "as the power of the future, as the God whose kingdom is
coming." And since freedom and personhood are intimately related,
God is "a personal reality of a supra-human kind . . . a pure act of
freedom." The idea of God as the source of radical personal freedom
does not prove the existence of God for Pannenburg. That question
will only be fully decided in the final revelation and even since
Christ, history is still moving toward that event. But in the present,
God is the one who is to come, the God of Jesus "who raises the dead
and is . . . the origin of freedom, which overcomes that which exists,
and redeems it."[55]

Edward Schillebeeckx, too, emphasizes the futurity of God as the
appropriate concept for Christianity in the new culture that is already emerging in our time. While the old culture was oriented toward the past, its concepts of God's transcendence projected into an

unchangeable, eternalized past, Schillebeeckx holds that the new culture of a "self-made world" recognizes the primacy of the future. Fundamental trust in life's meaning, experienced today primarily in terms of ethical responsibility for the future, means that believers not only connect God with a personal future but with the future of humanity as a whole. God is "the 'One who is to come,' the God who is *our* future." Formerly thought of as wholly Other, God should be conceived today as the wholly New. Such belief is grounded in the confidence that God is already beginning to make things new, that "hope is able *now* to change the course of history for the better."[56] God's act of creation, experienced in human trust, is "commitment to the task of militantly opposing all forms of injustice . . . the basis of trust that the future is the human task." God is at once memory, presence in absence, and the one "who goes ahead of us toward a future." For Schillebeeckx, history itself is the coming of God. The identity of this new concept of God with the original Christian message will come to light only indirectly in the activity of Christians themselves. Thus Schillebeeckx unites biblical eschatology with a pragmatic criterion: this symbol of God is a call "to transcend what *we* have made—war, injustice, the absence of peace, the absence of love," for the God who is to come will transform history "into a saving event *in and through* our freedom."[57] The old concept of a God who intervenes from outside human history, irrespective of human freedom, is dead. Schillebeeckx writes:

Those who believe in Christ know that the reality which we mean when we speak of "God" is not undialectically the ground of everything that is. It is the ground of what should be and will be, and so—dialectically—it is also the ground of present and past. Precisely for that reason God is not the ideological foundation of tradition and the *status quo,* but represents a threat to them. God is a God of *"change for the good"* and therefore judgment and grace, albeit in utter faithfulness.[58]

To reimagine and reconceptualize God as future is to think, in Rahner's terms, of Christianity as the religion of the *absolute* future, that "absolute future is . . . another name for what is really meant by God" who is the "sustaining ground of the dynamism toward the future. . . ."[59] Such themes fit the experience of contemporary women who struggle toward a future that still remains promise and hope. They fit women's experience of the abiding mystery of God.

The *unknown, hidden God* of mystery is a final way of speaking of the God who is always more than human images and concepts can suggest. "Incomprehensible mystery" reminds Christians always that they do not really grasp the one to whom the symbols point, the God who is dimly known as the mystery, source, fountainhead, and matrix of being that surrounds humankind in inexhaustible light. This God, of whom the mystics also speak, resonates in a special way to women today.[60] For how is it that women remain faithful, despite the negative official messages, to the one whom the church exists to proclaim? Women cling to their own experience of the one who is more, who is hidden, unknown, signified in always startling ways in the teaching of Jesus and in the parable of his life. The *via negativa*, which insists that God is not simply this or that, that all our images and concepts fall short, reaches its epitome in that blinding mystery that is named by the tradition as Trinity, God who is somehow a society, a community, a *perichoresis* of persons.

The symbol of the Trinity has taken on new meaning in liberation contexts today. Juan Luis Segundo writes that Latin America today is not so much confronted with "the death of God" as with the death of idols that hold that continent in bondage. One of these idols is the concept of God as absolutely independent of creatures, an impersonal abstraction that is contrary to the biblical understanding of God's involvement with persons in history and the preeminently personal character of God, Jesus Christ, and the Holy Spirit. Segundo interprets the Trinity as a community or society of persons in a way that leads to a socialized and interdependent understanding of human persons. It is a concept of God in which liberty, personality, and creativity take precedence over a supreme being of stability, permanence, and eternal order. His work is a "critical approach to the God of occidental society" in which the teaching about God as independent of history, society, and the world is really a projection onto God of the central limitations of Western society: individualism, passivity, and an other-worldly Christianity.[61]

The mystery of God as Trinity, as final and perfect sociality, embodies those qualities of mutuality, reciprocity, cooperation, unity, peace in genuine diversity that are feminist ideals and goals derived from the inclusivity of the gospel message. The final symbol of God as Trinity thus provides women with an image and concept of God that entails qualities that make God truly worthy of imitation, worthy of the call to radical discipleship that is inherent in Jesus' message. The Trinity includes all the suggestions of suffering and finally triumphant relationality when interpreted biblically and not simply metaphysically or abstractly: death and resurrection, relationship in God and so also in the human community of grace.[62]

Women's new understanding today of the superabundance of the gospel message of God's compassionate love finally transforms all notions of patriarchy, hierarchy, paternalism, and domination in the figure of suffering love and promise who is the God of Jesus Christ. New interpretations of the concept and reality of God, forged in relationship to contemporary experience, including the experience of women and other excluded groups, offers women a theological ground for their deepest struggle and for their final Christian peace and security in that struggle.

8. Feminism and Christology

This chapter begins an exploration of the mystery of Jesus Christ that will not be completed until the following chapter on the question of salvation, the church, and Mary. Its focus is on a Christology "from below," derived from what the stories of the New Testament reveal about the concrete patterns of the history of Jesus and the early churches. It also suggests the important work of feminist transformation of traditional symbols, a transformation that tries to take account of the contemporary experience of women and other marginalized groups. It is a transformation that has been occurring in the past decade and that continues in the present. Such transformation happens wherever Christian women gather to share their experience of the meaning of Jesus in their lives.

Several years ago, ethicist Daniel Maguire wrote: "Something profound is going on in our culture and feminization is its name."[1] Something profound is going on in grass roots Christianity and in Christian theology as well. The "something" is so deep and transformative that it cannot be attributed to a single source. In theology, there is the massive impact of the Enlightenment, its anthropology of autonomy and self-creation, entailing new political responsibility and the "end of God the Dominator." A new historical consciousness has pervaded scriptural and traditional authorities in Christianity and opened theology to self-consciously new interpretations.[2] There is the so-called second Enlightenment and the liberation movements and theologies of Latin America that strike many Christians as profoundly true in their vision of human responsibility as encompassing the social, political, and ecomomic frameworks of Christian freedom. There are European political theology, American black theology, and emerging voices in Asia and Africa struggling to name their own experience of the ultimate reality that Western traditions call God. There are urgent new theological and ethical perceptions attendent on technology and the rationality it bears: the terror of nuclear catastrophe on the one hand, ecological disaster on the other.

But perhaps no single movement, or theology, unites these strands and embodies the "something" so thoroughly as the international women's movement, the women's movement in the churches, and the theology to which it has given birth. Perhaps this is because women are not just one group among many today who are struggling for liberation, justice, peace, and wholeness, but are evenly distributed across all subordinated groups, across all races and classes. Women are a unique case: neither caste nor minority, women are more than half the human race. And women are everywhere. In the global solidarity of the women's movement, women are finding their plural political and theological voices in naming their experience of oppression and liberation—their experience of God and what it means to live justly in this world in relation to God.

In the Christian context, feminist theologians have retrieved old and formed new images and models of God and of the divine-human relationship that are nonpatriarchal, nonhierarchical, nondominating, images that stress interdependence, mutuality, reciprocity, cooperation. As we have seen, Sallie McFague has suggested the model of God as friend as more appropriate than father and the patriarchalism it has supported, in relation both to the message of the gospel and to the experience of contemporary women. Carter Heyward has proposed that God is better described in dynamic, relational terms, as the power of the mutual and just relation among individuals, groups, nations, and races. Born out of the experience that God is not male, not a king, not a warrior, not an omniscient, omnipotent tyrant, these and other models constitute a protest against the uses and effects of traditional models that support dominating modes of church structure, international relationship, and relations between women and men in society, church, and the family. Such revisioning entails new perceptions of providence, theodicy, salvation, ethics, ministry, and community. But at the heart of the Christian matter is Jesus Christ. That Jesus was male is not a negotiable issue. Mary Daly spoke truly of the effects of "Christolatry," although she also noted that Jesus was a free man; Dorothee Soelle warns us of the political consequences of "Christofascism."[3] Elisabeth Schüssler Fiorenza writes:

A feminist theologian *must* question whether the historical man Jesus of Nazareth can be a role model for contemporary women, since feminine psychological liberation means exactly the struggle of women to free themselves from all male internalized norms and models.[4]

Although some women who are critically conscious of the patterns of patriarchy, sexism, and androcentrism within the tradition have left the churches—perceiving its major symbol of the male Christ as destructive and exclusionary—many feminist women continue to call themselves Christian, to pray to Christ and with Christ to God. These are women who take the feminist critique seriously and struggle with the Christian symbols and their transformation. Both historically and in the present, the life, death, and resurrection of Jesus of Nazareth, the Christ event, has been, is, life-giving and liberating for women. How is this possible? Are they, we, simply unenlightened? Do such women labor under an unperceived burden of false consciousness? Or is the event of Jesus the Christ and the movement he set in motion not simply a history of oppression and victimization of women but also a history of liberation? Women's scholarship has demonstrated that Christianity has also been a source for the courage of self-affirmation, for significant historical leadership and personal agency, and for women's authorship of empowering theological perspectives that unite the personal and the political, the private and the public, in ways urgently needed today.[5]

That many of the new images of God offered by Christian feminist theology are modeled on Jesus as the revelatory exemplar of divine-human relationship suggests that Jesus Christ is *not* a symbol of patriarchal male supremacy for women but rather and precisely a powerful symbol of its subversion.[6] It is clear that patriarchy was not invented by Christianity but is much older and more pervasive in the human community.[7] *Uses* of the Christ symbol in theological anthropology, ecclesiology, and ministerial theology to support political, social, and ecclesiastical patriarchy are in fact a perversion of its positive religious content. These uses are a sobering reminder that no symbol, no tradition, is entirely pure but rather all are ambiguous, multivalent, open to both positive and negative human use. Hence there is need for *both* new interpretation *and* critical theory, a hermeneutics of generosity *and* suspicion, or both analogical *and* metaphorical theology. At the same time, I suspect that the central Christological tradition, in what David Tracy calls its "religious classics" as distinct from mere "period pieces," does not assert male superiority as a constitutive Christological principle, although it may imply or assume such a time-bound notion of the human.[8]

One can study the great tradition of Christology without even encountering the question of women. In the ordinary survey of New Testament and patristic Christologies one rarely meets the fundamental question raised by feminist women today: Can a male savior help women? The history of controversy that marks the ancient theological path to the formulation of Chalcedon never directly touches on the question of women; nor does the record after Chalcedon, when the meaning of its central affirmation—the unity of Christ's two natures, human and divine, joined without confusion, change, division, or separation in one person and one hypostasis—was the subject of continued debate. The classical doctrine of the Incarnation speaks of the divinity and humanity of Christ, *not* his maleness. The focus is on the fully human as a soteriological issue—God's redemption accomplished in a fully human history. "What was not assumed was not redeemed" according to the church fathers, who thus implicitly undermined their own negative appraisals of women in affirming the goodness of the flesh and the material realm with which women were associated. And so on through the tradition. Women have studied the Christologies of Anselm, Aquinas, Luther, Calvin, Schleiermacher, Barth, Bultmann, Tillich, Rahner, and Schillebeeckx and assumed they are included in the fully human that is Christ.[9]

Ever since women gained some access to theological study, and knowledge of women's own history, many have continued to find transcendent possibility, a community of mutuality and service in Jesus as the Christ, whether the stress is on his person as the mysterious unity of the divine and human, on the divine presence this historical figure bears as "God with us," or on the fully human "historical Jesus" of many contemporary Christologies. Women have accepted traditional affirmations that Jesus is like humans in all things except sin, that *all* of human nature was assumed by Christ—body, soul, flesh, intellect, will—and that he is the source of grace for all. Thus they have read themselves into the fullness of the Christian mystery in its classical and contemporary statements. Where the tradition speaks of "man," "all men," "human nature," "the Christian," women are obviously included by Baptism into the Christian community, so women have said, and thus share fully in the mystery of Christ.

THE FEMINIST PROBLEM

Reading other contexts in the New Testament and the theologians, however, one notices a difference between "man," "human nature," or "person," and "woman." In other contexts when the classical texts refer particularly to women, a shift occurs in which women are a special case, a marked class, usually valued as less (though sometimes as spiritually "more") than men. There is a not-so-subtle move from generic to sex-specific language in which women's special role, function, position, nature, character, psychology, or physiology are described in terms of distinct dangers. All that has been said about the human in Christ does not apply fully or in the same way to *all* persons. Women present a special case in Christianity, a problem, a question in theology and the life of the church. Consequently, some feminists question whether in the Christian view women really are persons, really are human, and really can be Christian. And they question in what sense Jesus Christ is the savior of women.

The massive distortion that women perceive within the Christian tradition appears in explicit denigration of women as inferior by nature, or as dangerously carnal and polluting, or as more moral and spiritual than men but passive and childlike, needing protection and ideally confined to the domestic realm because of motherhood or a delicate nature.[10] Such ideas, found throughout the tradition, are understood in feminist theory as ideologies, that is, ideas that elevate the interests of one group (men) to the level of the whole and legitimate unjust practice while masking the structures of domination and control that they support.[11] Because of such ideologies, women have been systematically excluded from the fullness of the Christian vision and the church's practical life. The specific Christological problem lies in the fact of a male savior, the significance of the maleness of Jesus, and the uses and effects of the male Christ symbol for the lives of women. Some religious feminists argue that because of the centrality of the male Christ, Christianity is intrinsically patriarchal and male-centered.[12] They claim that women who are now conscious of its oppressive effects should leave it behind as irredeemably harmful. Male symbols can be no help to women. "Christolatry," in Mary Daly's powerful language, chains women to an oppressive past that offered only passive roles of victim, scapegoat, or subordinate and to a tradition that continues to deny women's autonomy and equality while it supports an "unholy trinity of rape, genocide, and war."[13]

While Christian feminists believe that the doctrine of Christ is not intrinsically male-centered, that Christ can be shown, through new interpretations, to be supportive of the full humanity of women, they are aware that Christology is often used against women. Rosemary Ruether argues that, historically, the oppressive use of the Christ symbol finds its high point in Aquinas, who held that the male is the normative sex of the human species. Only the male represents full human potential; woman is a defective human being physically, morally, mentally, not merely after the Fall but in the original nature of things, and thus is legitimately confined to a subservient position in the social order. For Aquinas, the incarnation of the Word of God in the male Jesus is not simply an historical, contingent fact. The male represents the fullness of the image of God, in himself and as "head" of woman. Since women cannot represent "headship"— eminence, leadership—either in society or in the church, it is ontologically necessary that Christ be male.[14]

Little of this argument occurs in Aquinas's treatise on Christology but is derived from his discussions of human nature and sacramental priesthood.[15] Like the rest of the tradition, his Christological statements are general, and emphasize the fullness of the divine and human natures in Christ.[16] Yet when Aquinas's anthropology is incorporated with his Christology, the distortion is clear: the Christological emphasis on the truly human is skewed by androcentric bias. The logic of Aquinas's Christological pattern rests on the notion of "headship," which in one sense is an organic model in which Christ is the head of the body of the faithful; when considered in another way it is a hierarchical and dominating model that is used to justify the subordination of women. It is a clear instance of the way in which a symbol that is illuminating in one way—Christ as the head of the body of the Church ("Christ is the head of every man")—may be used falsely and with oppressive effect ("man is the head of women," I Corinthians 11:3). Because the headship motif functions as an important Christological symbol underlying Christian patriarchal systems, it can serve as an example of the ideological use of the Christ symbol.

THE MODEL OF HEADSHIP

When one examines the headship motif more closely, it becomes apparent how symbolic religious representations are linked to the social, political, and economic structures of the societies in which they arise. Thus the hierarchical patterns of medieval feudal society are reflected in Aquinas's use of the symbols of Christ as head of all men, of society, and the church. As Ruether points out, the Christological models of the imperial Christ that emerged in the context of imperial Rome, the androgynous Christ of the late medieval, apocalyptic thought of the Joachimites, and the synoptic model of the prophetic, iconoclastic Jesus, powerfully retrieved in our own day by political and liberation theologies, similarly reflect their respective social and political contexts.[17] That the Vatican declaration of 1976 on the question of women and priesthood presents arguments from medieval theology to insist on the necessity of a physical resemblance between the priest and the male Jesus suggests that the headship theme still operates (at least within the Roman Catholic Church) long after the cultural situation in which it was developed has passed.[18]

The model of headship, derived from letters of Paul in the New Testament and expanded in medieval theology, envisions Christ as head of the church, the universal head of all men, and the source of all grace, the "grace of headship." The motif is the center of a hierarchical scheme in which God's relation to human beings and Christ's relation to the church are analogous to the feudal religions of husband and wife, male and female, clergy and laity, a relationship of inferiority and subordination for the second term in each pair. The scheme embodies the hierarchical dualisms of patristic and medieval thought with their origins in Greek philosophy: spirit over flesh, soul over body, mind over matter. It is reformulated, but not essentially changed, in the later romantic pattern of head over heart, the so-called "complementarity" of husband and wife in the family and of masculine and feminine in popular Jungian psychological perspectives today.[19] In theology, the theme is present in Karl Barth's insistence on the secondary ordering of female to male as "B" to "A."[20] And as Anne Wilson Schaef has recently suggested, the motif informs the implicit "theology" of most Americans, believers or not, who describe subservient patterns of relationship between women and men as analogous to that between humans and God.[21]

The notion that the incarnation of the Word of God in the male sex is ontologically necessary, suggested in Aquinas, rests on the prior assumption of the defective and inferior nature of woman. The religious use of the headship model derives from imperial and monarchical patterns of past political structures. And it remains in official and popular use long after empirical studies in biology, psychology, sociology, anthropology, as well as common social experience have destroyed the first assumption about female inferiority and long after its originating political structures have disappeared. These foundations for the oppressive use of the headship symbol have been removed, yet the symbol remains operative in destructive fashion for women. It is a pattern of domination that, because of its exclusionary uses and effects, warrants the sharp feminist criticisms it has received.[22]

FEMINIST THEOLOGICAL REFLECTION

In Christology, as with any doctrine, theological reflection draws on a number of sources: the Scriptures both as history and as originating narrative context of symbolic representations of Jesus as the Christ; tradition as the ongoing historical interpretation of Scripture; knowledge derived from the natural and human sciences; contemporary experience as interpreted in literature, art, philosophy, popular movements, etc. Each category is important for feminist theology, which maintains the centrality of the experience of women and focuses on feminist interpretations of society, culture, history, religion. It is a complex enterprise in which the theologian searches for an interpretation that is critically adequate to tradition in acknowledging its oppressive as well as liberating effects for women and to the experience and needs of women in the present. Since the experience of women is particular and varied, feminist theology is radically pluralist. Each voice is only one in a wider conversation.

In my understanding, feminist theology requires some form of mutually critical correlation procedure in which Scripture and tradition, on one side, and contemporary experience, on the other, have equal voice.[23] This is so for at least two reasons, one theological, the other feminist. First, it is necessary because of the character of both Scripture and traditional texts as historically conditioned *theology*. Even as one considers Scripture and tradition as "revelation," it is revelation as revealed and witnessed in the historical experience of people, not exhaustively captured, in human language and symbols that both reveal *and* conceal in their limited human construction. As the record of the revelation of the living God, Scripture and tradition only live in continuing dialogue with contemporary questions, the two mutually illuminating and correcting each other. Only within this dialogue or conversation is tradition itself understood.[24] Thus, for example, Schillebeeckx writes that it is necessary "to have a constant movement to and fro between the biblical interpretation of Jesus and the interpretation of our present day experiences," that the story of Jesus is revelatory *only* if it effectively discloses the human wholeness that Christians seek in contemporary terms.[25] And in a feminist perspective, it is only through a critical correlation, whereby some parts of tradition are corrected by others or by contemporary experience, that a theology (and a faith) that is both Christian and feminist is possible. And some form of implicit feminism, at least, is required of every critically conscious woman today, lest she participate in and thereby support patriarchal theologies and structures that, in fact, deny her full dignity, agency, and responsibility as a human person. In a Christian framework, such a basic feminist perspective is more deeply required: by affirming herself as Christian, a woman implicitly claims such dignity as an autonomous and responsible agent who freely responds to the Christian message in faith.

All religious symbols, Tillich reminds us, emerge in a cultural revelatory situation in which they participate in the transcendent reality they signify. They are not identical with the divine: literal identification constitutes their idolatrous, indeed demonic possibility. Symbols are always ambiguous and display both progressive and regressive possibilities in their excess of meaning.[26] As McFague has argued, an analogical theology of likeness needs to be joined with a parabolic and metaphorical theology that insistently maintains the "and-it-is-not" of every likeness, every symbol.[27] Religious symbols thus demand both theological-spiritual sensitivity and ethical-critical interpretation.[28] The Christ symbol is no exception. In a Christian feminist perspective, critique of patriarchal, sexist, and androcentric ideology can be joined to positive reappropriation of Jesus as the Christ in a way that takes account of the experience of women within various social, racial, political, and class contexts today. Feminist theology, in its constructive moment, embodies especially the ethical ideals of cooperation, reciprocity, and mutuality for both church and society as suggested by the religious affirmations of the gospel and by its own image of "sisterhood." Where the "brotherhoods" of church and nation have represented exclusionary, dominating, competitive, and violent structures, the goals of feminist sisterhood entail the search for contrasting models of inclusion and reciprocity that incorporate all groups. As a form of liberation theology, feminist theology is part of those wider global movements that claim foundation in the gospel for emancipation from political, economic, and racial oppres-

sion.[29] In this context, woman is a symbol too, at once closely personal and political, a mirror as it were, reflecting a series of dominating
systems in society today.

The starting point for feminist theology is the present experience
of women in the church. In a Christological framework, this means
for many women the experience of Christ as risen, living, present. It
is Christ as mediated by church and tradition but also a presence
whose reality and power transcends those mediations. Women who
take the radical feminist critique seriously and yet remain in the
church offer witness to this presence of Christ as compelling and
transformative, within yet beyond present forms. For with full awareness of the church's "institutional aversion" to women, these women
refuse to be excluded.[30] Like Latin American perceptions of a liberating Jesus in and beyond the Christ of cult and dogma, women's perceptions of Christ are grounded in the church, its sacraments,
preaching, communal life, but have another source as well in the corporate and graced awareness of critical Christian feminism. In this
situation, women turn both to the Scriptures and to parts of the historical tradition that present Christ in ways that correspond to their
own experience of his transformative presence.

THE SCRIPTURAL WITNESS

In the Scriptures, women discover not only the motif of headship
that has had such a negative effective history, but liberating stories
about Jesus' relationships with women, his daring reversals of patriarchal family, religious, and societal orders in relation to the kingdom, the involvement of women in his ministry and in the early
missionary movements, and a pluralism of images of Christ that are
mutually corrective when viewed in connection with women's experience. Most contemporary feminist interpretations of Christ are
rooted in the gospel stories about Jesus, the parable of his life and
actions, the pattern of human life and divine-human relations suggested in the earliest witnesses about him. The stories disclose not
only who Jesus *is* (not was) for the communities of disciples, but who
God is and who we are. Contemporary women find transformative

truth in the witness of the New Testament to Jesus' remarkable freedom and openness to women. Accounts of his inclusion of women disciples, his friendship with Mary Magdalene and with Mary and Martha, his positive use of images of women in the parables, his breaking of taboos in speaking with the Samaritan and Syro-Phoenician women, and the position of women as the first witnesses of the resurrection are an important narrative foundation for feminist Christology. As Metz suggests, these are "dangerous stories," narratives whose retelling and further telling in the contemporary situation provide a continual "interruption of the system."[31] The theological symbols of Christian tradition are interpreted today by women within this narrative context that the New Testament stories provide. This is not to make particular historical claims about the details of Jesus' life, but rather to recognize the originating power of the biblical witness to him and of what that witness suggests about the general pattern of his life and the character of the early Christian tradition.

That women are presented by the gospel witness as among the marginalized groups (the poor, the sick, tax collectors, prostitutes) who were welcomed among Jesus' followers is the basis for the inclusive character of feminist Christology.[32] Christian feminists are conscious of the roots of their thought in the important stories of Jesus' acceptance of the oppressed groups of his own time, as well as in the orientation of early Christianity toward "the disinherited of the Roman Empire."[33] The complex fabric of oppression today, particularly of the global "feminization of poverty," places new demands on Christological interpretation. The contemporary experience of women as marginalized, poor, powerless, and subject to physical and psychological violence, means that feminist Christology must be radically inclusive in crossing all lines of social, racial, and class distinction. As a form of liberation theology, feminist Christology can adopt the Christ-liberator image of Latin American experience insofar as it self-critically transcends its own cause in fidelity to the marginalized everywhere.[34]

Some accounts of feminist Christology center on gospel narratives of the ministry and message of Jesus, particularly his inclusion of women, within the context of his prophetic reversals of familial, religious, and societal orders. Jesus' sayings appear to relativize patriarchal family relationships for himself and his followers. The earliest sources indicate an antipatriarchal ethos in the Jesus movement, that "Jesus and his followers broke with their families." A saying of Jesus predicts that his followers will experience family strife and persecution for the sake of the kingdom.[35] "Many of the New Testament writings, particularly the gospels and the historical Paul, were subversive toward the patriarchal family as it existed in Jewish and greco-Roman cultures."[36] Jesus' acceptance of women and his implicit criticism of family patriarchy are of a piece with his criticism of religious and societal orders in relation to the reign of God. One feminist reading suggests that it is precisely Jesus' antipatriarchal attitude that explains the depth of resistance to his teaching on the part of the religious and political establishments. Bernard Cooke writes:

It was the kind of God he was proclaiming which constituted the threat. . . . If God was as Jesus described . . . he threatened, not only the social power structure of his world, but the very notion of "society"; . . . he proposed and embodied a new approach to human relationship and human community, a new understanding of what it means . . . to be a person, a new foundation for evaluating humans and their behavior.[37]

Thus, while it is anachronistic to claim that Jesus was a feminist, Jesus' vision of God's inclusive and universal love transcends patriarchal gender valuation, "implicitly subverts" oppressive structures, and so corresponds with feminist and liberationist impulses today.[38]

Finally, there are Christological implications in the stories of women's participation in the early Christian communities. We have seen that women were active in the early communities as disciples, apostles, prophets, teachers, missionaries, patrons, and leaders of congregations.[39] These women, whom we know only through their names and provocative hints of their apostolic work, a work that apparently has been undervalued by an androcentric tradition and redaction process, represent an important heritage recovered by feminist scholarship. Elisabeth Schüssler Fiorenza argues that the tradition process attempted to suppress, but did not (could not?) entirely erase indication of the radical egalitarianism (inclusive of women and slaves) of the Jesus movement and the early Christian mission. The church's gradual accommodation to patriarchal culture is reflected in the later domestic codes of the late New Testament, understood as prescriptive, instructional texts, not simple description of the early communities. The evidence indicates not only the *fact* of women's equality but the persistence of the question of women. It suggests a struggle behind the scenes of the canonical New Testament in relation to an original impetus toward genuine equality whose roots lay in very old perceptions of the meaning of Jesus, the Christ—perceptions of the radical equality of all persons in Jesus' representation of God's universal love.[40]

Christologically, this universal love is the "something more" that Jesus meant for the community of his followers in the distant past and in the experience of Christian women through the centuries. This is the salvation, grace, and liberation for all people that is Christianity's central religious affirmation. Something more was happening with Christianity besides the denigration of women and despite ideological uses of Christology. That "more" was, and is, a message of God's universal love, of a transformation possible in the human community now and a hope for the future in the God who has taken up the human cause in Christ. This was the message that the Christological tradition sought to express as it struggled with the question: Who is Jesus? And this was the message it sometimes forgot in its focus on the metaphysics of Christ's inner being in abstraction from the community to whom he came and the God he proclaimed, its focus on the Jesus of the past with little reference to his present and future activity in the world and in the community of women and men that is his body.

FEMINIST INTERPRETATION

While it can be affirmed that, ultimately, Jesus' sex does not make any difference for women who seek to move beyond sex as a norm of valuation, this affirmation cannot be made too quickly. Explicit negation of certain Christological meanings and new interpretation needs to precede it. In Schubert Ogden's language, both de-ideologizing and political interpretation are required for a credible Christology today.[41] In looking at a few of the symbols of Christ that are difficult for women, some specific negations and affirmations can be suggested.

Schillebeeckx argues that the many Christologies in the New Testament are nevertheless structurally similar in uniting both mystical and political orientations—reflecting a conviction of the living presence of Christ in the community and of the ethical implications that this presence entails. The early communities freely adapted different Christological patterns appropriate to their situations; Schillebeeckx urges the church to continue this practice.[42] The pluralism of New Testament symbols and Christologies is not intellectually problematic for women; rather, it is liberating to find that different experiences of Christ were rendered in a variety of symbols, no one of which is exhaustive: word, sophia or wisdom, image, teacher, prophet, servant, shepherd, vine, door, bread, messiah, savior, lord. Christologies of adoption, conception, preexistence are functionally, religiously interchangeable insofar as they identify Jesus as the one through whom God is revealed and who is "of decisive significance for human existence."[43] Feminist theology interprets these and new images in ways that are critically empowering for women. Just as different images have been productive for religious life at different times in the past— for example, the poor and humble Jesus in the medieval Franciscan movement, Jesus as mother in the mysticism of the high Middle Ages—so reinterpretation of biblical images of Christ is necessary for the religious lives of contemporary Christian women.

Such interpretation attempts to view critically the *uses* to which symbols have been put in the past, to discern their practical effects for women and community generally, and to explore ways they might be retrieved by ethically and spiritually sensitive interpretation that is adequate both to their originary meaning and to contemporary experience. While some symbols may be irretrievable because of the weight of their destructive history for women, *any* symbol can be falsely used. No symbol is oppressive or nonoppressive in itself but only in its practical reverberations. A critical moment that takes account of racism, classism, elitism, sexism, homocentrism is needed in reinterpretation that is adequate for today.

Christ as the word of God, for example, is sometimes thought of as a purely male symbol, historically derived from the *logos* of Platonic and Stoic philosophy and bearing one-sidedly rationalistic connotations.[44] When considered in its other origins, however, in Hebrew experience of God's word as dynamic and performative and in its conjunction with the wisdom tradition's personification of a female divine principle, some new interpretations emerge.[45] In connection with women's experience of the centrality of verbal communication in personal relationships and of dialogue and participation in institutional contexts, the word can be an appropriate symbol of the mutuality and reciprocity that feminist theology seeks.[46] In the contemporary situation, liberation movements have demonstrated the importance of literacy campaigns among the poor as a first step toward the enhanced self-image that goes with genuine personhood and responsible historical agency. Feminist critics have spoken of women as deprived of the power of naming their own experience, of the male "theft of the word," "phallogocentrism."[47] In Latin America, it is the words of the poor woman Mary, in the Magnificat, that have inspired liberation movements (and their more recent women's movements) and are considered subversive, their public recitation forbidden by repressive governments.

Adela Yarbro Collins writes that "most of the things said about the Logos in the prologue (of the fourth Gospel) are things typically said about Wisdom, personified as a woman or goddess in the Jewish wisdom tradition. . . . In the Wisdom of Solomon and in Philo, Logos and Sophia are interchangeable." In other parts of the Gospel, Jesus' revelatory teaching is related to water and to bread, to eating and drinking. "In the wisdom literature food (bread) and drink (water and wine) are symbols for the instruction given by Wisdom and for Wisdom itself. Wisdom also invites her hearers to eat and drink" as Jesus did. While the prologue may be an attempt to masculinize traditional wisdom motifs, the text also portrays Jesus as incarnate Sophia.

If one can say that the Logos was God, then one can say that Sophia was God. The Gospel may not have intended to do so, but the prologue and the portrayal of Christ as Sophia imply ... a feminine dimension of divine reality.[48]

A similar Sophia-Christology, Schüssler Fiorenza maintains, pervades the early Christian missionary movement.[49] Clearly, the naming of Christ as the Word, Wisdom, or Sophia can be appropriated by feminist Christology, its critical edge subverting traditional masculine meaning in favor of those whose words have counted for little in the past but who have taken on the power of words in a new way today.

Images of Jesus as sacrificial victim and of his sacrificial love and self-surrender on the cross, shown by Mary Daly and Judith Plaskow as destructive for women, are among the most difficult for feminist Christians. At issue is the religious use of this Christological idea to legitimate family, church, and societal structures that support gender roles for women of nonassertiveness, passivity, and sacrifice of self. Male theologians have drawn from the experience of men in patriarchal culture to build models of the "imitation of Christ" that counteract *their* experience of sin as prideful self-assertion; the healing of grace is then understood as sacrificial love. Such models are no help for women, whose fundamental temptation has been described by feminist interpretation as failure to achieve selfhood and responsible agency—requirements for any mature Christian life. Religious self-transcendence first requires an authentic, responsible self. As Dorothee Soelle remarks, only a centered self-awareness can achieve religious selflessness.[50]

For women, the sacrificial love of Jesus on the cross requires reinterpretation in which Jesus' act is clearly seen as a free and active choice in the face of an evil that has been resisted.[51] It is not passive victimization. Nor did God require a sacrificial death. Jesus died because of the way he lived, because of the pattern of fidelity and commitment of his life and his liberating message. The ideal of self-sacrificial love is the ultimate Christ model, to be followed at extreme moments in human history, in martyrdom. "Imitation" of Jesus, discipleship, following, in relation to the Gospel witness of his message, ministry, and way of life, no longer connote passive self-sacrifice but an active, indeed even a subversive freedom in relation to God and to religious and societal structures.[52] For women who have little to lose in power and prestige, Jesus can be, as Metz says, a "dangerous memory" in the struggle for justice.[53]

Another ambiguous symbol for women and other marginalized groups is Jesus the servant. Women have long been servants in family, church, and society. Feminist criticism for over a century has analyzed woman's secondary roles as auxiliary, handmaid, helper, nurturer, and emotional caretaker for children and men. At the same time, such criticism has indicated the importance of choice with regard to traditional roles and women's values in love of children, men, home and the earth. There is nothing intrinsically oppressive about service to others, provided it is freely chosen in a social and economic framework that makes it a genuine option and not simply taken-for-granted, expected sacrifice of self. It is a high expression of human freedom to give of oneself for others, provided one has the freedom of choice. The model of servant presented by Jesus to his disciples in the New Testament stories is an unexpected reversal of roles, pointing to the paradox at the heart of the gospel: the grain of wheat, life through death, laying down one's life freely. It is the *man* Jesus who enacts the woman's role of servant.[54] Genuine service in discipleship of Jesus is not forced servitude but the radically free, intentional decision of a responsible human agent. Jesus' words, "I have not called you servants but friends," "I am in the midst of you as one who serves," and "anyone who wants to be great among you must be your servant," indicate the free self-transcendence that unites servanthood with the equality of friendship, and friendship with service.

The central designation of Jesus as the "son" of the God who is "father" is more problematic. It appears as a clear reflection of patriarchal culture in which men rule over wives, daughters, sisters, and the earth, of gender roles that are not equal but hierarchically valued. Feminist interpretation that accepts the Freudian reading of the ubiquity of the oedipal framework as descriptive of bourgeois family and cultural life under patriarchy, rejects this Christological symbol.[55] It epitomizes a long Christian history in which the correlate reference of son to God as father in heaven has legitimated the rule of fathers or men and the primacy of sons over daughters on earth.

The unconscious power of this gender dualism, reproduced continually in patriarchal society and taken for granted as "natural," bears a mighty weight, despite feminist criticism.

One biblical scholar argues that Jesus' name for God, "abba," connotes an intimacy and trust more commonly associated with motherhood and in connection with the Lord's Prayer, with God's sovereignty, compassion, liberation, reconciliation, faithfulness, and forgiveness. Robert Hamerton-Kelly argues that "abba" indicates that Jesus' special relationship to God is derivatively shared by his followers, who address God as "abba." Jesus' disciples are forbidden so to address anyone else: "Call no man your father on earth, for you have one father, who is in heaven" (Matthew 23:9). In the fourth Gospel, Jesus' status as son is characterized by his equality with and dependence on the father, and the "glory" of his unity with the father in the cross and resurrection is the same unity in which Christians share in loving one another as children in a single family. Read in connection with Freudian theory of murderous family relationships of parental possessiveness and sibling rivalry, where hate is masked as love and rebellion as submission, Jesus' sonship undermines patriarchal patterns in its offer of a spiritual relation to God that transcends these forms.[56]

Feminist criticism has shown, however, that a different effective history has been at play in the son-father correlation as *the* dominant metaphor in Christianity. In the name of the son and his father in heaven, wives have been subject to husbands and fathers, told to be silent, blamed for sin, denied the fullness of the image of God, and burned for witchcraft, even as they were told they share a glorious equality through baptism in the community of faith. Jesus' designation as son of the father and of Christians as brothers—"for us men and for our salvation" repeated each Sunday in the creed of the Catholic church—have effectively functioned to create and support a Christian patriarchy in which all authority and agency is in the hands of the fathers. Feminist analysis of traditional family structure has highlighted its inequity for women. While reformist trends seek to equalize male and female roles in marriage, to reinterpret fatherhood nonpatriarchally, and to adopt new forms of child rearing in which dualistic gender roles are replaced by a pluralism of qualities developed in children, radical separatist feminism encourages women to abandon male relationships entirely, even questioning women's relations to male children. Is the son and father symbolism irretrievable?

For today, perhaps so. Unlike the other symbols we have examined, sonship is specifically male. Schillebeeckx acknowledges the powerful patriarchal context of what he calls Jesus' "abba experience." While this experience led Jesus to proclaim the rule of God to the poor, the oppressed and excluded, it was nevertheless framed in a pattern of radical obedience of son to father, a context of emphatic paternal authority.[57] And Phyllis Trible points out that

to the extent that Jesus disavowed the earthly father in the name of the heavenly father . . . to that extent Jesus reenforced patriarchy by absolutizing the rule of the father. To transfer male dominance from earth to heaven is not to eliminate but to exacerbate it.[58]

Christologically, transformation of the masculinist connotations of sonship only occurs when the symbol is set in the narrative context of Jesus' life, death, and resurrection, only when it is read in conjunction with other symbols, of servant and sacrifice, for example. Taken together, these might set a Christological pattern for today. Confronted with the question raised by Christian women, the narrative pattern of the earliest witness about Jesus, about God, and about human persons precisely denies all hierarchical significance in its universal inclusion of all in intimacy with God and equal unity with one another. All notions of male supremacy associated with the sonship of Jesus must be explicitly rejected, corrected at every point by the use of many other images (including female and natural images) and by feminist criticism in theology, preaching, and church practices. Only then can the unity and intimacy expressed in the symbol of Jesus' sonship call feminist interpretation to self-criticism: radical separatism from or hatred of men and male children is as counter to the gospel as it is to practical feminist goals of social structures that are fully inclusive.

THEOLOGY AND PRACTICE

When contemporary Christians, aware of the possibility for change that lies within their agency, confront the "more" of the Christological tradition, the demand of the gospel is clear. When the maleness of Jesus does enter the tradition, it is as a distorted horizon that needs to be overcome. The destructive effects of a Christology that is not inclusive have been rehearsed frequently enough: violent antisemitism, murderous crusades, vicious psychological and political manipulation carried out in the name of Christ. Feminist criticism points out that if the "fully human" universality of the New Testament and classical tradition is maintained, then appeals to the maleness of Jesus, for whatever exclusionary purpose, are heretical. They are simply evil, unjust, even violent, and those who maintain such positions are no longer "invincibly ignorant" either about women or about the interests served by ideological Christology.[59]

The correctives, indeed major reversals, that emerge when the experience of women confronts the Scriptures and tradition—both the massive distortions and the transformative possibilities—measure the Christological tradition against its practical uses and effects in theological anthropology, ecclesiology, the theology of ministry and sacraments. Feminist interpretations of love, mutuality, reciprocity, and service, rooted in reflection on the parable of God in Jesus' life, death, and resurrection express a hope that the tradition is a transcendent horizon capable of overcoming itself in the living presence of the risen Christ.[60] Karl Rahner writes about a "searching Christology," in which Christians search for that historical bringer of salvation who corresponds to what they already know in graced experience.[61] Women do find that salvation in the story of Jesus carried by the Christian tradition. But Rahner's student, Johann Baptist Metz, cautions us about the crucial importance of historical practice: the historical race is not yet run.[62] A saying of Jesus in the oldest stratum of New Testament witness is "Why do you call me 'Lord, Lord' and not do what I say?"(Luke 6:46).[63]

Schillebeeckx says that the place of Jesus of Nazareth in our "whole history of human suffering in quest of meaning, liberation and salvation," that is, "Jesus' universal significance, cannot be affirmed unmediated or by some abstractly objectivizing argument, apart from the continuing, concrete effects of Jesus' history.[64] A pragmatic criterion of the future emerges when women put the question, "Can a male savior help women?" not just for more than half of humanity, but for that greater majority that is marginalized and poor and for the earth that is our common home. That theme is explored further in the following chapter.

9. The Salvation of Women: Christ, Mary, and the Church

The Christian understanding of salvation from sin—derived from the biblical metaphors of redemption, rescue, return, healing, atonement, re-creation, transformation—is a diverse and complex pattern in the Christian community. It represents a tightly woven fabric in which, nevertheless, the central threads are apparent and clearly named in the doctrines of Christ, the Holy Spirit, and the Church. In addition to exploring these major themes from the point of view of women and their experience, this chapter also gives special attention to the historical figure and symbol of Mary, the mother of Jesus. Mary has taken on new importance in the context of feminist thought since she represents the one real woman and one female figure of central symbolic importance who is named in the Christian story.

The meaning of salvation from sin is a profound mystery—the heart and center of the whole Christian scheme. And it is peculiarly so for women, who have traditionally been baptized into full membership in the redemptive community and yet are perceived as somewhat anomalous within that gathering of people that is, through the presence and work of the Holy Spirit, the unity of the "one body" of Christ.

Christian women today turn not only to the Gospel stories of the earthly Jesus but also to those of the risen, transcendent, and present Christ. For this Jesus Christ is seen as the manifestation, the re-presentation of God's all-inclusive and finally victorious love. While the human figure of Jesus is clearly male (just as many aspects of his earthly humanity are similarly contingent and historically conditioned), Jesus in his human history, as portrayed by the Gospels, reverses and transcends all the gender stereotypes against which women rightly protest in society and church. Further, in the victory of resurrection, the risen Christ is understood to have transcended all the particularities and limitations of earthly existence in the new life of resurrection, life with God, a life and energy that are extended by the action of the Holy Spirit into the earthly community, even now, in its "already but not yet" life of discipleship. Thus, Christian feminist women today search for Jesus the Christ whose reversals of the exclusionary patriarchal and masculinized patterns of culture, as witnessed in the Gospel reports of his inclusive message and ministry, are integrally one with the redemptive events of his death and resurrection and the sending of the Holy Spirit that forms the new and inclusive community that is the Church. Women find this Christ mediated by the New Testament, by some of the traditional symbols and teachings of the church, by their own prayer and ministries in the community, but not always by the structures, practices, and language of the "official" church.

In the relation to both the Jesus of the Gospels and to the trancendent, risen Christ—Christ as fully human and yet transcendent of the limitations of earthly existence in all its brokenness, especially that of patriarchy and all the other splits and fissures that prevail today in the exploitations of racism, classism, imperialism—Christian women have newly interpreted the salvation that is the heart of Christianity. For the painful question that women ask about whether they are really included in the Christian scheme leads to new depths as they search for the meaning of Christ's salvation in the light of their own experience. In this search, the symbol of Mary, as the religious figure who has come to embody many aspects of the feminine dimensions of God, of Christ, of the Holy Spirit, and especially of the Church, takes on particular significance. In the new appropriations of Mary that contemporary women are making, there is an important critical source for the renewal of the church itself. For as women call the church to repentance for its age-old sins of subordination and exclusion, there is a new consciousness that this call is also a powerful moment of grace for the church. It is a call for the church itself to become more fully conformed to its authentic Christian meaning as the community of equal disciples, of witness to salvation in Christ in a way that is not only responsive to the experience of women but to its own, very traditional, calling.

SALVATION IN CHRIST

When one probes the Bible to discern the meaning of salvation in Christ, one discovers a diversity of images and symbols that proclaim that all of humankind is redeemed, reconciled, cleansed, healed, restored to God, transformed into a new creation. Christians are one in the very body of Christ in a new wholeness and integrity as they are reunited with God in Christ beyond the ravages of sin. A similar diversity of explanatory theories pervades ongoing Christian history as the scriptural images were organized by theological thought. In this context a helpful typology suggests, however, that there are three major theories in the Christian tradition of the past that attempt to explain how human salvation is accomplished in Christ.[1] Each theory also implies a particular view of the meaning of sin as that "lostness" from which human persons and the human world itself needs salvation.[2]

Briefly, the first or classic view, best represented in the second-century church father St. Irenaeus, describes salvation in Jesus Christ as redemption in the sense of a ransom paid to the devil or a cosmic victory over the powers of evil that held human beings in bondage because of their sin. In Irenaeus's view, Jesus "recapitulated" the whole of human existence and history in his life, death, and resurrection and thereby broke the hold of the demonic powers that held human beings in sin. Redemption in Christ is a process from immaturity toward maturity. Humankind was not created in some original perfection but rather as destined for growth into God, for movement from being simply the "image" of God toward "likeness" to God. Sin for Irenaeus, therefore, is the failure to grow and mature that is induced by bondage to the devil or to evil "powers" beyond human control. The fragmentation, alienation, and disruption that is so marked a part of human experience is explained by the incomplete, as yet inadequate, growth that has occurred in human persons.[3]

The second view is the satisfaction theory, developed by St. Anselm, the eleventh-century monk and bishop whose thought exercised a strong influence on the church's later theology. This explanation holds that the sin of humankind constitutes a violation of the honor due to the infinite God; satisfaction or "doing enough" is the homage proper to repair that offense. Anselm deduces that humans are incapable of rendering such infinite satisfaction. Since only God can render the appropriate satisfaction and only a human being ought to do so, a God-man is required for the work of human salvation. This is the redemptive work of the sinless Jesus Christ in his freely chosen death. Sin, in Anselm's view, is the broken character of human relation to God, a brokenness that can be put in right order by one who is human and yet by being sinless transcends the human order as well. Thus the need for one who is both divine and human.[4]

The third theory is the subjective or moral influence perspective that is sometimes said to have emerged in Christian history with Peter Abailard, the famous twelfth-century logician and theologian who argued against both the classic idea, with its dualistic connotations of bondage to the devil, and the satisfaction theory, with its demanding God and its juridicial implications. In this view, Jesus is understood as the exemplary teacher and revelatory pattern of human life, whose life and death elicit responsive love on the part of Christians.[5] In some later formulations, even further stress is placed on the revelatory aspect of Jesus' message and ministry, his life, death, and resurrection. The pattern of Jesus' life shows God's way of working in the world of sin and conflict, and in this revelation Christians are called to model their lives in a pattern of loving imitation or discipleship.[6] Sin, in the perspective of this theory, is the failure of human beings to follow the way of love and self-giving that is fully revealed in the pattern of Jesus' life and death; it is the failure of love in the world.

When one views these types from the perspectives of Christian women today and explores the possibility of a critical retrieval that is responsive to women's needs, it becomes apparent that there is power and significance in all three traditional theories when they are reinterpreted in a contemporary and feminist way. But, before that reappropriation can occur, each theory bears the need for theological and feminist criticism as well.

From a general contemporary theological perspective, one can see the development that occurs from the first theory to the third. They are synthesized, in fact, in the work of Thomas Aquinas on the meaning of redemption.[7] There is genuine advance from the dualistic suggestion in the classical theory that there is a cosmic battle between God and the devil in which the devil holds humankind in bondage and in which God needs to pay a ransom for human release. Anselm's attempt to reason out the meaning of the death of Jesus, in the context of a feudal order of honor and justice, can be seen as a theological advance over the classical idea, at least insofar as it moved away from the dualism implicit in the notion of bondage to the devil. Nevertheless, there has been much criticism of the Anselmian satisfaction theory because it presents God in a "sinister" light: this idea of atonement seems to depict God as so jealous of the divine honor that God demands the death of Jesus, requires the satisfaction of suffering and death instead of expressing the compassion and love so prominent in the Gospel stories.[8] While recent scholarship has offered interpretations that show that the satisfaction theory was really meant to restore the *human* order and *human* dignity in a reflection of the medieval penitential system, it is yet apparent that the emphasis of the exemplary theory on Jesus' death as the revelatory expression and example of love restores a needed biblical balance.[9] Yet this theory, too, has been criticized for its tendency to reduce Christ's work to merely a moral example or model for Christian life, without pointing to the genuine transformation that it effects.

The mystery or "plan" of Jesus' salvific message and ministry, the saving meaning of his life, death, and resurrection as presented in the diversity of New Testament symbols, is placed in evolutionary and cosmic dimensions by the patristic idea of Christ's victory over the powers of sin that rule the world. These are terms that are inclusive of the whole of creation, animate and inanimate, and remind Christians that they face powers of evil, violence, and greed that are somehow beyond ordinary human intention and choice. In dealing with the social, political, and structural aspects of human existence, women are conscious of "powers" that are beyond reason and control, that the whole indeed is greater and more intractable than its individual parts. The struggle toward maturity and, in the case of feminist theology, the movement toward real inclusiveness are struggles with powers that transcend the reach of mere good will and reasoned discussion. That Christ has conquered these powers at root and continues to conquer in his broken body, in humankind, has powerful contemporary meaning.

Anselm's attempt to work out the significance of the death of Jesus can be newly appropriated today when the focus on the single moment of death as redemptive is integrated, as it is in much contemporary theology, with the whole of Jesus' life and with his resurrection.[10] The dual focus of women today is on the message and ministry of the Jesus of history, known "from below," and the risen Christ "from above" who in his body includes all baptized Christians and who transcends the limitations of history. Karl Rahner has argued that death is the most important moment of any human life precisely because it sums up and makes definitive all that goes before that death, a person's whole life.[11] Thus the meaning of the death of Jesus is derived from the meaning of his life, from his message of the radical inclusivity of God's love and the empowerment that he extended to the poor and the outcasts, the women. The death of Jesus and his resurrection to new life is the culmination, the vindication by God, of all that went before.[12]

Finally, the theory of the moral exemplarity of the love shown in the death of Jesus, the love of God and the love of Jesus, can be recast in a way that stresses precisely the transformative character of that divine and human love in the lives of the followers of Jesus. It is difficult today to separate completely the person and work of Jesus, Christology and soteriology, as earlier theology tended to do in its focus on the metaphysics of the person, *who* Jesus is. We know too well that who one is, is determined by what one does, that action determines being in a way that is not merely accidental, but genuinely transformative. While a classical metaphysics of substance, such as that of Thomas Aquinas, viewed human beings in an unchanging, static,

and cosmocentric framework, a contemporary historicized and process perspective holds that people are constituted, in fact, by their
relationships. As will be suggested below, the risen Jesus as the Christ
is constituted by his two-fold relationship to God and to people, to
the church in which he continues to live in the Spirit.

The experience of women and many men in the Christian community today calls for an approach to the question of sin and salvation that stresses the relational, communitarian, and pluralistic
character of each. Sin is not construed as a single past event tied to
"Adam" and "Eve" in a literal reading of the biblical story, especially
as centuries of preaching and theological interpretation of that story
have functioned to view sin as disobedience to an external command
and to blame Eve while opposing her to a sinless Mary. There has
already been feminist theological reinterpretation both of the Genesis 3 story of human sin and of the meaning of sin in relation to the
experience of women. Feminist thinkers have shown the androcentric character of traditional understandings and have suggested new
readings of the Genesis story that underscore the subjection of wom-
en as the consequence of sin, from which Christian salvation is
meant to liberate. They have shown how male theological perspectives have dominated understandings of sin as pride and rebellion
against God and have failed to attend to the sin of those who are powerless, who lack agency, selfhood, and responsibility, who have suffered violence and abuse. While women can sin in the ways of
"masculine"culture, especially in the new roles they have assumed
in that culture, their own "feminine" formation suggests sins of passive failure to develop a sense of self, a sense of agency and responsibility. Sin is understood, in a feminist perspective, as the breaking of
relationship with both God and with human beings that can take the
form of weakness as well as pride in its denial of the importance of
human responsibility in both the personal and the political realms.[13]

And salvation need not be thought of as a single, past event bound
up only with a male savior figure, important as Jesus the Christ is in
the perspectives of the community of his followers. Salvation, both as
a personal and political reality, is a matter of present and future solidarity, a solidarity that Jesus expressed in the past in what can be

known of his life and message, his death and resurrection, a solidarity with God and with people, all Jesus' members, that is meant to be continued through the action of the Spirit in the church. In the feminist perspective salvation is, as we have said, radically relational, communitarian, and pluralistic. It is a reality that Christians participate in now and for the future as they attend to the meaning of the Christ event. For salvation is the *event* of transformation, wherever that event occurs, in the liturgy of the church, in the inward soul of the individual, and in all the relationships of the human community, from the personal to the political.

While the question is sometimes asked, "Can a male savior help women?",[14] feminist women in the church insist that sexuality has nothing to do with saviorhood. The *uses* of the maleness of Jesus represent the more questionable issue. June O'Connor writes:

Because feminist theology takes seriously the full humanity and value of women, the affirmations that women and·men alike are made in the image and likeness of God, are called to responsibility and salvation in Christ, and are one in Christ (as are Greeks and Jews, slaves and lords), it sees no ultimate theological significance in the maleness of Jesus. Jesus' male identity is accepted as a feature of his person, not as a necessary condition of incarnation. Although there is no intrinsic theological significance in Jesus' maleness, there is admittedly "social symbolic significance." For Jesus undercuts the predominant mode of human relating and the foundational unit of society at his time: the first century Graeco-Roman male-favored patriarchal household.[15]

In following this Christian feminist perspective, women are led to a view of the importance of maintaining the unity of the person and the work of Jesus Christ, of holding his ministry and message of the radical inclusivity of God's love and empowerment of all in unity with the traditional doctrines of the incarnation, the saving death, and resurrection. Then the incarnation of Jesus as the Christ is seen, "from above," not only as a birth of God among us in the lowly form of the Christmas infant, but as the taking on of a fully human life.[16] The incarnation means that Jesus took on a wholly human history that can be understood, not in its detail or particular psychology perhaps, but surely in the central meaning of its story and pattern "from below," from the historicized faith narratives that are the Gospels. These stories make it plain that Jesus died because of the way he lived, because he ran afoul of the religious and political powers that were threatened by his message, that he was sent to his death by human beings very much like us. We can speak, with an older theology, of the death of Jesus as "God's plan" only in the sense that God willed for Jesus to live a truly human history; the unfolding of that history meant that his message of God's inclusive love was not accepted by those in power. God did not determine Jesus' death; human beings did. It came to be understood as *the* redemptive event because of its importance as the culmination of Jesus' life, because of its scandalous character, and because of the early Christians' need to integrate that death, and their experience of the resurrection of Jesus, into their understanding of the message of the Jesus of their experience. The result is the Pauline and Johannine interpretations of the paschal mystery, the "passing over" of the earthly Jesus to new life in God as the Christ of faith.

Finally, the resurrection of Jesus can be understood as the vindication of one whose life and purpose was lived out in commitment and fidelity both to God and to humankind and so is saving, that is, he is both a model and a representative for us precisely by the all-inclusive character of that commitment and fidelity. Francis Schüssler Fiorenza names that character of inclusive love, in line with many political and liberation theologies and the ideology critique of the Frankfurt School, emancipatory solidarity.[17] Jesus' death was suffered, just as his life was lived, in a twofold solidarity with God and with people, especially with the disenfranchised, with the outcasts, the poor, the sinful, the lost. And Jesus becomes the Christ in this double solidarity of fidelity and commitment that unites all those baptized in faith, all those actively and ethically committed to him in his solidarity with God and with humankind. Jesus is Christ in the church that is the gift of the Spirit, traditionally called the bond of unity, the Spirit given through the raising of the one who was faithful in this double solidarity to the end. It is confidence in the presence of Christ's Spirit that gives Christianity its unique hope in the eschatological future and that gives women their hope in the church of the future.

MARY

In the Eastern Orthodox and Western Catholic traditions of Christianity, Mary the mother of Jesus is intimately involved in the redemptive pattern. She is important to contemporary women not only because she is a particular historical woman who is named in the New Testament stories but because, as the mother of God, she is a religious symbol of enduring power in the tradition, especially as she is celebrated in the liturgy. And yet she is an ambiguous figure for women today. For Mary has been the subject of an idealizing Mariology that sought to venerate her at the expense of real women and that projected onto her the passive virtues of submission, humility, and docility that women, in a misogynist and patriarchal Christian culture, were expected to imitate.[18] Most of what has been understood about Mary in the art and the feasts and the words of the past has been the creation of men.[19]

Feminist scholars have shown that the tradition of Mariology was begun in the fourth century by church fathers who extolled Mary as the sinless virgin-and-mother, the epitome of spiritual motherhood, in contrast to Eve as the symbol of sin , the flesh, and matter. Only in ascetic virginity could women overcome their sinful and corrupt female nature in becoming "virtuous," "like men" or like Mary. Other women were identified with Eve in their sexuality and materiality.[20] Over the centuries Mary became the symbol of ideal womanhood that, on the one hand, holds motherhood as the fulfillment of women's whole purpose in life and, on the other, asserts that "virginity and celibacy are better and more blessed than the bond of matrimony."[21] Thus, for some feminist thinkers, Mary as virgin and mother represents an impossible ideal that no longer has any moral significance. All her representations, even recent ecclesial ones, are rooted in an androcentric and outmoded gynecology as this was built into the patriarchal frameworks of the past.[22] At the very least, contemporary women must be aware that Mary's depiction is part of the history of human thought about women, "a history of errors" that is not unique to Christianity and that calls for what Mary Gordon describes as a "forgiving vigilance."[23]

Many women today are reluctant to give up Mary as a present and still powerful female symbol in their religious lives. Devotion to her as refuge and protection developed as the figures of God and of Christ became masculinized and patriarchalized, distant and judgmental, in Christian history. It was Mary who came to embody the feminine dimension—the mercy, tenderness, and compassion—of the biblical God.[24] Centuries of Marian symbolism as *madonna, virgo, sponsa, pietà* reflect both the femininity of God and respond to important human and religious experiences.[25] Mary also absorbed the female, *sophia* or wisdom character of Jesus Christ for both women and men in Christian traditions.[26] And she came to represent the human, liberating side of the church.[27] In fact, the traditions about Mary suggest that she and the other figures, both women and men in the communion of saints with whom she is often pictured, represent a pluralism of redemptive role models in the full Christian vision. For "Christ" is not alone but includes all his members, all those who, even implicitly, belong to the Christian community, the people of God.

It has further been suggested that, while little is known about the historical Mary from the New Testament, her image has taken on a life of its own. Mary Daly, at least at an earlier stage, thought that the "sometimes God-like status" of Marian symbolism might be a prophetic sign of the new becoming of women. The doctrine of the virgin birth, for example, indicates that a woman need not be totally defined by her relationships with men, that virginity can be a symbol of integral female autonomy. Similarly, the doctrines of the immaculate conception and the assumption of Mary may suggest unintended double meanings for women, foretelling a future when women are fully seen as made in the image of God.[28] There is already indication that Mary Daly's prediction was, in general terms, accurate. For Mary is being reclaimed and newly envisioned today.

The Second Vatican Council, after long debate and the closest vote in its history of several years, chose to insert a chapter on Mary as part of its constitution on the church, *Lumen Gentium*. It chose what was then seen as a "minimalist" position over those who argued for a separate schema that would emphasize the glories and the special privileges of Mary. In doing so, the Council described Mary, although it did not use the phrase explicitly, as the mother of the church.[29] This choice meant that Mary was placed in a clearly secondary, and human, position in relation to Christ, the singular source of salvation. Protestant fears of an excessive Mariology were thus allayed, as were the hesitations of all who realized that very little of the Marian tradition had a solid basis in the Scriptures. The dogmas of the immaculate conception and the assumption were reaffirmed however, allaying the fears of those who believed that too many concessions were being made toward Protestantism. And the Council made use of patristic symbolism in a way that embodied many of the traditions of Eastern Christianity.[30] There is much to be said for the theological development in the Mary chapter of *Lumen Gentium*. The decision to see the meaning of Mary in the light of the church and in relation to Christ indicated that devotion to her was integrated into the whole of theology and the whole of the church's liturgical life. Novenas to Mary and the rosary, which in some places had assumed a place equal to or greater than the Eucharist and the sacraments, while not discouraged, were seen as secondary to the sacramental life of the church. Emphasis was placed in a new way on the Bible and on a vernacular liturgy that was intended to make the worship of the church more integrated for the benefit of all Christians who equally were called to holiness. For a time, devotion to Mary was diminished in the life of the church until feminists began to look at her with new, and critical, eyes.[31]

From the points of view expressed by contemporary women, the document on Mary at the Second Vatican Council remains ambiguous. Like the Council itself, which, except for a few passages in *Gaudium et Spes*, failed to deal with the question of women, the Mary chapter is uncritical in its use of the traditional Eve/Mary symbolism. This symbolism, which attributes sin and evil to Eve's disobedience in contrast to Mary's perfect obedience, still serves to cast all real women with the sinful Eve while rendering Mary as the ideal of perfection. This language of perfection is easily transferred to the church, understood triumphalistically as the perfect society of nineteenth- and early twentieth-century theology. The conflation of themes from Scripture with later dogma, which troubled Protestant observers at the time of the document's enactment, renders it problematic as the continuation of a past, idealizing Mariology.[32]

Women find a particular resource here in recent Scripture scholarship that demonstrates that what little can be known of the historical Mary shows her to be a very human figure. Mary, like the rest of Jesus' family, was probably not originally a follower of Jesus but, by the end of her life; came to have faith and to become a member of the believing community.[33] That Mary is the model of the church, indeed the mother of the church, suggests rather that she embodies the life of coming to faith, hope, and love that is the purpose of the human, indeed the sinful, pilgrim church on earth that is in constant need of reformation. Thus, in retrieving the model of Mary today, women can see her as a figure of faith and discipleship who grew through spiritual struggle, who walked in the obscurity and mystery of life. She is one whose history of trial and suffering included agonizing choices, from an unplanned pregnancy to the dark night of the cross of Jesus.[34] Mary, like Eve, is a sister to contemporary women.

The Second Vatican Council, in choosing to portray Mary as the model of the Church, opened the way to the new and surprising interpretations that are emerging today. Women are reclaimimg Mary, in her human role, as a female symbol of serious religious power. The dogmas of the immaculate conception and the assumption are newly seen as specifically female symbols of the created freedom and the final transformation of the world for which women hope. Mary is joined to the other Marys, especially Jesus' friend the apostle Magdalene, in ways that expand the symbol of the virgin and mother.[35] Mary Jo Weaver suggests:

We have now a woman who finds the divine within herself and so can participate in the extraordinary partnership with the heavenly powers; a woman whose poverty is attractive to God and whose voice is used to herald the messianic age; a woman who can command obedience from"a divine son," and yet, breaking the cultural limitations of her times, can dare to be disciple, a woman who . . . thrives with affirmation and attention, whose experience of Jesus' power transforms her into the most faithful of disciples. She is—to use some of the nameless women—no longer stooped, no longer bleeding, not at all shy about pressing her own claims. Poor herself, she still shares what she can with the poor, both bound and exalted by her solidarity with them.[36]

Similarly, Dorothee Soelle suggests the power of Mary and her Magnificat for the various contemporary liberation movements; she is a role model of resistance and a symbol that cannot be surrendered. Women who have loved Mary have not been blind or duped.[37] Thus Mary is reclaimed in new interpretations of her traditional titles, as queen of peace, as mirror of justice, as comforter of the afflicted. Her special significance as the virgin of Guadalupe particularly shows her power of assimilation and enculturation. For here she repeats, in a recent Mexican liberation context that is still very much alive not only in Mexico but in all the Americas, her ancient assimilation of the great goddesses of Hellenism.[38] While an ecumenically sensitive and historically critical Mariology today avoids making her a female goddess or equal to Christ or the Holy Spirit, her traditional symbol invites us to see the intimate relation that Mary, together with the whole communion of saints and all Christians, bears to God and to Christ in the salvation that is the continuing work of the Spirit in the church. In her many depictions Mary is black, brown, red, yellow, and white, just as she is Gentile and Jewish. Her symbol is given as an invitation to the participation of all, pointing those who love her to the divine. Her many feasts in the liturgy show this vividly.

Thus Mary continues to exercise her power over the Christian imagination, especially for women but also for men in contexts like Latin America, Africa, and Asia where she is seen as the poor one in whom God does great things, in her identification with the poor of Israel and with the Eves of this world, with the church's responsive and liberating tasks everywhere. Mary as virgin and mother need not be understood as an impossible double bind, an inimitable ideal, but as a central Christian symbol that signifies autonomy *and* relationship, strength *and* tenderness, struggle *and* victory, God's power *and* human agency—not in competition but cooperation. Mary *is* a utopian figure, a mystery. Her intimate place in the Christian pattern enables us to imagine a healed, reconciled, finally transformed world. While it is God who works human salvation in Christ and the Spirit who inspires the active response of the church, it is Mary who is the sign of the final transformation of the world.

THE CHURCH

The theology and the living images of Mary may tell us more about the church at a particular time than about Mary. The theology of Mary may be a way, carefully interpreted, to discern how the church understands itself. If this is so, then the treatment of Mary at Vatican Council II and its focus on her as mother of the church and model of Christian life witness to an important transition in ecclesial self-understanding, a transition that is by no means complete. The transition is from an idealized, divinized model of static perfection—the church as a perfect society that has all truth in advance—to a dynamic model of the earthly, human struggle from unbelief to faith in the ambiguities of history, the model of a pilgrim people in solidarity with God and with each other on their journey toward God's future. In feminist terms, the transition can be understood as the source of the acute tension that exists today between the patriarchal, hierarchical model of the church whose adherents are deeply threatened by an envisioned egalitarian, fully inclusive model of the Christian community of discipleship.[39]

Feminist women and men understand the church to be the gift of the Spirit, born of the life, death, and resurrection of Jesus. Biblical images of the union of the vine and the branches, of the stones in a living temple, of the unity of head and members in the one body have been interpreted by contemporary Christians as suggestive of commitment, fidelity, mutuality, service, and inclusive solidarity with God and with all others. The church is the enduring sign of Jesus' twofold solidarity with God and with humankind that is meant to be the sacrament, the visible and effective embodiment, of the salvation of the whole world in every aspect of the church's life, its inner communion, its worship, its mission, its governance. Like the unity of the divine and the human in Jesus Christ, however, the church bears its treasure in a human vessel that has taken many different forms in different places and times in its long history. The circular character of Christian experience and reflection in its living context *in history* indicates that no one model of the church is ever fully adequate or definitive. God's revelation in Christ, a mystery beyond full human comprehension, occurs in the changing currents of history. As revelation continues to meet the response of faith in different contexts (contexts shaped by their own history, traditions, culture, language, local concerns) the one revelation, the one church of Christ takes on a pluralism of manifestations.

This pluralism of models of the church is not new, though heightened consciousness of it is. New Testament scholars have shown the variety of forms in which the experience of salvation in Christ was expressed in the earliest Christian communities. For there was no single "early church" but rather a plurality of communities, many churches. All were one in their confession of faith in Christ, but each had its particular form and distinctive self-understanding. In studying the New Testament communities, Edward Schillebeeckx finds that a certain unity can be discerned within the rich and sometimes bewildering variety: each community manifested a particular "mystical-political" orientation. The mystical element refers to the community's inward experience of union with God through Christ and the Spirit (salvation); the political element refers to its outward relationships of love and service to others, to the world (liberation). Schillebeeckx urges the contemporary church to imitate the creativity of the New Testament communities in forging new models that fit the distinctive experience of Christian salvation in the variety of its geographical situations.[40]

In this context, the scholarly recovery of the "lost" history of women in the early Christian communities is significant. The importance of women in the circle of Jesus' disciples and as apostolic witnesses of Jesus' message and ministry, his death and resurrection, and of women's roles as apostles, prophets, teachers, and leaders of congregations in the original Jesus movement and the early Christian mission has been documented.[41] Elisabeth Schüssler Fiorenza's work is especially suggestive about the character of the earliest Christian churches as radically egalitarian, inclusive of marginal people (women and slaves), and counter-culture. She writes:

Only an egalitarian model for the reconstruction of early Christian history can do justice to both the egalitarian traditions of women's leadership in the church as well as to the gradual process of adaptation and theological justification of the dominant patriarchal Graeco-Roman culture and society.[42]

Thus feminist theology joins the theological critique of the church that is based in an historical awareness of pluralism. This pluralism is especially clear today, in the aftermath of Vatican Council II, a gathering that explicitly sought to renew the self-understanding of the church. In contrast to the post-Reformation church of the Council of Trent, organized to defend "Roman" Catholicism against the "heresies" of Protestantism, and in contrast to nineteenth-century "Roman School" ecclesiology that understood the church as the "perfect society" organized to defend itself against the onslaught of "modern thought" (expressed, for example, in the democratic movements of Europe and the Americas), Vatican II sought to renew the face of the church in the modern world. Taking account of biblical and patristic understandings of the church as the people of God, as pilgrim, as mystery, and of theological developments such as Karl Rahner's discussion of the church of sinners, the sinful church, the diaspora situation of the "little flock,"[43] the Council tried to synthesize old and new understandings in its two documents on the church, *Lumen Gentium* and *Gaudium et Spes*. The result, according to one ecclesiologist, was a "study in ambivalence."[44] On the one hand, a powerful renewal was set in motion with the vision of the church as the people of God, the sacrament of God's salvation in Christ, an exodus church on pilgrimage, attentive to the needs of the world and the signs of the times. And the international women's movement was affirmed as a Christian phenomenon. On the other hand, the juridical and hierarchical structure of the church, developed in the sixteenth century and more tightly bureaucratized in the nineteenth, was carefully reasserted, tempered somewhat by the principles of subsidiarity and collegiality. And the real questions of women in the church were ignored. Most theologians agree that the documents of Vatican Council II do not offer a coherent ecclesiology but a collection of diverse images that are in tension with one another if not contradictory.[45] Women find hope, but little concrete achievement, in the message of

Vatican Council II and since that time from the official Catholic church.

Avery Dulles summarized the situation in ecclesiology in 1974 in his popular *Models of the Church*.[46] He attributed many of the disputes within Catholicism to the conflicting notions of the church held by different groups. He described five central models: the church as institution, as mystical communion, as sacrament, as herald, and as servant. Each model bears its correlative understanding of Christ, revelation, and the function of the church in society. And each has its strengths and weaknesses according to its basis in Scripture and tradition, its capacity to give members a sense of corporate identity and mission, its ability to foster Christian virtues and values, its correspondence with contemporary religious experience, its theological fruitfulness, and its help in enabling members to relate to those outside the church. Dulles claimed that one model *cannot* be primary: the institutional model. Because of their very nature, institutions are subordinate to persons, structures are subordinate to life. While noting the special resonance of the servant model (one that is similar to the idea of the church today as mission), he believed the sacramental model had special merit because it preserved the values of each of the others. And he cautioned that the existence of many models should not give rise to a mere tolerance of a variety of views: the goal is a more adequate and helpful perspective on the church in our times.[47]

Dulles's choice of the sacramental model does not settle the issue. For while the sacramental model aptly symbolizes the church as a divine/human unity, a theological mystery, and a social reality, this model fails to express another key insight of biblical and conciliar understanding: the *dynamic* ralationship between the church and the kingdom or commonwealth of God.[48] At times in the history of the church, there has been a tendency to coalesce church and kingdom in the belief that the church already fully embodies the reign of holiness and love, justice and peace, equality and mutuality that was central in the preaching of Jesus. Images of the church as the perfect society and the mystical body of Christ are often interpreted this way. A more adequate view holds that the church exists for the sake of mission, for a task in the world. For God's grace is everywhere. Why then do we need the church? There is need today for a model that expresses, not only what the church is, but what it does, that clearly shows the purpose of the church, not as service to itself, but for the world to which it is sent.

In a later reflection, Dulles returned to the problem of the image of the church, concerned that the prevailing popular idea of the Catholic church especially, is institutional, hierarchical, paternalistic.

The Church is understood in terms of dogmas, laws, and hierarchical agencies which impose heavy demands of conformity. . . . Many think of the Church as a huge, impersonal machine set over against its own members. The top officers are regarded as servants of the institution, bound by a rigid party line, and therefore inattentive to the impulses of the Holy Spirit and unresponsive to the legitimate religious concerns of the faithful. . . . Following the inbuilt logic of all large institutions, they do what makes for law and order in the Church rather than what Jesus himself would be likely to do.[49]

In this context, Dulles reviewed his earlier models and found that none is widely accepted today. Thus he proposed, as a guiding image for the 1980's, the idea of the church as the "community of disciples," a designation that retrieves what is valid in the other models and that is especially congruent with everyday experience in the church. "The believer can identify rather easily with the early church as a company of witnesses engaged in a difficult mission." Most importantly, Jesus is central in this more modest and biblically fitting model that suggests the continual movement of the church toward the kingdom and the alteration of Christian experience "between being called together in the assembly and sent forth into the world."

As disciples we are initially gathered into unity; we sit at the feet of the Master for instruction and for intimate converse. We learn not only by receiving verbal instruction, but also by active participation in ministry and mission.[50]

Dulles's reference to the importance of mission recalls a statement of Oscar Romero shortly before his martyrdom. From his position as bishop in Central America and echoing Vatican Council II, he proposed to his European audience that the essence of the church lies in its mission of service to the world, in its mission of saving the world in its totality, and of saving it in history, here and now. The church exists to act in solidarity with the hopes and with the joys, with the anxieties and with the sorrows, of men and women. Like Jesus, the church was sent "to bring the good news to the poor, to heal the contrite of heart, to seek and save the lost" (*Lumen Gentium 8*).[51]

The experience of women in the life of the church over the last two decades has entailed this understanding of mission, a very old yet transformed pattern of service.

Christian feminists, both women and men, today see the church as a mystery that encompasses personal and political life, in which individual responsibility, risk, and courage for the public task are fostered through personal and liturgical prayer and through the authority of love and service. In their vision of the church, obedience is understood as participation in the obedience of Jesus, obedience to the revelation of Christ in the gospel as each one is empowered by the Spirit. Thus authority and obedience do not entail a pattern of domination and submission but rather signify a covenant in community that is meant to free individuals and groups for service. Christian feminists clearly recognize the importance of structure, law, authority, and proper order in the functioning of the church. But these structures are themselves ordered, through principles of subsidiarity and collegiality and of mutuality and respect for all, to an end beyond themselves—to the gospel as the mission of Jesus and the inclusive participation of all in that mission, to one another and to the world.

This feminist Christian vision thus opposes, as an inadequate expression of the church, the hierarchical, indeed very military, institutional model that stresses authority as command, not service, and obedience as submission or conformity, not Christian freedom. For this is a patriarchal model of the church in which the focus on authority and obedience is one of coercive power that suggests distrust of the members who are envisioned more as children than as responsible adults. This is the way women especially have been treated in the patriarchal church. This hierarchical, patriarchal, clerical, and military model of the church is simply in conflict with the gospel models of mystery, mystical communion, and mission. Thus the current conflict in the church is not surprising. It is an old conflict and is reflected in the ambiguity of the documents of Vatican Council II.

Christian feminist women are deeply involved in the transition from a patriarchal to an egalitarian model of the church. Many years ago, Karl Rahner argued that it is the task "of the church of women," supported by "the message of the Gospel and the power of the Spirit," not "the church of officialdom," to provide "the concrete model, the constructive pattern of life which is necessary for women in the present age." This task, he said, "cannot be taken away by the official authorities."[52] Today, women have bonded in the movement called "women-church" that, in its own pluralism, struggles to name its own experience of the gospel and that calls the official church to repentence and conversion.[53]

Women-church is the movement of various women's groups to join together in the search for ways of being church that are especially open to the experience of women. Their gatherings sometimes include men who share the hunger for more inclusive, relational, and communitarian expressions of Christian life. Activities take the form of new kinds of structure, decisionmaking, social action, and liturgy that can eventually be incorporated into ordinary parish communities. But at present, the existence of women-church simply allows for the time and space in which experimentation can occur and discoveries can be refined. The very existence of women-church signals the determination of women, as the symbol of all the other groups who have been excluded from the life of the church, to find a Christian life that is concretely expressive in today's world of the message of the gospel. It is, as well, an important expression of the feminist spirituality that has emerged in recent times. Thus the next chapter will explore the ways in which women's spiritual lives have been transformed in their active response to the Christian vision.

10. Christian Feminist Spirituality

It has been suggested that Christian spirituality is simply the human response to the salvation offered by God in Jesus Christ, a response that occurs through the working of the Spirit in the church.[1] It is the personal appropriation of the Christian mystery in its trinitarian, Christological, and ecclesial dimensions into the unity of human life as it is lived. As the characteristic way that different groups and individuals, in various times and places, have turned to God or to Christ in the Spirit, spirituality today names not only the interior life of Christians, especially the experience of prayer, but also the ways in which the Christian life is outwardly practiced in everyday life. It includes life-styles, attitudes, ideas, values, habits, and activities, images, stories, beliefs, even emotions and bodily expressions that are chosen as appropriate response to God and to the salvation, the life of love and union, that God continually offers. This chapter examines some of the ways in which a critical feminist consciousness informs and transforms the basic elements of Christian spirituality.

SPIRITUALITY

In its widest meaning, spirituality can be described as the whole of one's spiritual or religious experience, one's beliefs, convictions, and patterns of thought, one's emotions and behavior in respect to what is ultimate, or to God. Spirituality is holistic, encompassing all one's relationships to all of creation—to the self and to others, to society and nature, to work and leisure—in a fundamentally spiritual or religious orientation. Spirituality is broader than a theology or set of values precisely because it is so all-encompassing and pervasive. Unlike theology as an explicit pattern of cognitive or intellectual positions, spirituality reaches into one's physical, psychological, and religious depths, touches those surest human feelings and convictions about the way things really are. And while it shapes behavior and attitudes, spirituality is more than a consciously chosen moral code. In a religious perspective, in relation to God, it is who one really is, the deepest self, not entirely accessible to the most thoughtful self-scrutiny and reflection. And in a Christian perspective, as the experience of God's salvation in Christ and the response of individuals and groups to that salvation, spirituality can be understood as the source of both theology and morality. For it is the experience out of which both derive as a human response. At the same time, theology and morality can work back upon spirituality as sources of its criticism and transformation.[2]

Spirituality can be, for the most part, an unconscious pattern of relating that is seldom reflected on, activated only in certain "religious" situations, as a group might do at Sunday worship or an individual during a grave personal crisis. As such it is a dimension of life that is generally unexamined, resting on convention, upbringing, or conformity to social and religious expectations. But spirituality can also be made conscious, explicitly reflected on, developed, changed, and understood in a context of growth and cultivation of self or group in a particular setting of response and relationship. Christian spirituality entails the conviction that God is indeed personal and that human persons are in immediate personal relationship not only to others but to an Other who "speaks" and can be spoken to, who really affects human lives. Thus the emphasis in some discussions of spirituality is on the experience of prayer and the various forms of personal and communal prayer associated with specific groups.

Although it is deeply personal, spirituality is not, however, necessarily individualistic, because within the relationship to the ultimate, to God, it touches on everything: relations to the self both in body and spirit, to others, to community, to nature, to politics, society, the public world. Spirituality can be consciously oriented toward this inclusive social context, integrating the many inner and outer worlds in which all persons and all groups live.

Spirituality is expressed in everything one does. On the individual level, it is a style, unique to the self, that catches up all one's attitudes not only in personal and communal prayer but in behavior, bodily expressions, life choices, in what one supports and affirms, and what one protests and denies. As the life of the deepest self in relation to God, to the whole, and so literally to everything, spirituality changes and grows or diminishes in the whole context of life. Consciously cultivated and nourished, it often takes the character of a struggle as an individual or a group of people strive to integrate new perceptions, convictions, ideals, awareness. And it bears the character of grace for Christians as they experience themselves lifted beyond previous levels of integration by a power greater than their own, by the Holy Spirit.

Spirituality is deeply informed by family, teachers, friends, community, class, race, culture, sex, and by one's time in history, just as it is influenced by personal beliefs, intellectual positions, and moral options. Again, these influences may not be reflected on, but they can be made explicit through reading, reflection, conversation, conversion. And so spirituality may include and express a conscious and critical appraisal of one's situation in a particular place, in history, in human culture, in politics.

As a style of response, spirituality is individually patterned yet culturally shaped. Implicit metaphors, images, or stories drawn from one's culture are embodied in a particular spiritual style. And these stories can be made more explicit through reflection, journal keeping, conversation with others, through counseling or psychotherapy. Each individual lives a personal myth or story that is part of a wider network of symbols derived from familial, sexual, cultural, racial, and religious sources. When these myths are made conscious, they can be affirmed or denied; parts can be retained and others rejected as one grows in a widening and more inclusive relationship to the self, to God, to others, to society. These personal, familial, religious, cultural, racial, sexual stories help to answer the great questions: Where do I, or we, come from? How should I, or we, live? What is the meaning of the end, of death?[3] Making myths explicit means the possibility of, in some ways, moving beyond them as they become available for criticism and reconstruction. But even this move means that one has adopted a new story with implicit assumptions that need still further examination. Feminist consciousness, of course, is deeply aware of certain sexual myths that have informed both cultural and religious stories and raises critical questions especially about these and about their effects on the lives of women and of men.

WOMEN'S AND MEN'S SPIRITUALITIES

Even with affirmations of equality between women and men, of a single-nature anthropology in contrast to a dual-nature view, it seems clear that there are some differences between the sexes in basic styles of understanding and relationship to others and to God. The power of historical conditioning suggests that women have been socialized toward the roles and values of nurture and relatedness while men have been socialized toward the roles and values of autonomy and objectivity. It has been affirmed, though not without debate, that different ways of knowing and of moral judgment characterize the sexes in Western society.[4] And thus there are probably differences in women's and men's spiritualities as these involve both knowledge and moral judgment as well as other factors. Recognition of difference, while affirming real equality, need not always entail the notion of complementarity that involves the subordination or inferiority of one in relation to the other. Prescinding from the question (perhaps finally unanswerable) of whether they are the result of nature or nurture, what might some of these inherited or traditional differences be?

In her helpful book, *Women's Reality*, Anne Wilson Schaef describes the differences between what she calls the white male system and the emergent female system on the basis of her consultant experience with both women and men.[5] The white male system is the dominant one in American culture, she claims. While the culture includes other systems (black, Native American, Hispanic), the white male system views itself as (1) the only one, (2) innately superior, (3) knowing and understanding everything, and (4) believing that it is possible to be totally logical, objective, rational. Wilson Schaef lists a set of contrasts that might suggest some differences in women's and men's spirituality. These contrasts, of course, describe abstract types; no one is completely one type or the other. And some men are in fact in the female system while some women are in the white male system.[6]

But in sum, the white male system is analytic, concerned with definition, explanation, either/or categories, and is goal-oriented. The female system is synthetic, concerned with understanding, both/and categories, and is process-centered. Once could suppose that these broad distinctions would characterize the typical differences between men's and women's experience as approaches to God and to the life of the spirit. Wilson Schaef further performs an exercise with her groups (male, female, mixed) in which she asks participants to list characteristics of God (whether they believe in God or not) and of humankind; then characteristics of male and female. Invariably, she writes, the lists look something like this:[7]

God	Humankind	Male	Female
male	childlike	intelligent	emotional
omnipotent	sinful	powerful	weak
omniscient	weak	brave	fearful
omnipresent	stupid/dumb	good	sinful
eternal	mortal	strong	like children

She concludes that male is to female as God is to humankind. And this, she argues, is the religious mythology of the white male system. The basic hierarchical structure is God, men, women, children, animals, earth, in a system of dominance and dependence. Wilson Schaef says that traditional or popular theology supports this myth. Clearly feminist theology, and other forms of contemporary theology, do not.

Once could look at each system, with a view toward suggesting possible differences between men's and women's spiritualities, and decide that women's inherited patterns are to be more highly valued in a Christian perspective. Sandra Schneiders has, in fact, pointed out the "flip side" or positive spiritual effects of the experience of women in otherwise negative and demeaning Christian contexts.[8] Because of their secondary positions in the church and its ministry, Schneiders suggests that women more easily work and dream, pray and think in terms of nondominating and noncompetitive patterns and values. Because of women's long experience of lesser status, they more easily relate, not only to the immanence of God in ways that have been suggested earlier in this book, but also to God's transcendent otherness. Women have more experience in working with men and in knowing the meaning of shared ministry. They more easily relate to lack in their own social situations and are thus intuitively able to respond to need in a variety of ministerial situations. And Schneiders reports, from her work in spiritual direction, that because they have had little opportunity for the major roles of public leadership in the church, women have often developed deeply intense lives of affective prayer. While the secondary status of women is unjust and needs to be righted, the positive effects of women's historic experience will be of benefit to all in the transformed community that is envisioned by Christian feminism.

Thus, as critical of religious and cultural ideologies about gender that reach into one's very perception, thought, and language, feminist consciousness is a little suspicious of further stereotyping of traditional patterns of the "masculine" and the "feminine." Rather than delimiting a female spirituality to one side of the list, a critical feminist awareness would try to hold elements of both sides together in a measured correlation with one another. For there is need to preserve both the values of traditional female characteristics, especially as these relate to the concerns of home and family, and the strengths associated with traditional male traits, particularly the values of autonomy and agency that women have not been encouraged to develop in the patterns of the Christian past.[9]

FEMINIST SPIRITUALITY

A feminist spirituality would be distinguished as a spiritual orientation that has integrated into itself the central elements of feminist criticism of the patriarchal tradition. It is the spirituality of those who have experienced feminist consciousness raising and so have critical questions about inherited patterns and assumptions about gender differences and the implications of these for social and ecclesial roles and behavior. Feminist spirituality is thus different from women's spirituality, that is, the distinctive female relationship to the

divine in contrast to the male. Women's spirituality has been studied
across particular historical periods or within particular religions or in
certain racial or cultural groups (Puritan, Muslim, black, or as above,
white, middle class, Western), and certain "female" characteristics
delineated. For example, in contrast to male spirituality, women's
spirituality has been described as more related to nature and natural
processes and to the home and the domestic realm than to history
making and culture. It has been described as more diffuse, concrete,
personal, and general than focused, universal, abstract, as more emotional than intellectual.[10]

A specifically feminist spirituality, however, is simply that mode of
relating to God, and everyone and everything in relation to God, held
by anyone, female or male, who is deeply aware of the historical and
cultural restriction of women and their related gender roles to a narrowly defined "place" within the wider human "world." Such awareness would mean that feminists are particularly critical of the
cultural and religious ideologies that deny women full opportunities
for self-actualization and self-transcendence. This critical stance is
both negative and positive. Negatively, it bears a healthy suspicion
and vigilance toward taken-for-granted cultural and religious views
that, in a variety of open and subtle ways, continue to limit the expectations of women to passive, subordinate auxiliary roles and rewards.
Positively, this critical stance includes a vision of the world in which
genuine mutuality, reciprocity, and equality might prevail. A Christian feminist spirituality bears the traces of this feminist critical consciousness, integrated within a wider framework of Christian
response to God as it searches, in Dorothee Soelle's words, for "liberating strands" within the mainstream patriarchal tradition.[11]

Such a spirituality affirms and recognizes the realities of feminist
sisterhood as well as the broader solidarity of humankind. It therefore
acknowledges the importance of supportive networks among women
of all ages, races, and classes even as it envisions noncompetitive,
nonhierarchical, nondominating modes of relationship among all
human beings and in relation to nature. As critical, this spirituality
recognizes the dependent ways of relating to men and the competitive and nonsupportive ways in which women have sometimes relat-

ed to one another in the past, and it consciously struggles to achieve authentic, interdependent modes of relationship. As religious, and as Christian, such a spirituality strives to integrate the model of feminist solidarity into a wider vision of human community with men as brothers. Thus it is open to all people even as it does not cease calling the brothers to task for their failings, sometimes personal ones but more often the failures of the masculinist structures that have shaped the world. A Christian feminist spirituality calls everyone to wider visions of human mutuality, reciprocity, and interdependence before a God who seeks the unity and community of all.

A Christian feminist spirituality encourages the autonomy, self-actualization, and self-transcendence of all women (and men). For feminist thought today recognizes that the goals of human development and maturity go beyond mere convention and conformity to rules; these are goals that reach toward a spontaneous freedom that is both human and Christian in the universality of its compass.[12] More specifically, there is acknowledgement of the need of all human beings for the virtues associated with both autonomy (a traditional male trait) and relatedness (a traditional female characteristic).[13] Thus feminist spirituality recognizes the uniqueness of each individual as she tells her own story (for there is no single or universal women's experience) and affirms each one as she strives to make her own choices. As critical, a feminist spirituality recognizes the cultural and religious limitations placed on women in the past and present; and as self-critical, it recognizes the temptation of any particular feminist group, in its search for solidarity, to impose a new ideology as normative for all. A new ideology to which everyone must conform would be as oppressive as the old obedience to the fathers. Feminist spirituality consciously struggles to free itself from ideologies that mask the will to power or control in favor of the authentic freedom of the individual and the group as they attempt to be faithful to their own experience.[14] As religious, and as Christian, a feminist spirituality strives for an ever freer, but always human, embodied, and finite self-transcendence before a God who, in Christ, does not call humans servants but friends.[15]

In its encouragement of both solidarity and autonomy, feminist spirituality understands and probes more deeply into the wider dimensions of human oppression, especially the relationships among racism, classism, sexism, and elitism in society, and affirms the liberation of all oppressed groups. As critical—or better, as self-critical—it resists the limitation of the women's movement to a luxury that only the affluent or educated can afford and embraces the plight of women of all colors and all classes.[16] As religious, and as Christian, such a spirituality strives to become global in its compassion, in its prayer as in its action, to become truly inclusive of the whole of God's world, to pray and to act with the inclusive love of God, that is, to be self-transcendent.

A Christian feminist spirituality is universal in its vision and relates the personal struggle of the individual woman—black, brown, yellow or white, rich or poor, educated or illiterate—to the massive political problems the world faces today. For in recognizing the sin of human exploitation, whether that sin is expressed in physical or psychological violence, in militarism, in the domination of male over female, rich over poor, white over color, in-group over out-group, strong over weak, force over freedom, war over peace, man over nature, it sees the whole of the human problem through the part.[17] Such a spirituality strives not to be elitist but inclusive. It invites men, and all other oppressor groups, to conversion. Yet it remains critical, on guard against the easy cooptation that would dim its radical vision of human mutuality and cooperation. Wise as a serpent and cunning as a dove, Christian feminist spirituality lives in prayer as the hope for its vision even as it acts, in solidarity here and now, to bring that vision into reality.

Given the possible scope of feminist spirituality as it views the whole through the lens of the situation of women, what can be said about the female and male patterns indicated above? The first thing to be said is that each pattern has its values and limitations. It is clear that the emergent female system to which Wilson Schaef refers already bears strong, humanizing, and corrective elements for contemporary society. A specifically *feminist* spirituality is probably new. With the exception of some of the nineteenth-century feminists, the Christian feminist perspective that has been described in the preceding pages differs not only from male spirituality but from a good deal of female spirituality as well in its focus on the experience of women and its critical questions about gender expectations, about the relations between the personal and the political, the private and the public, the interior and the exterior. This spirituality flourishes in many reflective persons today, both female and male, and in various groups. It might be called "androgynous," if by that word is meant focus on the person as integrating the full range of human possibilities, with choices dependent on talent and attraction rather than the dreary stereotypes of race, class, and sex. In this sense, feminist thought recognizes that all are diminished, the oppressors are oppressed too, by limited horizons. Strictly feminist spirituality, with its particular stress on female bonding in sisterhood or solidarity, its affirmation of the self-actualization and self-transcendence of women, and its consciousness of the interrelationships among sexism, racism, and classism, is, one hopes, a temporary stage on the way to a fuller human and Christian spirituality.

It is a temporary stage, however, that has just begun to be explored, particularly in the movement called women-church.[18] For women have found it helpful, indeed necessary, to have a space apart that allows for free debate, experimentation, and both failures and successes in the probing and expression of their own religious experience. While most Christian feminists see the transformation of the structures of the whole church as the final aim of their vision, and so continue to maintain ties with the larger church in a variety of ways, they have also found valuable resources in groups dedicated solely to women's concerns. Yet often feminist men are a part of such groups. There are analogies with the experience of other oppressed or minority groups. One who has worked in and with any of these groups, shared in their struggle and their prayer, even if she is not a member of the group can, to some extent, know what their experience is, can be "converted." Such a person may be included in the work of the group, even as the group recognizes the need for times apart in its special task of self-discovery. So too any man who has identified with the struggle of women can participate in feminist experience, share in a feminist spirituality. Given the massive distortion of both the religious and the cultural traditions, justice and truth demand that any critical man should so participate in feminist experience and spirituality. All the spiritualities of liberation, notwithstanding the distinctive and never-to-be-totally-assimilated experience of the "minority," have a convergent unity within the Christian vision. But at the same time, it is precisely through the particularities of the individual group focus that some purchase on the broader unity can be had. Thus the importance of the small groups today in which women explore and express their long-muted experience of God, of Christ, and of their lives as Christians.

The feminist experience is unique in that it potentially covers the world, includes all races and all classes in every national group. This universality has led some feminists to maintain that male/female domination is not only the oldest but the source of all oppressor-oppressed relationships. Because of the close familial, personal, ethnic, and class ties involved, this form of domination is often seen as the most difficult to deal with. And yet the very closeness of male and female in all human groups may offer even stronger possibilities for overcoming the split, for healing the wound, particularly in the religious context that spirituality encompasses. For here, in the Christian framework at least, human beings understand themselves in relation not only to others but to God. This God who is ultimate, yet incarnate, whose name is love, calls everyone to unity and to the peace that is so urgent a task in today's world. The character of God is revealed in the message and ministry, the death and resurrection of Jesus, who is present in the Spirit in the church that human joy may be complete. This Spirit is the advocate and comforter yet is also the clarifier of sin and truth.

A feminist spirituality, with its sources in women's experience of friendship and solidarity, the search for interdependent autonomy and freedom, might express the experience of *joy* in the divine-human relationship, as suggested by Judith Plaskow in her study of Protestant theologies of sin and grace.[19] The experience of grace or the Spirit that she describes is neither "shattering" (Niebuhr) as by an authoritarian father-judge nor quietistic "acceptance" as by an understanding mother (Tillich); it is neither "subordination nor participation that threatens the boundaries of the individual self." Rather, it is an experience of grace or the Spirit that is "best expressed in words using the prefix 'co-'—co-creating, co-shaping, co-stewardship and in non-objectifying process words, aliveness, changing, loving, pushing, etc."[20] Plaskow's suggestion is similar to those made by other feminist theologians about the special value of the mystical tradition for the lives of feminist Christians and about the metaphor of friend/friendship as expressive of the divine-human relationship.

The mystical tradition bears special importance for women today, as Dorothee Soelle points out, because it is based on experience rather than authority, because it refers to God as one whose essence is not patriarchal power, might, and domination, and because it teaches the "great surrender."[21] Soelle claims, first, that the knowledge of God through experience that is taught by the mystical tradition has particular meaning for women who have been denied participation in the religious establishment and so have a different need to find God beyond the official, authoritarian structures. And she believes that mysticism is available to all, not just an elite group who are specially gifted with visions and trances. Mysticism colors the lives of many ordinary people who simply have never named their experience of personal union with God and its effects on their lives.

Second, the God of the mystics is both liberating and empowering. Soelle suggests that the images of the mystics are quite different from those that suggest that God demands obedience, sacrifice, and renunciation of the self. Images such as "fountainhead, source, spring of all goodness, living wind," "light, water, air," "ground, love, depth, sea" evoke God as seeking "not obedience but union," not as a distant other but as a loving and passionate God who desires human response and cooperation, the activity of genuine subjects.[22] Finally, Christian mysticism teaches the importance of the "great surrender" that is at the heart of all the religious traditions. This surrender is the giving up of self, in Soelle's feminist interpretation, giving up the depressed and empty self that women so often experience and even the paradoxical "giving up of God" in order that God be found in others. This final surrender, even of God and of familiar images of God, for God's sake, is "to learn solidarity."[23]

This theme of solidarity, which has run through the previous pages, emerges again when feminist thinkers suggest that God be imaged as friend. Far from a sentimentalizing view that might be suggested by this homely image, especially for those who insist that God is totally other than what human experience can discern, feminist perspectives suggest that friend and friendship are categories desperately needed on both the divine and the human levels today.[24] If God were envisioned as friend, even as a feminist friend, in addition to the images of father or mother, horizons would inevitably be widened. God would be understood as friend to humankind as a whole, and even more intimately as friend to every individual and every nation and every group in its particularities. A friend is one whose presence is joy, ever-deepening relationship and love, ever available in direct address, in communion and presence. A friend is one who remains fundamentally a mystery, inexhaustible, never fully known, always surprising. Yet a friend is familiar, comforting, at home. A friend is one who urges human freedom and autonomy in decision, yet one who is present in the community of interdependence. And this friend in fact continually strives to create that community. A friend is one who widens human perspectives daily and who deepens the Christian passion for freedom, one's own freedom and that of others. Jesus' relationship to his disciples, as the Gospel stories describe it, was that of chosen friends; he was rather critical of familial ties that emphasized blood relationships over the new ties of faith. Friendship transformed the lives of those disciples–both women and men–in ways beyond their wildest imagining as the Spirit pressed them forward. Can Christians pray to the God of Jesus, through the Spirit, as friends?

Feminist thinkers also suggest that God occasionally be imaged and worshipped as mother and sister, given the long effects of the dominant father image.[25] And they have shown that the risen Christ can be thought of, in a nonandrocentric way, as bearing the feminine qualities of the biblical Wisdom or Sophia as well as the masculine features of the Jesus of history and the Logos.[26] In these perspectives, the church is newly understood as the body, the very sacrament of humankind in God, as the risen Christ in all the female and male embodiments of the community of equal discipleship. The female figure of Mary as virgin and mother is newly appropriated as witnessing to both the strength of autonomy and the compassion of relatedness that human and Christian development implies. And Christian virtue, for both women and men, is newly conceived as both active and receptive strength, beyond conformity and obedience, in the solidarity of human community with God that is given in Christ and that is continually energized by the Spirit.

While it is clear that Christian feminism presents a challenge to the whole church, it has also become apparent that it offers a spiritual vision that derives, not solely from the experience of women, but from the Christian message itself. Thus Christian feminists persist in the project of finding liberating and empowering strands in an otherwise patriarchal tradition. Proximately, Christian feminism may concentrate on the experience of women and the other "others" who are on the margins of ecclesial life. But in a final sense, it is the demand of the Christian gospel that impels feminist women and men today to call the church to renewal. In this way, Christian feminism and the spiritual vision it entails is, indeed, a transforming grace for our times.

Notes

CHAPTER 1. COMING OF AGE IN CHRISTIANITY: THE WOMEN'S MOVEMENT AND THE CHURCHES

1. Protestant feminism emerged as early as 1948 with the formation of the World Council of Churches but it was not until 1969 that the Women's Caucus was formed within that group. See Judith Hole and Ellen Levine, *Rebirth of Feminism* (New York: Quadrangle Books, 1971), 374.

2. In the Roman Catholic Church alone, for example, such women's groups include the Leadership Council of Women Religious, the National Coalition of American Nuns, the National Assembly of Religious Women, Institute for Women, Women's Ordination Conference, and Catholics for ERA. Priests for Equality is an organization of priests who are supportive of women's concerns in the church. In addition, local chapters of some of these organizations and other local groups are organized around women's issues or include these concerns in their programs for justice and peace.

3. See Rosemary Radford Ruether, "Misogynism and Virginal Feminism in the Fathers of the Church," *Religion and Sexism,* ed. Rosemary Radford Ruether (New York: Simon and Schuster, 1974), 150-183 and George H. Tavard, *Women in Christian Tradition* (Notre Dame: University of Notre Dame Press, 1973), 97-121.

4. *Summa Theologiae* I, 92, I; note 18, in IV *Sent.* 25, 2, 1. See also Eleanor Commo McLaughlin, "Equality of Souls, Inequality of Sexes: Women in Medieval Theology," *Religion and Sexism,* 213-66.

5. See the anthology *Women and Religion: A Feminist Sourcebook of Christian Thought,* ed. Elizabeth Clark and Herbert Richardson (New York: Harper & Row, 1977). For the notion of "dangerous memory" see Johann Baptist Metz, *Faith in History and Society* (New York: Seabury Press, 1980), 100-18.

6. See, for example, *Women of Spirit,* ed. Rosemary Ruether and Eleanor McLaughlin (New York: Simon and Schuster, 1979). For instances of new interpretations of the biblical tradition, see Phyllis Trible, *God and the Rhetoric of Sexuality* (Philadelphia: Fortress Press, 1978), *Texts of Terror: Literary-Feminist Readings of Biblical Narratives* (Philadelphia: Fortress, 1984); Leonard Swidler, *Biblical Affirmations of Women* (Philadelphia: Westminster Press, 1979); Elisabeth Schüssler Fiorenza, *In Memory of Her: A Feminist Theological Reconstruction of Christian Origins* (New York: Crossroad, 1983); *Bread Not Stone, The Challenge of Feminist Biblical Interpretation* (Boston: Beacon Press, 1984); Letty M. Russell, ed., *Feminist Interpretation of the Bible* (Philadelphia: Westminster Press, 1985); Mary Ann Tolbert, ed., *Semeia 28: The Bible and Feminist Hermeneutics* (Society of Biblical Literature: 1983).

7. For a variety of examples of feminist theology, see *Theological Studies* 36:4 (December 1975); Sheila Collins, *A Different Heaven and Earth* (Valley Forge: Judson

Press, 1974); Alice L. Hageman, ed., *Sexist Religion and Women in the Church,* (New York: Association Press, 1974); Georgia Harkness, *Women in Church and Society* (Nashville: Abingdon Press, 1974); Rosemary Radford Ruether, *New Woman/New Earth* (New York: Seabury Press, 1975); *Sexism and God-Talk: Toward a Feminist Theology* (Boston: Beacon Press, 1983); Letty M. Russell, *Human Liberation in a Feminist Perspective—A Theology* (Philadelphia: Westminster Press, 1974); Letha Scanzoni and Nancy Hardesty, *All We're Meant to Be* (Waco, Texas: Word Books, 1974); Carrol Stuhlmueller, ed., *Women and Priesthood,* (Collegeville, MN: The Liturgical Press, 1978); Sallie McFague, *Metaphorical Theology: Models of God in Religious Language* (Philadelphia: Fortress Press, 1982) esp. ch. 5; Helen M. Luke, *Women, Earth and Spirit: The Feminine in Symbol and Myth* (New York: Crossroad, 1984); Marianne Katoppo, *Compassionate and Free: An Asian Woman's Theology* (Maryknoll: Orbis Books, 1979).

8. See Valerie Saiving Goldstein, "The Human Situation; A Feminine View," *Journal of Religion* 40 (April 1960): 100–112; Judith Plaskow, *Sex, Sin and Grace: Women's Experience and the Theology of Reinhold Niebuhr and Paul Tillich* (Washington, DC: University Press of America, 1980).

9. For an analysis of this theological method, see David Tracy, *Blessed Rage for Order* (New York: Seabury Press, 1975), 43–63; Leonard Swidler, ed., *Consensus in Theology?* (Philadelphia: Westminster Press, 1980), especially the essays by Küng, Schillebeeckx, and Tracy. In a feminist perspective, see Anne Carr, "What Are the Sources of My Theology?" *Journal of Feminist Studies in Religion* 1:1 (Spring 1985): 127–31.

10. See Marabel Morgan, *The Total Woman* (New York: Pocket Books, 1973).

11. See Mary Daly, *Beyond God the Father* (Boston: Beacon Press, 1973); *Gyn/Ecology: the Metaethics of Radical Feminism* (Boston, Beacon Press, 1978); *Pure Lust: Elemental Feminist Philosophy* (Boston: Beacon Press, 1984); Naomi Goldenberg, *Changing of the Gods* (Boston: Beacon Press, 1979); the essays in section IV, "Creating New Traditions," of *Womanspirit Rising,* ed. Carol P. Christ and Judith Plaskow (New York: Harper & Row, 1979), 193–287. Rosemary Ruether has written several important essays on feminist Wicca religion, "Goddesses and Witches: Liberation and Countercultural Feminism," *The Christian Century* (September 10-17, 1980): 842-47, "A Religion for Women: Sources and Strategies," *Christianity and Crisis* 38:19 (December 10, 1980): 307-311; and "Female Symbols, Values, and Context," *Christianity and Crisis* 46:19 (January 12, 198): 460-64.

12. See *The Feminist Papers,* ed. Alice S. Rossi (New York: Bantam Books, 1974), 241-50.

13. See William O'Neill, *Everyone Was Brave: The Rise and Fall of Feminism in America* (Chicago: Quadrangle Books, 1969); Eleanor Flexner, *Century of Struggle: The Women's Rights Movement in the United States* (New York: Atheneum, 1949, 1973).

14. Ann Douglas, *The Feminization of American Culture* (New York: Avon Books, 1977). See also Ann Taves, "Mother and Children and the Legacy of Mid-Nineteenth Century American Christianity," *Journal of Religion* 67:2 (April 1987), 203–219.

15. See Rosemary Ruether, *New Woman/New Earth.*

16. Swidler, *Biblical Affirmations of Women,* 49.

17. Plaskow, *Sex, Sin and Grace,* 162-167.

18. See Juliet Mitchell, *Psychoanalysis and Feminism* (New York: Vintage Books,

1975); Judith Van Herik, *Freud on Femininity and Faith* (Berkeley: University of California Press, 1982).

19. Elisabeth Schüssler Fiorenza, "Why Not a Category of Friend/Friendship?" *Horizons* 2:1 (Spring 1975): 117–18; Sallie McFague, *Metaphorical Theology*, 145–94.

20. Sacred Congregation for the Doctrine of the Faith, "Declaration on the Question of Admission of Women to the Ministerial Priesthood" (Vatican City, 1976).

21. See the essays in *Women Priests: A Catholic Commentary on the Vatican Declaration*, ed. Leonard Swidler and Arlene Swidler (New York: Paulist Press, 1977).

22. Mary Jo Weaver, *New Catholic Women: A Contemporary Challenge to Traditional Religious Authority* (San Francisco: Harper & Row, 1985), 109–144.

23. See Elizabeth Janeway, *Man's World, Woman's Place* (New York: Dell Publishing Co., 1971).

24. For a discussion of this cultural process on the psychological level see Nancy Chodorow, *The Reproduction of Motherhood* (Berkeley: University of California Press, 1978).

25. See Helen Fuchs Ebaugh, *Out of the Cloister* (Austin: University of Texas Press, 1977) for a sociological study that demonstrates the relation between educational level and the democratizing of institutional structures in American Catholic religious communities of women.

CHAPTER 2. THE CHURCH IN PROCESS: ENGENDERING THE FUTURE

1. See Karl Rahner, "Theology and Anthropology," trans. Graham Harrison in *Theological Investigations* (New York: Herder and Herder, 1973), IX:28–45; Paul Tillich, *Systematic Theology* (Chicago: University of Chicago Press, 1951), I:3–5; David Tracy, *Blessed Rage for Order: The New Pluralism in Theology* (New York: Seabury, 1971), 32–42; idem. *The Analogical Imagination: Christian Theology and the Culture of Pluralism* (New York: Crossroad, 1981), 47–98.

2. See Emily C. Hewitt, "Anatomy and Ministry: Shall Women Be Priests?" *Women and Orders*, ed. Robert J. Heyer (New York: Paulist Press, 1974), 39–55; Emily C. Hewitt and Suzanne R. Hiatt, *Women Priests: Yes or No?* (New York: Seabury Press, 1973), 57–70.

3. See Karl Rahner, "Scripture and Tradition," *Theological Investigations*, trans. Karl H. and Boniface Kruger (Baltimore: Helicon, 1969), VI:98–103.

4. See "Dogmatic Constitution on the Church," *The Documents of Vatican II*, ed. Walter M. Abbott, S. J. (New York: Guild Press, 1966), 14–37.

5. René Laurentin, "The New Testament and the Present Crisis of Ministry," *Office and Ministry in the Church*, Concilium 80, ed. Bas Van Irsel and Roland Murphy (New York: Herder and Herder, 1972), 7–18; Richard McBrien, *Church: The Continuing Quest* (Paramus, New Jersey: Newman Press, 1970), 5–21; Avery Dulles, *Models of the Church* (New York: Doubleday, 1974), 7–30; Edward Schillebeeckx, *Christ: The Experience of Jesus as Lord* (New York: Seabury, 1980), 631–44.

6. Dulles, 43–96. See also Dulles's suggestions of a new model, "the community of disciples," as more adequate for the times in his "Imaging the Church for the 1980's," *A Church To Believe In* (New York: Crossroad, 1982), 1–18.

7. Karl Rahner, *The Shape of the Church to Come*, trans. and intro. Edward Quinn

(New York: Seabury Press, 1974), 59–63, 93–132. In describing such a church, Rahner advocates the "relative" ordination of married men, and of women, in relation to particular Christian communities.

8. See Richard McBrien, review of Haye van der Meer's, *Women Priests in the Catholic Church?, Commonweal,* 101:2 (October 11, 1974): 44–45.

9. See Committee on Pastoral Research and Practices of the National Conference of Catholic Bishops, "Theological Reflections on the Ordination of Women," *Review for Religious* 32:2 (March 1973): 221.

10. Rahner, *The Shape of the Church to Come,* 24.

11. John McKenzie, "Ministerial Structures in the New Testament," *The Plurality of Ministries,* Concilium 74, ed. Hans Küng and Walter Kasper (New York: Herder and Herder, 1972), 13.

12. Hans Küng, *The Church* (New York: Sheed and Ward, 1967) 385, 393–406.

13. Geoffrey Kelly, "Priesthood in the Context of Brotherhood," *Priestly Brothers* (Wheaton, Maryland: National Assembly of Religious Brothers, 1975), 11. On the question of who presided at the Eucharist, see Myles Bourke, "Reflections on Church Order in the New Testament," *Catholic Biblical Quarterly* 30:4 (October 1968): 499–507; Raymond Brown, *Priest and Bishop, Biblical Reflections* (New York: Paulist Press, 1970), 40–45. Bourke distinguishes the first two models and implicitly allows for the third.

14. Brown, 13.

15. Küng, *The Church,* 370–80. But see also Brown, 14–15, who maintains that I Peter 2:9 "does not primarily concern priestly function (in particular, cultic sacrifice) but priestly holiness. ... One cannot argue from the royal priesthood of Christians against the existence of a Christian specialized cultic priesthood." Brown argues that all Christians share in priesthood through baptism and confirmation but that the ordained priesthood is a different thing.

16. Hans Küng, *Why Priests?,* trans. Robert C. Collins, S. J. (New York: Doubleday, 1972); Alexandre Ganoczy, " 'Splendours and Miseries' of the Tridentine Doctrine of Ministries," *Office and Ministry in the Church,* 84.

17. Brown, 16–20; Kelly, 7, 16, nn. 3,4. See also Bourke, 505, on the New Testament appropriation of the Jewish ordination rite in relation to the celebration of the Christian Eucharist, and Daniel Donovan, "Brown, Küng and the Christian Ministry," *The Ecumenist* 10 (September–October, 1970), 88–94, on these thinkers' divergent approaches to the issue of priesthood and ministry.

18. Küng, *Why Priests?,* 39.

19. Ibid., 39–40; Peter Kearney, "New Testament Incentives for a Different Ecclesiastical Order?" *Office and Ministry in the Church,* 57. See Brown, 27–28, on the notion of service as primarily service to Jesus Christ.

20. Bourke, 495–498.

21. Küng, *Why Priests?*; McKenzie, 14–15.

22. Küng, *The Church,* 405–6; Bourke, 504–505.

23. Bourke, 503.

24. Ernst Niermann, "Priest," *Sacramentum Mundi* 5, ed. Karl Rahner et al. (New York: Herder and Herder, 1970), 97.

25. André Lemaire, "From Services to Ministries: 'Diakoniai' in the first Two Centuries," *Office and Ministry in the Church,* 48.

26. Küng, *Why Priests?,* 55.

27. Ibid., 50.

28. Lemaire, 48; compare Kearney, 61–63.

29. Küng, *Why Priests?*, 55.

30. Niermann, 99.

31. Ibid.

32. Ganoczy, 75–86.

33. "Decree on the Ministry and Life of Priests," *Documents of Vatican II*, 538–46.

34. "Decree on the Church's Missionary Activity," *Documents of Vatican II*, 605; "Constitution on the Church," *Documents of Vatican II*, 55.

35. "Constitution on the Church," 24–37, 77, 30, 50.

36. "Pastoral Constitution on the Church in the Modern World," *Documents of Vatican II*, 202.

37. Eugene Kennedy, *The People are the Church* (New York: Doubleday, 1969), 25.

38. Sister Albertus Magnus McGrath, O. P., *What a Modern Catholic Believes About Women* (Chicago: Thomas More Press, 1972), 5.

39. George H. Tavard, *Women in Christian Tradition* (Notre Dame: University of Notre Dame Press, 1973), 8.

40. Mary Jo Weaver, "Women in the Church: Some Historical Perspectives," unpublished paper.

41. See Constance F. Parvey, "The Theology and Leadership of Women in the New Testament," in *Religion and Sexism*, ed. Rosemary Radford Ruether, 132–36.

42. Ibid., McGrath, 29–42.

43. Compare Krister Stendahl, *The Bible and the Role of Women* (Philadelphia: Fortress Press, 1966); Alicia Craig Faxon, *Women and Jesus* (New York: United Church Press, 1973); Leonard Swidler, "Jesus was a Feminist," *Catholic World* (January 1971): 177–83; Rachel Conrad Wahlberg, *Jesus According to Women* (New York: Paulist, 1975).

44. See especially Elisabeth Schüssler Fiorenza, *In Memory of Her: A Feminist Theological Reconstruction of Christian Origins* (New York: Crossroad, 1983); Charles R. Meyer, "Ordained Women in the Early Church," *Chicago Studies* 4:3 (Fall 1965): 285–309; Charles R. Meyer, *Man of God: A Study of the Priesthood* (New York: Paulist 1975), 58–85.

45. Rosemary Ruether, "Misogynism and Virginal Feminism," *Religion and Sexism*, 150–183.

46. Eleanor Commo McLaughlin, "Equality of Souls, Inequality of Sexes: Women and Medieval Society," *Religion and Sexism*, 213–66; Kari Elisabeth Borresen, *Subordination and Equivalence: The Nature and Role of Women in Augustine and Thomas Aquinas* (Washington, DC: University Press of America, 1981), 339–41.

47. McLaughlin, 260.

48. See Clara Maria Henning, "Canon Law and the Battle of the Sexes," *Religion and Sexism*, 267–91; Ida Raming, *The Exclusion of Women from the Priesthood: Divine Law on Sex Discrimination*, trans. Norman R. Adams (Metuchen, NJ: Scarecrow Press, 1974); James Coriden, ed., *Sexism and Church Law* (Ramsey, NJ: Paulist Press, 1971). For commentary on the position of women in the 1985 code, see Elizabeth McDonough, "Women and the New Church Law," *Canon Law: Church Reality*, Concilium 185, ed. James Provost and Knut Walf (Edinburgh: T. and T. Clark, 1986), 73–81.

49. Mary Daly, *The Church and the Second Sex* (New York: Harper & Row, 1968), 95–98. See Kari Vogt, "Becoming Male: One Aspect of an Early Christian Anthropology," *Women—Invisible in Theology and Church*, Concilium 182, ed. Eli-

sabeth Schüssler Fiorenza and Mary Collins (Edinburgh: T. and T. Clark, 1985), 72–83.

50. *The Documents of Vatican II,* 227–28.

51. John XXIII, *Pacem in Terris* (New York: America Press, 1963), 14:14.

52. *The National Catholic Reporter* 11:29 (May 16, 1975): 5.

53. Daly, *The Church and the Second Sex,* 107–17.

54. Mary Daly, *Beyond God the Father: Toward a Philosophy of Women's Liberation* (Boston: Beacon Press, 1973). In another vein, C. S. Lewis, *God in the Dock: Essays on Theology and Ethics,* ed. Walter Hooper (Grand Rapids, MI: Eerdmans, 1970), 230–39, maintains that patriarchal and sexual role models are so central to Christianity that their removal from doctrine and practice would result in a new religion.

55. See, for example, Letty M. Russell, *Human Liberation in a Feminist Perspective* (Philadelphia: Westminster Press, 1974); Alice L. Hageman, ed., *Sexist Religion and Women in the Church* (New York: Association Press, 1974); Sarah Bentley Doely, ed., *Women's Liberation and the Church* (New York: Association Press, 1970); Arlene Swidler, *Woman in a Man's Church* (New York: Paulist, 1972); Fran Ferder, *Called to Break Bread,* (Mt. Rainier, MD: Quixote Center, 1978); Denise Lardner Carmody, *Feminism and Christianity: A Two-Way Reflection* (Nashville: Abingdon Press, 1982); Mary Jo Weaver, *New Catholic Women* (San Francisco: Harper & Row, 1985), 109–144.

56. See June O'Connor, "Liberation Theologies and the Women's Movement," *Horizons* 1:2 (Spring 1975): 103–13.

57. Rosemary Radford Ruether, "Women, Blacks and Latins: Rivals or Partners in Liberation Theology?" address given at the University of Chicago, May 1975.

58. See Karl Rahner, "The Position of Women in the New Situation in Which the Church Finds Herself," *Theological Investigations,* trans. David Rourke (New York: Herder and Herder, 1971), VIII: 75–93.

59. Harvey Cox, "Eight Theses on Female Liberation," *Christianity and Crisis* 31:16 (October 4, 1971): 199.

60. See Rosemary Ruether, "Sexism and the Theology of Liberation," *Christian Century* 90:49 (December 12, 1973), 1224–29; Letty M. Russell, *Household of Freedom: Authority in Feminist Theology* (Philadelphia: Westminster Press, 1987).

61. Mary Daly, *The Church and the Second Sex,* 202–3.

62. Dorothy Donnelly, "The Gifted Woman: New Style for Ministry," *Women in a Strange Land,* ed. Clare Benedicks Fischer, Betsy Brenneman, and Anne McGrew Bennett (Philadelphia: Fortress Press, 1975), 90.

63. See Marie Augusta Neal, "Social Encyclicals: Role of Women," *Network Quarterly* 3:2 (Spring 1975).

64. Russell, *Human Liberation,* 73.

65. Gregory Baum, "Ministry in the Church," *Women and Orders,* 57–66.

66. See Karl Rahner, "Priestly Existence," *Theological Investigations,* trans. Karl H. and Boniface Kruger (Baltimore: Helicon Press, 1967), III:239–62.

67. See Haye van der Meer, *Women Priests in the Catholic Church?* (Philadelphia: Temple University Press, 1973).

68. Ann Kelley and Anne Walsh, "Ordination: A Questionable Goal for Women," *Women and Orders,* 67–74.

69. Mary Daly, *The Church and the Second Sex,* 207; Nelle Morton, "Preaching the

Word," *Sexist Religion and Women in the Church,* 29–45 and *The Journey is Home* (Boston: Beacon Press, 1985), 40-61.

70. See Anne E. Patrick, "Conservative Case for the Ordination of Women," *New Catholic World* 18:1305 (May-June 1975): 108–11.

CHAPTER 3. ORDINATION FOR WOMEN AND CHRISTIAN THOUGHT: HISTORY, THEOLOGY, ETHICS

1. The notion of the "seriously imaginable" from David Kelsey, *The Uses of Scripture in Recent Theology* (Philadelphia: Fortress Press, 1975), chap. 8, is used by Margaret A. Farley, "Sources of Sexual Inequality in the History of Christian Thought," *Journal of Religion* 56:2 (April 1976): 162.

2. See Elizabeth Janeway, *Man's World, Woman's Place* (New York: Dell Publishing Co., 1971); Karl Rahner, "The Position of Women in the New Situation in Which the Church Finds Herself," *Theological Investigations,* trans. David Bourke (New York: Herder and Herder, 1971), VIII: 75–93.

3. Valerie Saiving, "Androcentrism in Religious Studies," *Journal of Religion* 56:2 (April 1976): 177-97; and the classic text, Simone de Beauvoir, *The Second Sex,* trans. and ed. H. M. Parshley (New York: Vintage Books, 1974).

4. Mary Daly, *Beyond God the Father.*

5. See, for example, Letha Scanzoni and Nancy Hardesty, *All We're Meant to Be* (Waco, Texas: Word Books, 1975).

6. See the review of feminist theology by Carol Christ, "The New Feminist Theology: A Review of the Literature," *Religious Studies Review* 3:4 (October 1977): 203-212. While Christ's distinctions between reformist and revolutionary approaches is valid from one perspective, it should not be allowed to divide women's religious scholarship and search. Each position has strengths that are important to the ongoing discussion.

7. Judith Hole and Ellen Levine, *Rebirth of Feminism* (New York: Quadrangle Books, 1973), 374.

8. Ibid., 375.

9. See, for example, "Vatican Declaration: Women in the Ministerial Priesthood," *Origins* 6:33 (February 3, 1977): 517-24. See also the bibliographies of Anne E. Patrick, "Women and Religion: A Survey of Significant Literature, 1965-1974," *Theological Studies* 36:4 (December 1975): 737-65; and "Studies on Women Priests," *Women Priests: A Catholic Commentary on the Vatican Declaration,* ed. Leonard Swidler and Arlene Swidler (New York, Ramsey, Toronto: Paulist Press, 1977), 771-73.

10. See the important and detailed study of Gerda Lerner, *The Creation of Patriarchy* (New York: Oxford University Press, 1986), which examines patriarchy as an ancient, but historical creation.

11. See George H. Tavard, *Women in Christian Tradition,* 3-26; Elizabeth Carroll, "Women and Ministry," *Theological Studies* 36:4 (December 1975): 660-87, especially 673.

12. See, for example, Elisabeth Schüssler Fiorenza, *In Memory of Her,* 97-342; C. E. Cerling, "An Annotated Bibliography on the New Testament Teaching about Women," *Journal of Evangelical Theology Society* 16 (1973): 47-53; Raymond E.

Brown, "Roles of Women in the Fourth Gospel," *Theological Studies* 36:4 (December 1975): 688–99; Leonard Swidler, "Jesus Was a Feminist," *New Catholic World* 214 (1971): 771–73; Elizabeth M. Tetlow, *Women and Ministry in the New Testament* (New York: Paulist Press, 1980).

13. Farley, 163; Bernadette J. Brooten, *Women Leaders in the Ancient Synagogue: Inscriptional Evidence and Background Issues,* Brown Judaic Studies 36 (Chico, CA: Scholars Press, 1982).

14. Farley, 166; see also Bernard Prusak, "Woman: Seductive Siren and Source of Sin?", *Religion and Sexism,* ed. Rosemary Radford Ruether, 89–116.

15. See Robin Scroggs, "Paul and The Eschatological Woman," *Journal of the American Academy of Religion* 40:3 (September 1972): 283–303; idem. "Paul and the Eschatological Woman: Revisited," ibid., 42:3 (September 1974): 532–37; Elaine Pagels, "Paul and Women: A Response to Recent Discussion," ibid., 538–49.

16. See Rosemary Radford Ruether, "Misogynism and Virginal Feminism in the Fathers of the Church," *Religion and Sexism,* 157–58

17. Developments in the medieval period are discussed in Eleanor Commo McLaughlin, "Equality of Souls, Inequality of Sexes: Women in Medieval Theology," *Religion and Sexism,* 213–66.

18. See, for example, Elizabeth Schüssler Fiorenza, "Women Apostles: The Testament of Scripture," *Women and Catholic Priesthood: An Expanded Vision,* ed. Anne Marie Gardiner (New York, Paramus, Toronto: Paulist Press, 1976), 94–102; idem, "The Apostleship of Women in Early Christianity," *Women Priests,* ed. Swidler, 135–40; idem, "The Twelve," ibid., 114–22; J. Massyngberde Ford, "Women Leaders in the New Testament," ibid., 132–34; Madeleine I. Boucher, "Women and the Apostolic Community," ibid., 152–55; Pheme Perkins, "Peter's Pentecost Sermon: A Limitation on Who May Minister?", ibid., 156–58; Adela Yarbro Collins, "The Ministry of Women in the Apostolic Generation," ibid., 159–66; Elizabeth Carroll, "Women and the Ministry," *Theological Studies,* 660–87.

19. Hans Küng, *The Church* (New York: Sheed and Ward, 1967), 385, 393–406; Myles Bourke, "Reflections on Church Order in the New Testament," *Catholic Biblical Quarterly* 30:4 (October 1968): 504–505.

20. See the statement of the National Conference of Catholic Bishops, "Theological Reflections on the Ordination of Women" (Washington: USCC, 1972), also published in *The Journal of Ecumenical Studies* 10 (1973): 695–99; Sacred Congregation of the Doctrine of the Faith, "Declaration on the Question of the Admission of Women to the Ministerial Priesthood," Rome, 1976, reprinted in *Women Priests,* 35–49, *Origins* 6:33 (February 1977): 517–24, and *New Women, New Church* 10:1 (January-February 1987): 9–13.

21. Mary Aquin O'Neill, "Toward a Renewed Anthropology," *Theological Studies* 36:4 (December 1975): 725–36; see also *Research Report: Women in Church and Society,* ed. Sara Butler (Catholic Theological Society of America, 1978), 32–40.

22. See Orthodox-Anglican Consultation, "A Reaction to the Proposed Ordination of Women," June 25, 1973; Archbishop Athenagoras, "The Question of the Ordination of Women," *L'Osservatore Romano* (July 3, 1975): 9–10 (weekly edition in English).

23. Pope Paul VI, "Address to Committee for the International Women's Year," *Origins* 4:45 (May 1, 1975): 718–19.

24. Pope John XXIII notes that it is those nations with a Christian tradition that have

experienced a more rapid emergence of women into positions of equality in public life, in *Pacem in Terris* (New York: America Press, 1962), 14 n. 14.

25. See Pope Paul VI, *Pacem in Terris,* 719; "Vatican Declaration," 523; David Burrell, "The Vatican Declaration: Another View," *America* 136:13 (April 2, 1977): 289–91.
26. For a review of the literature see Mary Brown Parlee, "Review Essay: Psychology," *Signs* 1:1 (Autumn 1975): 119–38; Martha T. Schuch Mednick, "Some Thoughts on the Psychology of Women," *Signs* 1:3, pt. 1 (Spring 1976): 763–70.
27. "Vatican Declaration on the Admission of Women," 523.
28. See the report of the Catholic Theological Society of America, *Women in Church and Society,* 37.
29. O'Neill, p. 735, highlights especially the importance of "embodiment" in discussions of human nature.
30. See the anthology *New French Feminisms,* ed. Elaine Marks and Isabelle de Courtivron (New York: Shocken Books, 1981).
31. See Phyllis Trible, "Depatriarchalizing the Biblical Interpretation," *Journal of The American Academy of Religion* 41:1 (March 1973): 30–48; Sallie McFague, *Metaphorical Theology,* 145–92.
32. See Margaret Farley, "New Patterns of Relationship: Beginnings of A Moral Revolution," *Theological Studies* 36:4 (December 1975): 627–46.
33. "Vatican Declaration," 522.
34. John R. Donahue, "Women, Priesthood and the Vatican," *America* 136:13 (April 2, 1977): 285–89.
35. Edward J. Kilmartin, "Bishop and Presbyter as Representative of the Church and Christ," *Women Priests,* ed. Swidler, 295–302.
36. Anne E. Patrick, "Conservative Case for the Ordination of Women," *New Catholic World* 218:1205 (May-June 1975): 108–11.
37. See National Conference of Catholic Bishops, "Theological Reflections on the Ordination of Women," 69: "The Catholic priesthood is a unique phenomenon springing solely from the faith, the doctrine, the history, the growing self-consciousness of the Church, not from the religious needs of the Catholic people, certainly not from any principles or theories concerning the rights of men and women. . . ." See also Jon Sobrino, *Christology at the Crossroads: A Latin American Approach,* trans. John Drury (Maryknoll: Orbis Books, 1976), 295–305.
38. Elisabeth Schüssler Fiorenza, *Bread Not Stone: The Challenge of Feminist Biblical Interpretation* (Boston: Beacon Press, 1984), 10–15.
39. "Vatican Declaration," 519–22.
40. See chapter 2 above.
41. See Karl Rahner, "Theology II, History," *Sacramentum Mundi,* 6:243; "Man (Anthropology) III, Theological," ibid., 3:366–67.
42. See Schubert Ogden's criticism of this view of theology in his "Response to Dorothee Soelle," in *The Challenge of Liberation Theology,* ed. Brian Mahan and L. Dale Richesin (Maryknoll: Orbis Books, 1981), 17–20.
43. See Anne Carr, "Authentic Theology in the Service of the Church," *Women Priests,* ed. Swidler, 221–26.
44. Emily Hewitt, "The Justice of the Gospel Narrative," *Women and Catholic Priesthood,* ed. Gardiner, 64. See also Daniel C. Maguire, "The Exclusion of Women from Orders: A Moral Evaluation," *Cross Currents* 34:2 (Summer 1984): 141–52.
45. Patricia Hughes, "Who Are These Women? The Answer Takes Shape," *Women*

and Catholic Priesthood, ed. Gardiner, 174–81; Fran Ferder, *Called to Break Bread?* (Mt. Rainier, MD: Quixote Center, 1978), especially 91–95.

46. Valerie Saiving Goldstein, "The Human Situation: A Feminine View," *Journal of Religion* 40 (1960): 100–112; Judith Plaskow, *Sex, Sin and Grace: Women's Experience and the theologies of Reinhold Niebuhr and Paul Tillich* (Washington, DC: University Press of America, 1980).

47. Margaret Farley, "Moral Imperatives for the Ordination of Women," *Women and Catholic Priesthood,* ed. Gardiner, 35–51; see also her *Personal Commitments* (San Francisco: Harper & Row, 1986) for a more general ethical discussion that integrates a feminist perspective.

48. See *Women's Consciousness, Women's Conscience: A Reader in Feminist Ethics,* ed. Barbara Hilkert Andolsen, Christine E. Gudorf, and Mary L. Pellauer (Minneapolis: Winston Press, 1985); Beverly Wildung Harrison, *Making the Connections,* ed. Carol S. Robb (Boston: Beacon Press, 1985); Christine E. Gudorf, "To Make a Seamless Garment, Use a Single Piece of Cloth," *Cross Currents* 34:4 (Winter 1984–85): 473–91; and Judith Vaughn, *Sociality, Ethics, and Social Change* (Lanham, MD: University Press of America, 1983) for examples of feminist ethics that emphasize the relation of the private and the public.

CHAPTER 4. THE SCHOLARSHIP OF GENDER: WOMEN'S STUDIES AND RELIGIOUS STUDIES

1. Virginia Woolf, *A Room of One's Own* (Harmondsworth: Penguin, 1972), 28–29.
2. Florence Howe, "Feminist Scholarship: The Extent of the Revolution," *Change: A Magazine of Higher Learning* 14:3 (April 1982): 14. See also Marilyn J. Boxer, "For and About Women: The Theory and Practice of Women's Studies in the United States," *Signs* 7:3 (Spring 1982): 661–95.
3. Howe, "Feminist Scholarship," 14.
4. Gerda Lerner, "The Challenge of Women's History," *The Majority Finds its Past* (New York: Oxford University Press, 1979), 168–80; Carl Degler, "What the Women's Movement Has Done to American History," *Soundings* 64:4 (Winter 1981): 417–19; Joan Kelly-Gadol, "The Social Relations of the Sexes: Methodological Implications of Women's History," *Signs* 1:4 (1976): 812–17; Jane Tibbetts Schulenberg, "Clio's European Daughters," *The Prism of Sex,* ed. Julia A. Sherman and Evelyn Torton Beck (Madison: University of Wisconsin Press, 1979), 33–53.
5. Kelly-Gadol, "The Social Relations of the Sexes," 811.
6. Ibid., 810.
7. Lerner, "The Lady and the Mill Girl," *The Majority Finds its Past,* 15–30.
8. Lerner, "The Challenge of Women's History," 169.
9. Ibid., 177.
10. Ibid., 180.
11. "Autobiographical Notes: By way of an Introduction," ibid., xiv.
12. Ibid., xv.
13. Ibid., xxx–xxxi.
14. Carl Degler, *At Odds: Women and Family in America from the Revolution to the Present* (New York: Oxford University Press, 1980). See John Schilb, "Men's Studies and Women's Studies," *Change,* 38–41.

15. Carl Degler, "What the Women's Movement Has Done to American History," 406–408. He points out that only slowly did women begin to exercise the power of the vote as individuals and not simply as wives.
16. An observation made by Professor DeAne Lagerquist in conversation.
17. Margaret McIntosh of the Wellesley Center for Research on Women, quoted in Edward B. Fiske, "Women's Studies Now Challenge Scholars' Long-Held Beliefs," *New York Times* (November 23, 1981): 12.
18. Carol Gilligan, *In a Different Voice: Psychological Theory and Women's Development* (Cambridge: Harvard University Press, 1982).
19. Anthropologist Sally Slocum of the University of Montana, quoted in Fiske, *New York Times.*
20. See *Critical Inquiry* 8:2 (Winter 1981), a special number on "Writing and Sexual Difference" edited by Elizabeth Abel.
21. See Myra Jehlen, "Archimedes and the Paradox of Feminist Criticism," *Signs* 6:4 (Summer 1981): 575–601, and the responses in "Letters/Comments," *Signs* 8:1 (Autumn 1982): 160–76; Carolyn Heilbrun, "A Response to Writing and Sexual Difference," *Critical Inquiry* 8:3 (Summer 1982): 805–811.
22. See Mary Vetterling-Braggin, Frederick A. Elliston, and Jane English, eds., *Feminism and Philosophy* (Totowa, NJ: Littlefield, Adams, and Co., 1981); Mary Vetterling-Braggin, *"Feminity," "Masculinity," and "Androgyny"* (Totowa, NJ: Littlefield, Adams, and Co., 1982); Janet Radcliffe Richards, *The Sceptical Feminist: A Philosophical Inquiry* (London: Routledge and Kegan Paul, 1980); see also Jane English, "Review Essay: Philosophy," *Signs* 3:4 (Summer 1978): 823–31.
23. English, "Review Essay," 828.
24. Elizabeth Mannich, quoted in Fiske, *New York Times.*
25. "Introduction," *Yale French Studies* 62 (1981): 2–5.
26. Ibid., 3–4.
27. Elaine Showalter, "Towards a Feminist Poetics," *Women Writing and Writing About Women,* ed. Mary Jacobus (London: Croom Helm, 1979), 39, quoted in *Yale French Studies,* 4.
28. Heilbrun, "A Response," *Critical Inquiry* 8:4 (Summer 1982): 806.
29. Ruth Hubbard, quoted in Fiske, *New York Times.* See "A Feminist Critique of Scientific Objectivity," *Science for the People* (July-August 1982): 5–8, 30–33; Evelyn Fox Keller, "Feminism and Science," *Feminist Theory: A Critique of Ideology,* ed. Nannerl O. Keohane, Michelle Z. Rosaldo, and Barbara C. Gelpi (Chicago: University of Chicago Press, 1982), 113–126; Anne Wilson Schaef, *Women's Reality* (Minneapolis: Winston Press, 1981), 16–20, on science and scientific methods.
30. See, for example, the special issue "A Feminist Perspective in the Academy: The Difference it Makes," *Soundings* 64:4 (Winter 1981), which surveys several disciplines.
31. Howe, "Feminist Scholarship," 15–17; Mariam Chamberlain, "A Period of Remarkable Growth-Women's Studies Research Centers," *Change* 14:3 (April 1982): 24–29.
32. Howe, "Feminist Scholarship," 19.
33. Judith B. Walzer, "New Knowledge or a New Discipline: Women's Studies at the University," *Change* 14:3 (April 1982): 22.
34. Elaine Showalter, "Feminist Criticism in the Wilderness," *Critical Inquiry* 8:2 (Winter 1981), 197ff.

35. Judith Van Herik, *Freud on Femininity and Faith* (Berkeley: University of California Press, 1982), 116. But see p. 114, where Van Herik indicates that gender is not only distinguishable from sex but also *less* malleable than sex, given the possibility of sex-change surgery today. Her discussion of the concept of gender provides a survey of the major issues and distinctions, pp. 112–19. See also Ann Oakley, *Sex, Gender and Society* (New York: Harper & Row, 1972), 158–72; John Archer and Barbara Lloyd, *Sex and Gender* (Cambridge: Cambridge University Press, 1985).
36. Judith Shapiro, "Anthropology and the Study of Gender," *Soundings* 64:4 (Winter 1981), 448.
37. Rita Gross, "Androcentrism and Androgyny in the Methodology of History of Religions," *Beyond Androcentrism: New Essays on Women and Religion* (Missoula, MT: Scholars Press, 1977), 9.
38. Van Herik, 29–30.
39. Shapiro, 448.
40. Robert Stoller, *Sex and Gender,* (New York: Jacob Aronson, 1968), I:9, cited in Van Herik, 114.
41. Van Herik, 116.
42. Inge K. Broverman, Donald M. Broverman, and Frank E. Clarkson, "Sex-Role Stereotypes and Clinical Judgments of Mental Health," *Journal of Consulting and Clinical Psychology* 34:1 (1970): 1–7, cited in Shapiro, 447.
43. Shapiro, 450–56. Other anthropologists have used economic theories (control of marriage, colonialism, capitalism, class) but Shapiro finds them unsatisfying in relation to the data. See the collections *Woman, Culture and Society,* ed. Michelle Zimbalist Rosaldo and Louise Lamphere (Stanford, CA: Stanford University, 1974); *Sexual Meanings: The Cultural Construction of Gender and Sexuality,* ed. Sherry B. Ortner and Harriet Whitehead (Cambridge: Cambridge University, 1981); and the studies by Peggy Reeves Sanday, *Female Power and Male Dominance: On the Origins of Sexual Inequality* (Cambridge: Cambridge University, 1981) and Nancy Chodorow, *The Reproduction of Motherhood: Psychoanalysis and the Sociology of Gender* (Berkeley: University of California, 1978).
44. Shapiro, 457.
45. Ibid., 458–59.
46. Lecture, "When Cosmologies Lie," Divinity School of the University of Chicago, October 1982.
47. Degler, "What the Women's Movement Has Done to American History," 412.
48. Elisabeth Schüssler Fiorenza, " 'You Are Not To Be Called Father,' " *Cross Currents* 29 (1979): 301–23; see also Schüssler Fiorenza, *In Memory of Her,* 245–342.
49. Edwin Ardener, "Belief and the Problem of Women," in *The Interpretation of Ritual,* ed. J. S. LaFontaine (London: Tavistock, 1972), reprinted in S. Ardener, *Perceiving Women* (New York: Wiley, 1975).
50. Shapiro, 459–62.
51. Kelly-Gadol, "The Social Relation of the Sexes," 814–16.
52. Ibid., 816–17.
53. Ibid., 822–23. Kelly-Gadol cites the work on the family of Philippe Ariés, Nancy Chodorow, David Hunt, the Frankfurt School, Wilhelm Reich, and Eli Zaretsky. See also Marc Poster, *The Critical Theory of the Family* (New York: Seabury, 1980).
54. Boxer, "Theory and Practice of Women's Studies," 683.

55. Namascar Shaktini, "Displacing the Phallic Subject: Monique Wittig's Lesbian Writing," *Signs* 8:1 (Autumn 1982): 30.
56. Ibid., 31–32.
57. Julia Kristeva, "Women's Time," trans. Alice Jardine and Harry Blake, *Signs* 7:1 (Autumn 1981): 21. See also Julia Kristeva, *The Kristeva Reader* ed. Toril Moi (New York: Columbia University Press, 1986).
58. Alice Jardine, "Introduction to Julia Kristeva's 'Women's Time,'" *Signs,* 11. A fascinating introduction to and interpretation of French feminism is Alice Jardine, *Gynesis: Configurations of Women and Modernity* (Ithaca and London: Cornell University, 1985). See also Hester Eisenstein and Alice Jardine, eds., *The Future of Difference* (New Brunswick, NJ: Rutgers University Press, 1985).
59. Boxer, 687.
60. See, for example, Elizabeth Clark and Herbert Richardson, eds., *Women and Religion: A Feminist Sourcebook of Christian Thought* (New York: Harper & Row, 1977); Rosemary Radford Ruether, *New Woman/New Earth: Sexist Ideologies and Human Liberation* (New York: Seabury, 1975); Rosemary Radford Ruether, ed., *Religion and Sexism*; Margaret A. Farley, "Sources of Sexual Inequality in the History of Christian Thought," 177–97.
61. Rita Gross, "Androcentrism and Androgyny in the Methodology of History of Religions," 9.
62. Valerie Saiving, "Androcentrism in Religious Studies," *The Journal of Religion* 56:2 (April 1976): 185; Mircea Eliade, *Rites and Symbols of Initiation* (New York: Harper & Row, 1965), 45. See Saiving's "The Human Situation: A Feminine View," *The Journal of Religion* (April 1960), reprinted in Carol P. Christ and Judith Plaskow, eds., *Womanspirit Rising*, 25–42.
63. Ibid., 189–91; Eliade, 132.
64. Saiving, 191.
65. Eliade, 101.
66. Saiving, 192–95.
67. Elisabeth Schüssler Fiorenza, "Discipleship and Patriarchy: Early Christian Ethos and Christian Ethics in a Feminist Theological Perspective," in *The Annual of the Society of Christian Ethics: Selected Papers, 1982*, ed. L. Rasmussen, (Waterloo: The Council of the Study of Religion, 1982), 132–36. See also Schüssler Fiorenza, *In Memory of Her,* 251–84.
68. Schüssler Fiorenza, "Discipleship and Patriarchy," 143.
69. Ibid., 146
70. Ibid., 148.
71. Ibid., 149–61.
72. Susan Moller Okin, *Women in Western Political Thought* (Princeton: Princeton University Press, 1979), 276, cited in Schüssler Fiorenza, "Discipleship and Patriarchy," 164.
73. Rosemary Radford Ruether, "The Feminist Critique in Religious Studies, *Soundings* 64:4 (Winter 1981): 391.
74. See, for example, *Women of Spirit*, ed. Rosemary Ruether and Eleanor McLaughlin.
75. Janet Wilson James, *Women in American Religion* (Philadelphia: University of Pennsylvania Press, 1980), 24–25.
76. See Denise Lardner Carmody, *Women and World Religions* (Nashville: Abingdon,

1979) for a very general survey from a Christian theological perspective.

77. Rita M. Gross and Nancy Auer Falk, eds., *Unspoken Worlds* (San Francisco: Harper & Row, 1980), xvi.

78. Rosemary Radford Ruether, "A Religion for Women: Sources and Strategies," *Christianity and Crisis* 21:19 (December 10, 1979): 310. But see also her "Female Symbols, Values, and Context," *Christianity and Crisis* 46:19 (January 12, 1987): 460-64.

79. Judith Ochshorn, *The Female Experience and the Nature of the Divine* (Bloomington: Indiana University Press, 1981); reviewed by Joan O'Brien, *Theological Studies* 43:3 (December 1982): 743-44.

80. *Beyond God the Father,* see also *Pure Lust: An Elemental Feminist Philosophy* (Boston: Beacon Press, 1984).

81. Carol P. Christ, "Spiritual Quest and Women's Experience," *Womanspirit Rising,* ed. Carol P. Christ and Judith Plaskow, 228-45; see also Christ's *Diving Deep and Surfacing* (Boston: Beacon Press, 1980).

82. Carol P. Christ, "Why Women Need the Goddess," *Womanspirit Rising,* 275.

83. Naomi Goldenberg, *The Changing of the Gods;* "Dreams and Fantasies as Sources of Revelation," *Womanspirit Rising,* 219-27. See also the relevant essays in *The Politics of Women's Spirituality,* ed. Charlene Spretnak (New York: Doubleday, 1982).

84. Caroline Walker Bynum, *Jesus as Mother: Studies in the Spirituality of the High Middle Ages* (Berkeley: University of California Press, 1982), 173, n. 10.

85. Review of *Womanspirit Rising* and *The Changing of the Gods* in *Signs* 6:2 (Winter 1980): 333, citing Clifford Geertz, *Islam Observed* (Chicago: University of Chicago Press, 1968), 2.

86. See Landes; Rosemary Radford Ruether, "Goddesses and Witches: Liberation and Countercultural Feminism," *Christian Century* 97:28 (September 10-17, 1980): 842-47.

87. Landes, 333-34.

88. Schüssler Fiorenza, "Discipleship and Patriarchy," 133-36 and "Feminist Theology as a Critical Theology of Liberation," *Theological Studies* 36:4 (December 1975): 605-26; Ruether, "Goddesses and Witches," 846; Ruether, *New Woman/New Earth,* 186-214; Ruether, *Sexism and God-Talk: Toward a Feminist Theology* (Boston: Beacon Press, 1982), 72-92; Phyllis Trible, *God and the Rhetoric of Sexuality* (Philadelphia: Fortress Press, 1978) and *Texts of Terror: Literary-Feminist Readings of Biblical Narratives* (Philadelphia: Fortress Press, 1984); Margaret A. Farley, "New Patterns of Relationship: Beginnings of a Moral Revolution," *Theological Studies* 36:4 (December 1975): 627-46.

89. Mary R. Lefkowitz, "Princess Ida, the Amazons and a Women's College Curriculum," *Times Literary Supplement* 4104 (November 27, 1981): 1399-1401, argues forcefully, in the context of her work in classics, for the importance of careful exploration of women's status in nonanachronistic terms through the use of new sources (for example, gravestones, boundary markers, wills, marriage contracts), the sophisticated use of epic and drama, and for comparative analysis with the status of men in appropriate class and period contexts. Margaret R. Miles, *Image as Insight: Visual Understanding in Western Christianity and Secular Culture* (Boston: Beacon Press, 1985) urges the study of images (art, architecture, artifacts) as a way to understand the experience of nonliterate members of historical societies.

CHAPTER 5. THE POSSIBILITY OF A CHRISTIAN FEMINIST THEOLOGY

1. Carol P. Christ, "The New Feminist Theology: A Review of the Literature," 203–212; see Mary Daly, *Beyond God the Father.*
2. Christ, 211, 205.
3. See Zsuzsanna Budapest, *The Feminist Book of Lights and Shadows* (Luna Publications, 1976); Starhawk (Miriam Simos), *The Spiral Dance: The Rebirth of the Ancient Religion of the Great Goddess* (San Francisco: Harper & Row, 1979); Carol P. Christ, *Diving Deep and Surfacing: Women Writers on Spiritual Quest* (Boston: Beacon Press, 1980); Naomi Goldenberg, *Changing of the Gods*; Penelope Washburn, *Becoming Woman* (New York: Harper & Row, 1977), *Seasons of Women* (San Francisco: Harper & Row, 1979); and the essays in part IV of *Womanspirit Rising*, ed. Carol P. Christ and Judith Plaskow.
4. Rosemary Ruether, "A Religion of Women: Sources and Strategies," 310. It is important to note, however, that advocates of Goddess symbolism are not deeply concerned about historical origins. Carol Christ suggests that the symbol is as much "created" or "invented" by contemporary women as it is "remembered." See her article "Why Women Need the Goddess" in *Womanspirit Rising,* 277.
5. Rosemary Radford Ruether, "Goddesses and Witches: Liberation and Countercultural Feminism," 842–47, quote at 846. See also, however, her "Female Symbols, Values, and Context," 460–64.
6. Ibid., 847.
7. *Beyond God the Father,* 13–63, 44–68, 69–71; *Gyn/Ecology,* 37–38. See also Simone de Beauvoir, *The Second Sex,* xixff. for the concept of the "other." Dorothee Soelle uses the arresting term "Christofacism"; see Tom F. Driver, *Christ in a Changing World: Toward an Ethical Christology* (New York: Crossroad, 1981), 3.
8. *Beyond God the Father,* 11–12, 69–97; see also *Pure Lust,* 1–32.
9. See *Women of Spirit,* ed. Rosemary Ruether and Eleanor McLaughlin.
10. See Judith Plaskow, *Sex, Sin and Grace,* 162–67.
11. Hans-Georg Gadamer, *Truth and Method,* trans. ed. Garret Barden and John Cumming (New York: Seabury Press, 1975), especially section II of part II, 235–344, and supplement II, 491–98; see also Paul Ricoeur, *Interpretation Theory: Discourse and the Surplus of Meaning* (Fort Worth: Texas Christian University Press, 1976), 39–95.
12. Jürgen Habermas, *Knowledge and Human Interests,* trans. Jeremy J. Shapiro (Boston: Beacon Press, 1986), 311; Thomas McCarthy, *The Critical Theory of Jürgen Habermas* (Cambridge: MIT Press, 1981), 169–93. The phrase "ethical and productive distance" is Paul Ricoeur's, in "Ethics and Culture: Habermas and Gadamer in Dialogue," *Philosophy Today* 17 (1973): 164–65, cited in McCarthy, 192. The debate between Gadamer and Habermas is clarified in their respective articles in *Continuum* 8:1 (Spring 1970): 77–95, 122–33.
13. Habermas, *Knowledge and Human Interests,* 317. Mary Knutsen, whose forthcoming study, *Shrieking Heaven: Resources in Critical Social Theory, Psychoanalysis, and Interpretation Theory for Feminist Theology* will provide a thorough discussion of these issues, provided helpful criticism in this context. For another use of critical theory, see Francis Schüssler Fiorenza, "Critical Social Theory and Christology: Toward an Understanding of Atonement and Redemption as Emancipatory

Solidarity," *Proceedings of the Catholic Theological Society of America* 30 (1975): 63-110.

14. Ricoeur, "Ethics and Culture," ibid.

15. Paul Tillich, *Theology of Culture,* ed. Robert C. Kimball (New York: Oxford University Press, 1964), 53-67 and *Systematic Theology,* (Chicago: University of Chicago Press, 1951), I:238-41.

16. Tillich, *Theology of Culture,* 67.

17. Paul Ricoeur, *Freud and Philosophy: An Essay on Interpretation,* trans. David Savage (New Haven and London: Yale University Press, 1970), 3-56, 494-551; *Interpretation Theory,* 45-69.

18. *Freud and Philosophy,* 496; *Interpretation Theory,* 45-46. The unpublished work of Patricia Harrington on the symbol of the virgin of Guadalupe was particularly important in suggesting the helpfulness of Tillich and Ricoeur for a feminist theory of symbolism.

19. See David Tracy, *Blessed Rage for Order,* 32-34, 43-48; "Particular Questions Within General Consensus," *Consensus in Theology?* ed. Leonard Swidler (Philadelphia: Westminster Press, 1980), 33-39; *The Analogical Imagination: Christian Theology and the Culture of Pluralism* (New York: Crossroad, 1981), 238-47; Edward Schillebeeckx, *Interim Report on the Books Jesus and Christ,* trans. John Bowden (New York: Crossroad, 1981) 56-62.

20. Ruether, "A Religion for Women," 309: "All significant works of culture have depth and power to the extent that they have been doing something else besides justifying sexism. They have been responding to the fears of death, estrangement and oppression and the hopes for life, reconciliation and liberation of humanity."

21. Elisabeth Schüssler Fiorenza, "Sexism and Conversion," *Network* 9:3 (May-June, 1981): 15-22; see also Rosemary Radford Ruether, *New Woman/New Earth,* 115-33, 162-85; *Sexism and God-Talk,* 214-34.

22. See, for example, *Women of Spirit,* ed. Ruether and McLaughlin and *Women in American Religion,* ed. Janet Wilson James (Philadelphia: University of Pennsylvania Press, 1980); *Women and Religion,* ed. Elizabeth Clark and Herbert Richardson; *Religion and Sexism,* ed. Rosemary Radford Ruether; Margaret A. Farley, "Sources of Sexual Inequality in the History of Christian Thought," 162-76. Ruether, *New Woman/New Earth,* 24-31; see also Elizabeth Janeway, *Man's World, Woman's Place: A Study in Social Mythology* (New York: Dell Publishing Co., 1971) and *Women, Culture and Society,* ed. Michelle Zimbalist Rosaldo and Louise Lamphere (Stanford, CA: Stanford University Press, 1974).

23. Christ, 206.

24. Trible, *God and the Rhetoric of Sexuality,* 4. See also Trible's *Texts of Terror.*

25. *God and the Rhetoric of Sexuality,* 7.

26. Ibid., 22; see also Ricoeur, *Interpretation Theory,* 64.

27. Trible, *God and the Rhetoric of Sexuality,* 201-202; see also Phyllis Bird, "Images of Women in the Old Testament," *Religion and Sexism,* 41-88; Leonard Swidler, *Biblical Affirmations of Women* (Philadelphia: Westminster Press, 1979), 75-159.

28. Elisabeth Schüssler Fiorenza, "Interpreting Patriarchal Traditions," *The Liberating Word,* ed. Letty M. Russell (Philadelphia: Westminster Press, 1976), 49; see also her *In Memory of Her* and *Bread Not Stone.*

29. "Interpreting Patriarchal Traditions," 52; *In Memory of Her,* 105-59; see also Swidler, *Biblical Affirmations,* 161-35

30. "Interpreting Patriarchal Traditions," 53.

31. See Elisabeth Schüssler Fiorenza, "Word, Spirit, and Power: Women in Early Christian Communities," *Women of Spirit,* 30–70 and "Women in the Early Christian Movement," *Womanspirit Rising,* 84–92.

32. Elisabeth Schüssler Fiorenza, " 'You Are Not To Be Called Father'," 301–23.

33. It is important to distinguish here between a cultural and a religious tradition and each of these within both Judaism and Christianity. Religious tradition in each case represents a transcendent horizon. Countercultural Christianity is not to be seen over against Judaism as a patriarchal unity; the Jewish religious tradition reveals its own transcendent dynamic. I am grateful to Professor Susan Shapiro, who brought this important distinction to my attention. See also Judith Plaskow, "Christian Feminism and Anti-Judaism," *Cross Currents* 28:3 (Fall 1978): 306–9; Susanna Heschel, ed., *On Being a Jewish Feminist: A Reader* (New York: Shocken Books, 1983).

34. Elisabeth Schüssler Fiorenza, " 'You Are Not To Be Called Father'," 318.

35. Elisabeth Schüssler Fiorenza, "Interpreting Patriarchal Traditions," 61. Similar approaches are followed, in the evangelical tradition, by Letha Scanzoni and Nancy Hardesty, *All We're Meant to Be* (Waco, Texas: Word Publishers, 1974) and in the Roman Catholic ordination discussion in the essays in *Women and Catholic Priesthood: An Expanded Vision,* ed. Ann Marie Gardiner; see Schubert M. Ogden, *The Point of Christology* (San Francisco: Harper & Row, 1982), 164 ff. for another view.

36. See especially Rosemary Radford Ruether, *Sexism and God-Talk.*

37. See Valerie Saiving, "The Human Situation: A Feminine View," *Womanspirit Rising,* 23–42; Plaskow, *Sex, Sin and Grace*; Margaret Farley, "New Patterns of Relationship: Beginnings of a Moral Revolution," *Theological Studies* 36:4 (December 1975), 627–46; on women and ministry, see the bibliography by Hyang Sook Chung Yoon in *Women and Priesthood,* ed. Carroll Stuhlmueller (Collegeville, MN: Liturgical Press, 1978), 178–85; Elizabeth M. Tetlow, *Women and Ministry in the New Testament* (New York: Paulist, 1980); Elisabeth Schüssler Fiorenza, *In Memory of Her,* 97ff.

38. Trible, *God and the Rhetoric of Sexuality,* 200–201.

39. Elisabeth Schüssler Fiorenza, " 'You Are Not To Be Called Father'," 317.

40. Ruether, *New Woman/New Earth,* 65; see *Sexism and God-Talk,* 47–71.

41. See Edward Schillebeeckx, *God the Future of Man,* trans. N. D. Smith (New York: Sheed and Ward, 1968), 181–86.

42. See David Bakan, *And They Took Themselves Wives: The Emergence of Patriarchy in Western Civilization* (San Francisco: Harper & Row, 1979); Robert Hamerton-Kelley, *God the Father: Theology and Patriarchy in the Teaching of Jesus* (Philadelphia: Fortress Press, 1979). Diane Tennis, in "The Loss of the Father God: Why Women Rage and Grieve," *Christianity and Crisis* 41:10 (June 8, 1981): 164–70, makes too literal and direct a move, I believe, from human fatherhood to God, bypassing the moments of negation or relativization in interpreting the symbol; see also her *Is God the Only Reliable Father?* (Philadelphia: Westminster Press, 1985).

43. Elizabeth A. Johnson, "The Incomprehensibility of God and the Image of God Male and Female," *Theological Studies* 45:3 (September 1984): 441–80; Anne Carr, "The God Who Is Involved," *Theology Today* 38:3 (October 1981): 314–28. See Thomas J. J. Altizer, *Total Presence: The Language of Jesus and the Language of Today* (New York: Seabury Press, 1980), 25–36.

44. See, for example, Karl Rahner, *Foundations of Christian Faith,* trans. William V. Dych (New York: Seabury Press, 1978), 24–89; Edward Schillebeeckx, *God and Man,* trans. Edward Fitzgerald and Peter Tomlinson (New York: Sheed and Ward, 1969) and *God the Future of Man;* Wolfhart Pannenberg, *The Idea of God and Human Freedom,* trans. R. A. Wilson (Philadelphia: Westminster Press, 1973), *What Is Man?* (Philadelphia: Fortress Press, 1970) and *Anthropology in Theological Perspective,* trans. Matthew J. O'Connell (Philadelphia: Westminster Press, 1985); Jürgen Moltmann, *The Theology of Hope,* trans. James W. Leitch (New York: Harper & Row, 1967); Langdon Gilkey, *Naming the Whirlwind: The Renewal of God-Language* (Indianapolis: Bobbs-Merrill, 1969), *Reaping the Whirlwind: A Christian Interpretation of History* (New York: Seabury Press, 1979); David Tracy, *Blessed Rage for Order; The Analogical Imagination;* Schubert M. Ogden, *The Reality of God and Other Essays* (New York: Harper & Row, 1965); Hans Küng, *Does God Exist?* (New York: Doubleday, 1980).

45. See, for example, Johannes B. Metz, *Theology of the World,* trans. William Glen-Doepel (New York: Herder and Herder, 1969); *Faith in History and Society,* trans. David Smith (New York: Seabury Press, 1980); Juan Luis Segundo, *Our Idea of God,* trans. John Drury (Maryknoll, Orbis Books, 1974); Gustavo Gutierrez, *A Theology of Liberation: History, Politics, and Salvation,* trans. Sr. Caridad Inda and John Eagleson (Maryknoll, Orbis Books, 1973).

46. Elisabeth Schüssler Fiorenza, "Feminist Theology as a Critical Liberation Theology," *Theological Studies* 36:4 (December 1975): 605–26.

47. See Margaret Farley, "New Patterns of Relationship: Beginnings of a Moral Revolution, and Anne Wilson Schaef, *Women's Reality.*

48. Karl Rahner, *Foundations of Christian Faith,* 295ff.; John B. Cobb, Jr., *Christ in a Pluralistic Age* (Philadelphia: Westminster Press, 1975); Jürgen Moltmann, *The Crucified God,* trans. R. A. Wilson and John Bowden (New York: Harper & Row, 1973); Jon Sobrino, *Christology at the Crossroads;* Frans Josef van Beeck, *Christ Proclaimed: Christology as Rhetoric* (New York: Paulist, 1979); Rosemary Radford Ruether, "Christology and Feminism," *To Change the World: Christology and Cultural Criticism* (New York: Crossroad, 1981), 45–56, *Sexism and God-Talk,* 116–38.

49. Schillebeeckx, *Jesus: An Experiment in Christology,* trans. Hubert Hoskins (New York: Seabury Press, 1979), 606–12; *Christ: The Experience of Jesus as Lord,* trans. John Bowden (New York: Seabury Press, 1980), 76.

50. Schillebeeckx, *Jesus,* 623; *Christ,* 76.

CHAPTER 6. THEOLOGICAL ANTHROPOLOGY AND THE EXPERIENCE OF WOMEN

1. Paul Tillich, *Systematic Theology* (Chicago: University of Chicago, 1951), I:3–5; Karl Rahner, *Theological Investigations,* trans. Graham Harrison (New York: Herder and Herder, 1973), IX:28–45.

2. David Tracy, "Particular Questions within General Consensus," *Consensus in Theology?* ed. Leonard Swidler (Philadelphia: Westminster Press, 1980), 34; *The Analogical Imagination: Christian Theology and the Culture of Pluralism* (New York: Crossroad, 1981), 238–40.

3. Judith Plaskow, *Sex, Sin and Grace,* 6, 9–50.

4. Mary Aquin O'Neill, "Toward a Renewed Anthropology," *Theological Studies* 36:4 (December 1975): 725–36.
5. Elizabeth Janeway, *Man's World, Woman's Place*, 51–57, cited in O'Neill, 732.
6. See Sherry B. Ortner, "Is Female to Male as Nature Is to Culture?" *Women, Culture, and Society*, ed. Michelle Zimbalist Rosaldo and Louise Lamphere (Stanford, CA: Stanford University Press, 1974), 67–87.
7. Rosemary Radford Ruether, *New Woman/New Earth*, 3–23. See her *Sexism and God-Talk*, 47–54.
8. Carol Christ, "Margaret Atwood: The Surfacing of Women's Spiritual Quest and Vision," *Signs* 2:2 (Winter 1976): 327.
9. Shulamith Firestone, *The Dialectic of Sex* (New York: William Morrow, 1971).
10. Simone de Beauvoir, *The Second Sex*, trans. H. M. Parshley (New York: Vintage Books, 1974).
11. Rosemary Radford Ruether, "Motherearth and the Megamachine: A Theology of Liberation in a Feminine, Somatic and Ecological Perspective," *Womanspirit Rising*, ed. Carol Christ and Judith Plaskow, 51.
12. Judith Plaskow, "On Carol Christ: Some Theological Reflections," *Signs* 2:2 (Winter 1976): 336.
13. O'Neill, 735.
14. *Research Report: Women in Church and Society*, ed. Sara Butler (Mahwah, NJ: Catholic Theological Society of America, 1978).
15. Ibid., 37.
16. Historical study has also demonstrated that patriarchy is an historical creation. See Gerda Lerner, *The Creation of Patriarchy*.
17. *Research Report*, 39.
18. Mary Buckley, "The Rising of the Woman is the Rising of the Race," *Proceedings of the Catholic Theological Society of America* 34 (1979), 48–63.
19. Ibid., 59.
20. See Carolyn Osiek, *Beyond Anger: On Being A Feminist in the Church* (New York: Paulist, 1986).
21. See, for example, Karl Rahner, "The Experiment with Man," and "The Problem of Genetic Manipulation," *Theological Investigations* IX:205–24, 225–52.
22. Karl Rahner, "The Position of Women in the New Situation in Which the Church Finds Herself," *Theological Investigations*, VIII:75; see p. 88 for reference to "the church of women."
23. See the essays in *Women: Invisible in Church and Theology*, Concilium 182, eds. Elisabeth Schüssler Fiorenza and Mary Collins (Edinburgh: T. and T. Clark, 1985); Rosemary Radford Ruether, *Women-Church: Theology and Practice* (San Francisco: Harper & Row, 1986).

CHAPTER 7. FEMINIST REFLECTIONS ON GOD

1. Sallie McFague, *Metaphorical Theology* (Philadelphia: Fortress Press, 1982), 147–48.
2. Gordon Kaufman, *The Theological Imagination: Constructing the Concept of God* (Philadelphia: Westminster Press, 1981), 35–39, 274–79.
3. Karl Rahner, "The Concept of Mystery in Catholic Theology," *Theological Investigations*, trans. Kevin Smith (Baltimore: Helicon Press, 1966), IV:57.
4. See John L. McKenzie, *The Two Edged Sword* (New York: Bruce, 1956), 93–94:

"God is of course masculine, but not in the sense of sexual distinction. ..."

5. See Mary Daly, *Beyond God the Father*; Carol P. Christ, "The New Feminist Theology: A Review of the Literature," 203-12.

6. McFague, 145-92; Daly, 13-43. But see Sandra M. Schneiders, *Women and the Word* (New York: Paulist, 1986).

7. See Rosemary Radford Ruether, *New Woman/New Earth.*

8. Mary Daly, *Beyond God the Father,* 132-54; *Gyn/Ecology,* 37-89; Naomi Goldenberg, *Changing of the Gods.*

9. See Judith Van Herik, *Freud on Femininity and Faith,* 107-39; Gerda Lerner, *The Creation of Patriarchy,* 212-29.

10. See the essays in Michelle Zimbalist Rosaldo and Louise Lamphere, eds., *Woman, Culture and Society*; Ruether, *New Woman/New Earth,* 63-85; and Susan Rubin Suleiman, ed., *The Female Body in Western Culture: Contemporary Perspectives* (Cambridge and London: Harvard University Press 1986).

11. John R. Thompson, "Women and Religion: Psychic Sources of Misogyny," *Christianity and Crisis* (April 2, 1979): 72-77; Mary O'Brien, *The Politics of Reproduction* (Boston: Routledge and Kegan Paul, 1981); Nancy Jay, *Throughout Your Generations Forever: A Sociology of Blood Sacrifice* (unpublished Ph.D. dissertation, Brandeis University, 1981); Nancy Jay "Sacrifice as Remedy for Having Been Born of Women," in *Immaculate and Powerful: The Female in Sacred Image and Social Reality,* ed. Clarissa W. Atkinson, Constance H. Buchanan, and Margaret R. Miles (Boston: Beacon Press, 1985), 283-309.

12. Nancy Chodorow, *The Reproduction of Mothering: Psychoanalysis and the Sociology of Gender* (Berkeley: University of California, 1978).

13. Carol P. Christ, "Why Women Need the Goddess," in Carol P. Christ and Judith Plaskow, eds, *Womanspirit Rising,* 275.

14. See Daniel O'Hanlon, "The God Beyond," *Commonweal* CXI: 9 (May 4, 1984): 271-75.

15. McFague, 31-66.

16. Paul Tillich, *Theology of Culture,* ed. Robert C. Kimball (New York: Oxford University, 1964), 53-67. See also Sandra M. Schneiders, *Women and the Word,* 1-37.

17. Paul Ricoeur, *Freud and Philosophy,* 459-551; *Interpretation Theory,* 45-69.

18. Karl Rahner, "Observations on the Doctrine of God in Catholic Dogmatics," *Theological Investigations,* trans. Graham Harrison (New York: Herder and Herder, 1972) IX:127.

19. See Sallie McFague, "An Epilogue: The Christian Paradigm," in Peter C. Hodgson and Robert H. King, eds., *Christian Theology: An Introduction to Its Transitions and Tasks* (Philadelphia: Fortress Books, 1982), 323-36.

20. Anita Röper, *Ist Gott ein Mann? Ein Gespräch mit Karl Rahner* (Düsseldorf: Patmos, 1979), 34-65; Nicholas Lash, " 'Son of God': Reflections on a Metaphor," in E. Schillebeeckx and J. Metz, eds., *Jesus, Son of God* Concilium 153 (New York: Seabury Press, 1982), 11-16.

21. Christ, "Why Women Need the Goddess," 278-86.

22. See, for example, Marilyn Chapin Massey, *The Feminine Soul* (Boston: Beacon Press, 1985).

23. See Carol Gilligan, *In a Different Voice* (Cambridge: Harvard University, 1982).

24. McFague, 192-94.

25. Rosemary Radford Ruether, *Sexism and God-Talk,* 71.

26. Mary Daly, *Beyond God the Father,* 33-34. This early description of God by Daly

demonstrates the influence of Jacques Maritain in her thought at this stage.

27. Isabel Carter Heyward, *The Redemption of God: A Theology of Mutual Relation* (Lanham, MD: University Press of America, 1982).

28. McFague, 177–94, especially 179.

29. See Edward Farley, "God as Dominator and Image-Giver: Divine Sovereignty and the New Anthropology," *Journal of Ecumenical Studies* 6:3 (Summer 1969): 354–75.

30. See Carol Ochs, *Women and Spirituality* (Totowa, NJ: Rowman and Allanheld, 1983); Virginia Ramey Mollenkott, *The Divine Feminine: The Biblical Imagery of God as Female* (New York: Crossroad, 1981).

31. See Mary E. Giles, ed., *The Feminist Mystic* (New York: Crossroad, 1982).

32. See Mary O'Brien, *The Politics of Reproduction*, 19–64.

33. Elisabeth Schüssler Fiorenza, *In Memory of Her*, parts II and III.

34. Madeleine Boucher, "The Image of God as Father in the Gospels: Toward a Reassessment," an unpublished paper presented to the Catholic Biblical Society of America, New Orleans, August 12, 1984.

35. Rosemary Radford Ruether, "An Unrealized Revolution," *Christianity and Crisis* 43:17 (October 31, 1983): 398–400; Robert Hamerton-Kelly, *God the Father: Theology and Patriarchy in the Teaching of Jesus* (Philadelphia: Fortress Press, 1979), 52–104; Gerd Theissen, *Sociology of Early Christianity*, trans. John Bowden (Philadelphia: Fortress Press, 1977), 8–16.

36. Bernard Cooke, "Non-Patriarchal Salvation," *Horizons* 10:1 (1983): 22–31.

37. See Jürgen Moltmann, *The Crucified God*, 126–45; Leonardo Boff, *Jesus Christ Liberator*, trans. Patrick Hughes (Maryknoll: Orbis Books, 1978), 100–120.

38. Elisabeth Schüssler Fiorenza, "Feminist Theology as a Critical Liberation Theology," *Theological Studies* 36 (1975), 605–26.

39. See Gustavo Gutierrez, "Faith as Freedom: Solidarity with the Alienated and Confidence in the Future," in Francis A. Eigo, ed., *Living with Change, Experience, Faith* (Villanova, PA: Villanova University, 1976), 37; Juan Segundo, *Grace and the Human Condition* (Maryknoll: Orbis Books, 1973), 14–57.

40. Johann Baptist Metz, *Faith in History and Society: Toward a Practical Fundamental Theology*, trans. David Smith (New York: Seabury Press, 1980), 60–77.

41. Langdon Gilkey, *Reaping the Whirlwind: A Christian Interpretation of History* (New York: Seabury Press, 1976), 248–49, 279–81.

42. Karl Rahner, "On the Theology of the Incarnation," *Theological Investigations*, trans. Kevin Smith (Baltimore: Helicon Press, 1966), IV: 177.

43. Thomas Aquinas deals with this precise problem in his discussion of the theological virtue of charity in the *Summa Theologiae* II–II, q. 23, art. 1, where he argues against Aristotle and cites John's Gospel as his authority.

44. See the writings of Charles Hartshorne, John Cobb, Schubert Ogden. For a Catholic appropriation of the concept of the dipolarity of God, see David Tracy, *Blessed Rage for Order*, 175–87.

45. Heyward, *The Redemption of God*, especially 149–78.

46. See Richard Rubenstein, *After Auschwitz* (Indianapolis: Bobbs-Merrill, 1966).

47. Thomas F. Tracy surveys the positions of Langdon Gilkey, Gordon Kaufman, and Schubert Ogden and offers his own resolution to the question of God's activity in history in *God, Action, and Embodiment* (Grand Rapids, MI: Eerdmans, 1984).

48. Alfred N. Whitehead, *Adventures of Ideas* (New York: Macmillan, 1933), 213.

49. Whitehead, *Process and Reality: An Essay in Cosmology* (New York: Harper & Row, 1937), 532. See Ronald Goetz, "The Suffering God: The Rise of a New Orthodoxy," *The Christian Century* 103: 13 (April 16, 1986): 385–89; Warren McWilliams, *The Passion of God: Divine Suffering in Contemporary Protestant Theology* (Macon, GA: Mercer University Press, 1985).

50. Moltmann, *The Crucified God*, 235–48.

51. Jon Sobrino, *Christology at the Crossroads*, 179–235.

52. Sandra Schneiders, "Women and Power in the Church: A New Testament Reflection," *Proceedings of the Catholic Theological Society of America* 37 (New York, 1982), 127–28.

53. Elisabeth Schüssler Fiorenza, *Bread Not Stone*, 10–11.

54. Jürgen Moltmann, *The Theology of Hope*, trans. James W. Leitch (New York: Harper & Row, 1967).

55. Wolfhart Pannenberg, *The Idea of God and Human Freedom*, 95–115.

56. Edward Schillebeeckx, *God the Future of Man*, 181, 183.

57. Ibid., 77, 81, 184–85, 91.

58. Edward Schillebeeckx, *Christ: The Experience of Jesus as Lord*, 808.

59. Karl Rahner, "Marxist Utopia and the Christian Future of Man," *Theological Investigations*, trans. Karl H. and Boniface Kruger (Baltimore: Helicon Press, 1969) VI:62.

60. See Dorothee Soelle, "Mysticism— Liberation—Feminism" in *The Strength of the Weak: Toward a Christian Feminist Identity*, trans. Robert and Rita Kimber (Philadelphia: Westminster Press, 1984), 79–105; Elizabeth A. Johnson, "The Incomprehensibility of God and the Image of God Male and Female," *Theological Studies* 45:3 (September 1984): 441–80.

61. Juan Segundo, *Our Idea of God* (Maryknoll: Orbis Books, 1974), 49, 178–79. See also Richard E. Creel, *Divine Impassibility: An Essay in Philosophical Theology* (Cambridge: Cambridge University Press, 1986).

62. Patricia Wilson-Kastner, *Faith, Feminism and the Christ* (Philadelphia: Fortress Press, 1983), 121–37; Moltmann, *The Crucified God*, 200–290; idem, *The Trinity and the Kingdom: The Doctrine of God*, trans. Margaret Kohl (San Francisco: Harper & Row, 1981). For a recent historical and theological study and further bibliography see Robert W. Jenson, *The Triune Identity: God According to the Gospel* (Philadelphia: Fortress Press, 1982).

CHAPTER 8. FEMINISM AND CHRISTOLOGY

1. Daniel C. Maguire, "The Feminization of God and Ethics," *Christianity and Crisis* 42:4 (March 15, 1982): 59.

2. Edward Farley, "God as Dominator and Image-Giver: Divine Sovereignty and the New Anthropology," *Journal of Ecumenical Studies* 6:3 (Summer 1969) 354–75.

3. Sallie McFague, *Metaphorical Theology*, 354–375; Isabel Carter Heyward, *The Redemption of God*; Mary Daly, *Beyond God the Father*, 69–81; Dorothee Soelle, cited in Tom Driver, *Christ in a Changing World: Toward an Ethical Christology* (New York: Crossroad, 1981), 3.

4. Elisabeth Schüssler Fiorenza, "Toward a Feminist Biblical Hermeneutic," in *The Challenge of Liberation Theology*, ed. Brian Mahan and L. Dale Richesin (Maryknoll: Orbis Books, 1981), 107 (italics mine).

5. See *Women of Spirit,* ed. Rosemary Ruether and Eleanor McLaughlin; Elisabeth Moltmann-Wendel and Jürgen Moltmann, *Humanity in God* (New York: Pilgrim Press, 1983), 1-50.

6. See, for example, McFague, *Metaphorical Theology,* 18-81; Heyward, *The Redemption of God,* 9-11; Sandra M. Schneiders, *Women and the Word,* 50-71.

7. Mary O'Brien, *The Politics of Reproduction* (Boston, London, and Henley: Routledge and Kegan Paul, 1981); Gerda Lerner, *The Creation of Patriarchy.*

8. On religious classics, see David Tracy, *The Analogical Imagination* 99-153; on the constitutive Christological assertion see Schubert M. Ogden, *The Point of Christology,* 64-85.

9. See the summary of Christological issues in Madeleine Boucher (drafter), "Authority and Community in Christian Tradition," (A Study Document of the Commission on Faith and Order, National Council of Churches of Christ) in *Midstream: An Ecumenical Journal* 21 (1982), 402-17, esp. 411-14.

10. See Rosemary Radford Ruether, *New Woman/New Earth,* 24-31; Margaret Farley, "Sources of Sexual Inequality in the History of Christian Thought," 162-76.

11. See Raymond Geuss, *The Idea of a Critical Theory: Habermas and the Frankfurt School* (Cambridge: Cambridge University Press, 1981), 4-44, on the several uses of the term "ideology." For the negative use of the term in relation to theology, see Schubert Ogden, *The Point of Christology,* 96; 150ff; 164ff. Juan Luis Segundo uses "ideology" in a positive sense in *The Liberation of Theology* (Maryknoll: Orbis Books, 1976) and *Jesus of Nazareth Yesterday and Today* vol. 1, *Faith and Ideologies* (Maryknoll, NY: Orbis Books, 1984).

12. See Carol Christ, "The New Feminist Theology: A Review of the Literature," 203-12.

13. Mary Daly, *Beyond God the Father,* 69-81, 114-24.

14. Rosemary Radford Ruether, *To Change the World: Christology and Cultural Criticism,* 45.

15. *Summa Theologiae,* part I, q. 92, art. 1 and 2; part III, supplement, q. 39, a. 1.

16. *Summa Theologiae,* part III, q. 1-59. In q. 31, art.4, Aquinas argues for the fittingness, not the necessity, of the Incarnation in the male sex: "The male sex is more noble than the female, and for this reason He took flesh in the male sex. But lest the female sex should be despised, it was fitting that he should take the flesh of a woman." The inequality that Aquinas assumes is apparent.

17. Ruether, *To Change the World,* 48-56; *Sexism and God-Talk,* 122-26.

18. *Declaration on the Question of the Admission of Women to the Ministerial Priesthood,* Vatican City, October 15, 1976.

19. See Rosemary Radford Ruether, "Misogynism and Virginal Feminism in the Fathers of the Church" and Eleanor Commo McLaughlin, "Equality of Souls, Inequality of Sexes: Women in Medieval Theology," in *Religion and Sexism,* ed. Ruether, 150-83, 216-66.

20. Karl Barth, "The Doctrine of Creation," *Church Dogmatics,* ed. G. W. Bromiley and T. F. Torrance (Edinburgh: T. and T. Clarke, 1961), III:150-81.

21. Anne Wilson Schaef, *Women's Reality,* 161-69.

22. See Elisabeth Schüssler Fiorenza, "Word, Spirit and Power: Women in Early Christian Communities," *Women of Spirit,* 37 and 65 n.25 for an extensive bibliography on the Pauline texts. Paul K. Jewett, *Man as Male and Female* (Grand Rapids, MI: Eerdmans, 1975), 44-119 traces the headship theme in Paul, Aquinas, Luther, Calvin, Barth.

23. See the essays by Küng, Tracy, and Ruether on *Consensus in Theology?* ed. Leonard Swidler (Philadelphia: Westminster Press, 1980) and Ogden, *The Point of Christology,* 1-4, on appropriateness and credibility as criteria of adequacy; see also Edward Schillebeeckx, *Christ: The Experience of Jesus as Lord,* 71-79.
24. See above, chapter 5.
25. Edward Schillebeeckx, *Jesus: An Experiment in Christology,* 606-12; *Christ,* 76.
26. Paul Tillich, *Theology of Culture,* 55-67 and *Systematic Theology* (Chicago: University of Chicago, 1951), I:238-41. See also Paul Ricoeur, *Freud and Philosophy,* 3-56, 459-551; *Interpretation Theory,* 45-69.
27. McFague, *Metaphorical Theology,* 1-29.
28. See Sandra Schneiders, "The Paschal Imagination: Objectivity and Subjectivity in New Testament Interpretation," *Theological Studies* 43:1 (March 1982): 52-68; Driver, *Christ in a Changing World,* 12-31.
29. Elisabeth Schüssler Fiorenza, "Feminist Theology as a Critical Theology of Liberation," *Theological Studies* 36:4 (December 1975), 605-26
30. Daniel Maguire refers to the church's "institutionalized aversion to women" in "The Feminization of God and Ethics," 64.
31. See, for example, Elizabeth Caroll, "Women and Ministry," and Raymond E. Brown, "Roles of Women in the Fourth Gospel," *Theological Studies* 36 (December 1975), 660-86, 688-99; Elisabeth Schüssler Fiorenza, "Interpreting Patriarchal Traditions," *The Liberating Word,* ed. Letty M. Russell (Philadelphia: Westminster Press, 1976), 39-61; Ruether, *New Woman/New Earth,* 63-66. On narrative as the permanent and practical origin and context of all argumentative theology, see Johann Baptist Metz, *Faith in History and Society: Toward a Practical Fundamental Theology* (New York: Seabury Press, 1980), 208-17.
32. Elisabeth Schüssler Fiorenza, *In Memory of Her,* 122-30.
33. John Gager, *Kingdom and Community* (Englewood Cliffs, NJ: Prentice-Hall, 1975), 94; Gerd Theissen, "Itinerant Radicalism: The Tradition of Jesus Sayings from the Perspective of the Sociology of Literature," in *The Bible and Liberation* (Berkeley, CA: Community for Religious Research and Education, 1976), 89, cited in Lee Cormie, "The Hermeneutical Privilege of the Oppressed: Liberation Theologies, Biblical Faith, and Marxist Sociology of Knowledge," *Proceedings of the Catholic Theological Society of America* 33 (1978), 165. Theissen further suggests the continuity between Jesus himself and the traditions of the early Jesus movement after Easter and "the ethical requirements of the idea of discipleship—a correspondence between Jesus and his followers" in *Sociology of Early Palestinian Christianity* (Philadelphia: Fortress Press, 1978), 3-4, 26.
34. Cormie, "The Hermeneutical Privilege of the Oppressed," 180-181, argues that the privileged point of view of the oppressed sets an absolute limit to the claims of pluralism: it is not simply a methodological starting point but a practical commitment, a life-style, "a whole way of doing theology" as well.
35. Robert Hamerton-Kelly, *God the Father: Theology and Patriarchy in the Teaching of Jesus,* 64-68; Theissen, *Sociology of Early Palestinian Christianity,* 10-12, on "homelessness" and "lack of family" as characteristic of Jesus' followers.
36. Rosemary Radford Ruether, "An Unrealized Revolution," *Christianity and Crisis* 43:17 (October 31, 1983): 399.
37. Bernard Cooke, "Non-Patriarchal Salvation," *Horizons* 10:1 (Spring 1983): 26.
38. Elisabeth Schüssler Fiorenza, *In Memory of Her,* 142.
39. Elisabeth Schüssler Fiorenza, "Word, Spirit and Power," 30-44.

40. Elisabeth Schüssler Fiorenza, " 'You Are Not To Be Called Father'," 301-23.

41. Ogden, *The Point of Christology*, 89-96.

42. Schillebeeckx, *Christ*, 631-34, 643-44.

43. Ogden, *The Point of Christology*, 76.

44. Rosemary Radford Ruether, "Christology and Feminism: Can a Male Savior Help Women?" *Occasional Papers* 1:13 (Methodist Board of Higher Education and Ministry: December 1976), 3: "In the New Testament the Logos-Christ is specifically identified with the masculine divine principle which is related to the female church as head over body." See also Ruether's *To Change the World*, 45-49, and *Sexism and God-Talk*, 125.

45. See John L. McKenzie, "The Word of God in the New Testament," *Theological Studies* 21:2 (June 1960): 183-206; Adela Yarbro Collins, "New Testament Perspectives: The Gospel of John," *Journal for the Study of the Old Testament* 22:1 (1982): 47-53; Elizabeth A. Johnson, "Jesus, the Wisdom of God: A Biblical Basis for Non-Androcentric Christology," *Ephemerides Theologicae Lovanienses* LX 1:4 (December 1985): 261-94.

46. Schaef, *Woman's Reality*, 99-145.

47. Daly, *Beyond God the Father*, 8-11; Claudine Hermann, *Les voleuses de langue* (Paris: des femmes, 1976); Nanascar Shaktini, "Displacing the Phallic Subject," *Signs* 8:1 (Autumn 1982): 30.

48. Yarbro Collins, "New Testament Perspectives," 50-51; Johnson, "Jesus, the Wisdom of God," 291-294.

49. Elisabeth Schüssler Fiorenza, *In Memory of Her*, 189-99.

50. Daly, *Beyond God the Father*, 75-77; Plaskow, *Sex, Sin and Grace*, 149-74. Dorothee Soelle, *Beyond Mere Obedience* (New York: Pilgrim, 1982), 54-59.

51. Sandra Schneiders, "Women and Power on the Church: A New Testament Reflection," 123-28.

52. See Jon Sobrino, *Christology at the Crossroads*, 57-61, 126-29, 132-33, 405-12 on "discipleship" as a reinterpretation of "imitation"; Hans Küng, *On Being a Christian* (New York: Doubleday, 1976) 544ff; Johann Baptist Metz, *Faith in History and Society*, 176.

53. Johann Baptist Metz, *Faith in History and Society*, 88ff., 200-204.

54. Diane Tennis, "Reflections on the Maleness of Jesus," *Cross Currents* 28 (1978): 137-40; Schneiders, *Women and the Word*, 55-62.

55. Juliet Mitchell, *Psychoanalysis and Feminism* (New York: Vintage, 1975); Judith Van Herik, *Freud on Femininity and Faith*.

56. Hamerton-Kelly, *God the Father*, especially 70-81, 91-97.

57. Schillebeeckx, *Jesus*, 256-71.

58. Phyllis Trible, review of Robert Hamerton-Kelly's *God the Father* in *Theology Today* 37 (1980): 116-19.

59. See Schneiders, "Women and Power in the Church: A New Testament Reflection," 123, 127.

60. For further discussion and bibliography on Jesus as parable see Schillebeeckx, *Jesus*, 626-74 and McFague, *Metaphorical Theology*, 51-54.

61. Karl Rahner, *Foundations of Christian Faith*, 318-21.

62. Johann Baptist Metz, *Faith in History and Society*, 158-63.

63. See Ogden, *The Point of Christology*, 167.

64. Schillebeeckx, *Jesus*, 623.

CHAPTER 9. THE SALVATION OF WOMEN: CHRIST, MARY, AND THE CHURCH

1. See Gustaf Aulén, *Christus Victor: An Historical Study of the Three Main Types of the Idea of Atonement,* trans. A. G. Herbert (New York: Macmillan, 1966), 1–7, 143–54.

2. Lee E. Snook, *The Anonymous Christ: Jesus as Savior in Modern Theology* (Minneapolis: Augsburg, 1986), 13–35. For a series of "parables" and "analogues" descriptive of alienation and atonement see F. W. Dillistone, *The Christian Understanding of Atonement* (London: James Nisbet, 1968).

3. Irenaeus, *Adversus Haereses,* ed. and trans. Alexander Roberts and W. H. Rambaut (Edinburgh: T. and T. Clark, 1868), for example III:18, 1, 7; I:10, 1–2, V:21,1; see also H. E. Turner, *The Patristic Doctrine of Redemption* (London: A. R. Mowbray, 1952); Francis Schüssler Fiorenza, "Critical Social Theory and Christology," especially 63–66.

4. Anselm, "Cur Deus Homo," *Basic Writings,* trans. S. N. Deane (LaSalle, IL: Open Court, 1962), 171–288, especially I:7, 11, 12; II:1–18.

5. Aulén, 95–97. Aulén's thesis about Abailard's view of redemption has been disputed. Nevertheless, the *theory* of the moral exemplarity of Christ's redemption remains important as a type. See, for example, Richard E. Weingart, *The Logic of Divine Love: A Critical Analysis of the Soteriology of Peter Abailard* (Oxford: Clarendon Press, 1970), 202ff., where it is maintained that Abailard's own view is not "pelagian" as the exemplary theory would seem to imply but in fact theocentric: God does the work of redemption in Christ, not human beings. An excerpt of Abailard's "Exposition of the Epistle to the Romans," trans. Gerald E. Moffatt, is available in English in *A Scholastic Miscellany: Anselm to Ockham,* ed. Eugene R. Fairweather (Philadelphia: Westminster Press, 1956, The Library of Christian Classics), 276–87.

6. See, for example, Roger Haight, *An Alternative Vision: An Interpretation of Liberation Theology* (Mahwah, NJ: Paulist, 1985), 121–37; 147–49.

7. *Summa Theologiae* III, q. 46, 49.

8. Joseph Ratzinger, *Introduction to Christianity,* trans. J. R. Foster (New York: Seabury Press, 1969), 172–74.

9. See Edward Schillebeeckx, *Jesus,* 567–69 and notes 24 and 25, p. 731.

10. Francis Schüssler Fiorenza, "Critical Social Theory and Christology," 97–110.

11. See "The Comfort of Time," *Theological Investigations,* trans. Karl H. and Boniface Kruger (Baltimore: Helicon Press, 1967), III:149–50; see also "Theological Considerations concerning the Moment of Death," *Theological Investigations,* trans. David Bourke (New York: Seabury Press, 1974), II:309–21, and "Ideas for a Theology of Death," *Theological Investigations,* trans. David Bourke (New York: Seabury Press, 1975), XIII:169–86.

12. Karl Rahner, "On the Spirituality of the Easter Faith," *Theological Investigations,* trans. Margaret Kohl (New York: Crossroad, 1981), XVII: 8–15; Wolfhart Pannenberg, *Jesus— God and Man,* trans. Lewis L. Wilikins and Duane A. Priebe, 2d ed. (Philadelphia: Westminster Press, 1977), 67, 225–44.

13. See Phyllis Trible, *God and the Rhetoric of Sexuality,* 72–143; Valerie Saiving, "The Human Situation: A Feminine View," in *Womanspirit Rising,* ed. Carol P. Christ and Judith Plaskow, 42; Judith Plaskow, *Sex, Sin and Grace;* Wanda War-

ren Berry, "Images of Sin and Salvation in Feminist Theology," *Anglican Theological Review* LX (January 1978): 25–54. I am indebted to Linda Lee Nelson for the formulation of "relational, communitarian, and pluralistic" as the requirements of a feminist soteriology.

14. Rosemary Radford Ruether, *To Change the World*, 45–56; *Sexism and God-Talk*, 116–38.

15. "Feminism and Christology," *Newsletter of the Currents in Contemporary Christology Group of the AAR*, (Fall 1986), 14.

16. See Leo J. O'Donovan, "The Word of the Cross," *Chicago Studies* 26:1 (1986): 95–110.

17. Francis Schüssler Fiorenza, "Critical Social Theory and Christology," 101–110; Jon Sobrino, *Christology at the Crossroads*, 201–35.

18. Mary Gordon, "Coming to Terms with Mary," *Commonweal* CIX (January 25, 1982): 11.

19. Donal Flanagan, *The Theology of Mary* (Hales Corners, WI: Clergy Book Service, 1976), 97.

20. Rosemary Radford Ruether, "Misogynism and Virginal Feminism in the Fathers of the Church," *Religion and Sexism*, Ruether, 150–83.

21. Cited from the Council of Trent in Marina Warner, *Alone of All Her Sex: The Myth and Cult of the Virgin Mary*, (New York: Alfred A. Knopf, 1976), 336.

22. Kari Borresen, "Mary in Catholic Theology," *Mary in the Churches*, ed. Hans Küng, and Jürgen Moltmann, Concilium 168 (New York: Seabury Press, 1983), 48–56.

23. Gordon, 12. See also Barbara Corrado Pope, "Immaculate and Powerful: The Marian Revival in the Nineteenth Century," *Immaculate and Powerful: The Female in Sacred Image and Social Reality*, ed. Clarissa W. Atkinson, Constance H. Buchanan, and Margaret Miles (Boston: Beacon Press 1985), 173–200.

24. Elisabeth Schüssler Fiorenza, "Feminist Spirituality, Christian Identity, and Catholic Vision," *Womanspirit Rising*, 138–39.

25. Andrew M. Greeley, *The Mary Myth: On the Femininity of God* (New York: Seabury Press, 1977).

26. Joan Chamberlain Engelsman, *The Feminine Dimension of the Divine* (Philadelphia: Westminster Press, 1979), 122–33, 139–48.

27. Ibid., 133–39; Rosemary Radford Ruether, *Mary—the Feminine Face of the Church* (Philadelphia: Westminster Press, 1977).

28. Mary Daly, *Beyond God the Father*, 81–90.

29. Borresen, 53–54. The title was conferred by Pope Paul VI in his speech of November 21, 1964, when he promulgated *Lumen Gentium*.

30. Anne Carr, "Mary in the Mystery of the Church: Vatican Council II," *Mary According to Women*, ed. Carol Frances Jegen (Kansas City: Leaven, 1985), 5–32.

31. See the essays in *Mary According to Women*, 33ff.

32. Carr, "Mary in the Mystery of the Church," 20–26. For an analysis of the changes in the theological understanding of Mary, see Elizabeth A. Johnson, "Mary and Contemporary Christology: Rahner and Schillebeeckx," *Eglise et Théologie* 15 (1984), 155–82 and idem. "The Marian Tradition and the Reality of Women," *Horizons* 12:1 (Spring 1985) 116–35.

33. *Mary in the New Testament*, ed. Raymond E. Brown, Karl P. Donfried, Joseph A. Fitzmyer, and John Reumann (Philadelphia: Fortress Press, 1978), 284, 286.

34. Richard Kugelman, "Presenting Mary to Today's Catholics," *Marian Studies* 22

(Dayton: Mariological Society of America, 1971), 53.

35. Elisabeth Moltmann-Wendel, "Women Experiencing God," *Humanity in God*, ed. Elisabeth Moltmann-Wendel and Jürgen Moltmann (New York: Pilgrim Press, 1983), 3–16.

36. Mary Jo Weaver, *New Catholic Women: A Contemporary Challenge to Traditional Religious Authority* (San Francisco: Harper & Row, 1985), 209.

37. Dorothee Soelle, *The Strength of the Weak: Toward a Christian Feminist Identity*, trans. Robert and Rita Kimber (Philadelphia: Westminster Press, 1984), 42–48.

38. See Virgil Elizondo, "Mary and the Poor: A Model of Evangelizing," *Mary and the Churches*, 59–65; Mary DeCock, "Our Lady of Guadalupe: Symbol of Liberation?" *Mary According to Women*, 113–41.

39. Carr, "Mary in the Mystery of the Church," 27–29; see Anne E. Patrick, "Narrative and the Social Dynamics of Virtue," *Changing Values and Virtues*, ed. Dietmar Mieth and Jacques Pohier, Concilium 191 (Edinburgh: T. and T. Clark, 1987).

40. Edward Schillebeeckx, *Christ*, 19–79, 463–670.

41. Elisabeth Schüssler Fiorenza, *In Memory of Her*.

42. " 'You Are Not To Be Called Father'," 318.

43. See Karl Rahner, "The Church of Sinners" and "The Sinful Church in the Decrees of Vatican II," *Theological Investigations*, trans Karl H. and Boniface Kruger (Baltimore: Helicon Press, 1969), VI: 253–69, 270–94.

44. Richard McBrien, *Church: The Continuing Quest* (New York: Newman, 1970), 23–41.

45. For example, McBrien, *ibid.*; Karl Rahner, "Theology and Anthropology," *Theological Investigations*, trans. Graham Harrison (London: Darton, Longman & Todd, 1972), IX:38.

46. Avery Dulles, *Models of the Church* (New York: Doubleday, 1974).

47. Ibid., 182.

48. McBrien, 67–85.

49. Avery Dulles, "Imaging the Church for the 1980s," *A Church to Believe In* (New York: Crossroad, 1982), 3.

50. Ibid., 10.

51. Oscar Romero, "The Political Dimension of Christian Love," *Commonweal* CIX (March 26, 1982): 169–72.

52. Karl Rahner, "The Position of Women in the New Situation in Which the Church Finds Herself," *Theological Investigations* trans. David Bourke (New York: Herder and Herder, 1971) VIII: 75–93.

53. See Rosemary Radford Ruether, *Women-Church*.

CHAPTER 10. CHRISTIAN FEMINIST SPIRITUALITY

1. See William M. Thompson, *The Jesus Debate: A Survey and Synthesis* (New York: Paulist, 1985), 361–63.

2. Sandra M. Schneiders, "Theology and Spirituality: Strangers, Rivals, or Partners?" *Horizons* 13:2 (Fall 1986): 253–74.

3. See Mircea Eliade, *Myth and Reality*, trans. Willard R. Trask (New York and Evanston: Harper & Row, 1963), especially 1–20.

4. Mary Field Belenky, Blythe McVicker Clinchy, Nancy Rule Goldenberger, and Jill Mattuck Tarule, *Women's Ways of Knowing: The Development of Self, Voice,*

and Mind (New York: Basic Books, 1986); Carol Gilligan, *In A Different Voice: Psychological Theory and Women's Development* (Cambridge and London: Harvard University Press, 1983); John M. Broughton, "Women's Rationality and Men's Virtues: A Critique of Gender Dualism in Gilligan's Theory of Moral Development," *Social Research* 50:3 (Autumn 1983): 597–642; Patricia Wilson-Kastner, *Faith, Feminism and the Christ* (Philadelphia: Fortress Press, 1983), 39–54.

5. Anne Wilson Schaef, *Women's Reality* (Minneapolis: Winston Press, 1981).

6. Ibid., 99–145.

7. Ibid., 163.

8. Schneiders, "The Effects of Women's Experience on Their Spirituality," *Spirituality Today* 35:2 (Summer 1983): 100–116, reprinted in *Women's Spirituality: Resources for Christian Development,* ed. Joann Wolski Conn (New York: Paulist, 1986), 31–48.

9. Joann Wolski Conn, "Women's Spirituality: Restriction and Reconstruction," *Cross Currents* (Fall 1980): 293–308, reprinted in Wolski Conn, *Women's Spirituality,* 9–30.

10. See Carol Christ, "Spiritual Quest and Women's Experience," *Womanspirit Rising,* ed. Carol P. Christ and Judith Plaskow, 228–45; Amanda Porterfield, *Feminine Spirituality in America: From Sarah Edwards to Martha Graham* (Philadelphia: Temple University Press, 1980).

11. Dorothee Soelle, "Mysticism, Liberation and the Names of God," *Christianity and Crisis* 41:11 (June 22, 1981): 179–85, phrase quoted at p. 179.

12. See Joann Wolski Conn, "Introduction," *Women's Spirituality,* 1–5. The significance of human and Christian freedom is a constant theme in Karl Rahner's theology; for a brief treatment that is specifically related to spirituality see his "Experiencing the Spirit," in Karl Rahner, *The Practice of Faith: A Handbook of Contemporary Spirituality,* ed. Karl Lehmann and Albert Raffelt (New York: Crossroad, 1986), 77–84.

13. See Mary Buckley, "The Rising of the Woman is the Rising of the Race," 63, especially 59–63 on the question of gender and virtue.

14. This is not to assert that all power is wrong but that power that is manipulative or coercive is. Power that enables oneself or others to act as effective subjects is good, as similar forms of ambition are good. See the important study of Rollo May, *Power and Innocence: A Search for the Sources of Violence* (New York: W. W. Norton, 1972), in which he describes the form of powerlessness or pseudo-innocence that can deny its own complicity in evil and is a naive, childish sort of romanticism.

15. See the important study by James B. Nelson *Embodiment: An Approach to Sexuality and Christian Theology* (Minneapolis: Augsburg, 1978). The theme of the body is developed in a paper as yet unpublished by Susan A. Ross, "The Body: Reflections on the Sacramental and Feminist Perspectives," that deals with the ways in which both the sacramental and the feminist approaches attempt to overcome the traditional dualism between mind and body with a positive concern for the body. Another helpful study, from a cross-disciplinary perspective, is *The Female Body in Western Culture,* ed. Susan Rubin Suleiman (Cambridge and London: Harvard University Press, 1986).

16. See the important collection *This Bridge Called My Back: Writings by Radical Women of Color,* ed. Cherrie Moraga and Gloria Anzaldua (New York: Kitchen Table: Women of Color Press, 1981); Audre Lorde, *Sister Outsider* (Trumansville, NY: Crossing Press, 1984); Delores S. Williams, "Womanist Theology: Black

Women's Voices," *Christianity and Crisis* 47:3 (March 2, 1987): 66–70; Marianne Katoppo, *Compassionate and Free: An Asian Woman's Theology* (Maryknoll: Orbis Books, 1980); Mercy Oduyoye, "The Christ for Africa: Observations and Reflections," *Newsletter* of the Currents in Contemporary Christology Group of the American Academy of Religion (1986): 35–45, especially 40–41 on "A Woman's Christ".

17. These connections are especially clear in Rosemary Radford Ruether, *New Woman/New Earth*; Carol Frances Jegen, *Jesus the Peacemaker* (Kansas City, MO: 1986); Juliana Casey, *Where Is God Now? Nuclear Terror, Feminism and the Search for God* (Kansas City: MO: 1987).

18. See Rosemary Radford Ruether, *Women-Church*.

19. Judith Plaskow, *Sex, Sin and Grace*.

20. Ibid., 172.

21. Soelle, "Mysticism, Liberation and the Names of God," 179; see also *The Feminist Mystic,* ed. Mary E. Giles (New York: Crossroad, 1982).

22. Ibid., 183–84. See Warren McWilliams, *The Passion of God: Divine Suffering in Contemporary Protestant Theology* (Macon, GA: Mercer University Press, 1985).

23. Ibid., 185.

24. Sallie McFague, *Metaphorical Theology,* 177–90; Elisabeth Schüssler Fiorenza, "Why Not the Category Friend/Friendship?" *Horizons* 2:1 (Spring 1975): 117–18.

25. Ibid.; see also Gail Ramshaw Schmidt, *Christ in Sacred Speech: The Meaning of Liturgical Language* (Philadelphia: Fortress Press, 1986) and her earlier "De Divinis Nominibus: The Gender of God," *Worship* 56:2 (March 1982): 117–31; Pamela Payne Allen, "Taking the Next Step in Inclusive Language," *The Christian Century* 103:12 (april 23, 1986): 410–13.

26. Elizabeth A. Johnson, "Jesus, the Wisdom of God: A Biblical Basis for Non-Androcentric Christology," *Ephemerides Theologicae Lovianienses* 61:4 (December 1985): 261–94; Susan Cayd, Marian Ronan, and Hal Tausig, *Sophia: The Future of Feminist Spirituality* (San Francisco: Harper & Row, 1986).

Selected Bibliography

Abel, Elizabeth and Emily K. Abel, eds. *The Signs Reader: Women, Gender, and Scholarship.* Chicago: The University of Chicago Press, 1983.

Agonito, Rosemary, ed. *History of Ideas on Women: A Source Book.* New York: Putnam, 1977.

Al-Hibri, Azizah. *Women and Islam.* Elmsford, NY: Pergamon Press, 1982.

Allen, Pamela Payne. "Taking the Next Step in Inclusive Language." *The Christian Century* 103:12 (April 23, 1986): 410–13.

Andolsen, Barbara Hilkert. *Daughters of Jefferson, Daughters of Bootblacks: Racism and American Feminism.* Macon, GA: Mercer University Press, 1986.

Andolsen, Barbara Hilkert et al., eds. *Women's Consciousness, Women's Conscience: A Reader in Feminine Ethics.* Minneapolis: Winston Press, 1985.

Archer, John and Barbara Lloyd. *Sex and Gender.* Cambridge: Cambridge University Press, 1985.

Ardener, Edwin. "Belief and the Problem of Women." *The Interpretation of Ritual.* Ed. J. S. LaFontaine. London: Tavistock, 1972. Reprinted in: S. Ardener. *Perceiving Women.* New York: Wiley, 1975.

Ariés, Philippe and Andre Bejin, eds. *Western Sexuality: Practice and Precept in Past and Present Times.* Trans. Anthony Forster. Oxford: Basil Blackwell Ltd., 1985.

Armstrong, Karen. *The Gospel According to Woman: Christianity's Creation of the Sex War in the West.* New York: Anchor Press–Doubleday, 1987.

Atkinson, Clarissa W., Constance H. Buchanan and Margaret Miles, eds. *Immaculate and Powerful: The Female in Sacred Image and Social Reality.* Boston: Beacon Press, 1985.

Bakan, David. *And They Took Themselves Wives: The Emergence of Patriarchy in Western Civilization.* San Francisco: Harper & Row, 1979.

Barker, Paula S. Datsko. "The Motherhood of God in Julian of Norwich's Theology." *Downside Review* (October 1982): 290–304.

Baum, Charlotte, Paula Hyman and Sonya Michel. *The Jewish Woman in America.* New York: Dial Press, 1976.

Beauvoir, Simone de. *The Second Sex.* Trans. and ed. H. M. Parshley. New York: Vintage Books, 1974.

Beck, Lois and Nikki Keddie, eds. *Women in the Muslim World*. Cambridge, MA: Harvard University Press, 1978.

Belenky, Mary Field et al. *Women's Ways of Knowing: The Development of Self, Voice and Mind*. New York: Basic Books, 1986.

Bell, Linda A., ed. *Visions of Women: An Anthology of Philosophers' Views of Women from Ancient to Modern Times*. Clifton, NJ: Humana Press, 1983.

Bettenhausen, Elizabeth. "Personal and Political, Private and Public." *Christianity and Crisis* (October 29, 1984): 394–96.

Bianchi, Eugene C. and Rosemary R. Ruether. *From Machismo to Mutuality: Essays on Sexism and Woman-Man Liberation*. New York: Paulist Press, 1976.

Bleier, Ruth, ed. *Feminist Approaches to Science*. New York: Pergamon Press, 1986.

Borresen, Kari Elisabeth. *Subordination and Equivalence: The Nature and Role of Women in Augustine and Thomas Aquinas*. Washington, DC: University Press of America, Inc., 1981.

Bowles, Gloria and Renate Duelli Klein. *Theories of Women's Studies*. London: Routledge & Kegan Paul, 1983.

Boys, Mary. "A Religious Educator's Perspective." *Proceedings of the Catholic Theological Society of America* 38 (June 15–18, 1983): 58–62.

Bridenthal, Renate and Claudia Koonz, eds. *Becoming Visible: Women in European History*. Boston: Houghton Mifflin Company, 1977.

Brooten, Bernadette J. *Women Leaders in the Ancient Synagogue: Inscriptional Evidence and Background Issues*. Diss. Brown Judaic Studies. Chico, CA: Scholars Press, 1982.

Brown, Raymond E. et al., eds. *Mary in the New Testament: A Collaborative Assessment by Protestant and Roman Catholic Scholars*. Philadelphia: Fortress Press, 1978.

Bruns, J. Edgar. *God as Woman, Woman as God*. New York: Paulist Press, 1973.

Buckley, Mary. "Rediscovering the Christian God: A Feminist Perspective." *Proceedings of the Catholic Theological Society of America* 33 (June 7–10, 1978): 148–54.

Buckley, Mary. "The Rising of the Woman is the Rising of the Race." *Proceedings of the Catholic Theological Society of America* 34 (1979): 48–63.

Buckley, Mary. "Women, Power and Liberation." *Proceedings of the Catholic Theological Society of America* 37 (June 10–13, 1982): 109–11.

Budapest, Zsuzsanna. *The Feminist Book of Lights and Shadows*. Luna Publications, 1976.

Bulkin, Elly and Barbara Smith. *Feminist Perspectives on Antisemitism and*

Racism: Two Essays. Brooklyn, NY: Long Haul Press, 1983.

Bunch, Charlotte et al. *Building Feminist Theory: Essays from "Quest—A Feminist Quarterly."* New York: Longman, 1981.

Burghardt, Walter, ed. *Woman: New Dimensions.* New York: Paulist Press, 1977. (Essays originally published in *Theological Studies* 36:4, December 1975.)

Buvinic, Mayra, ed. *Women and Poverty in the Third World.* Baltimore: Johns Hopkins University Press, 1983.

Bynum, Caroline Walker. *Holy Feast and Holy Fast: The Religious Significance of Food to Medieval Women.* Berkeley: University of California Press, 1987.

Bynum, Caroline Walker. *Jesus as Mother: Studies in the Spirituality of the High Middle Ages.* Berkeley: University of California Press, 1982.

Bynum, Caroline Walker, Stephen Harrell and Paula Richman, eds. *Gender and Religion: On the Complexity of Symbols.* Boston: Beacon Press, 1986.

Cady, Susan, Marian Ronan and Hal Tausig. *Sophia: The Future of Feminist Spirituality.* San Francisco: Harper & Row, 1986.

Cahill, Lisa Sowle. *Between the Sexes: Foundations for a Christian Ethics of Sexuality.* Philadelphia: Fortress Press. New York: Paulist Press, 1985.

Cannon, Katie G. et al. (The Mud Flower Collection). *God's Fierce Whimsy: Christian Feminism and Theological Education.* New York: The Pilgrim Press, 1985.

Carmody, Denise Lardner. *Feminism and Christianity: A Two-Way Reflection.* Nashville: Abingdon Press, 1982.

Carmody, Denise Lardner. *Women and World Religions.* Nashville: Abingdon Press, 1979.

Carmody, Denise Lardner. "Summary of the Discussion: The Role of Women in Theology." *Proceedings of the Catholic Theological Society in America* 38 (June 15–18, 1983): 74–6.

Carr, Anne. "Summary of the Discussion: Women and Power in the Church." *Proceedings of the Catholic Theological Society of America* 37 (June 10–13, 1982): 128–29.

Carroll, Bernice A., ed. *Liberating Women's History: Theoretical and Critical Essays.* Urbana, IL: University of Illinois Press, 1976.

Casey, Juliana. *Where is God Now? Nuclear Terror, Feminism and the Search for God.* Kansas City, MO: Sheed and Ward, 1987.

Catholic Biblical Association. Madeline Boucher et al. "Women and Priestly Ministry: The New Testament Evidence." *Catholic Biblical Quarterly* 41:4 (October 1979): 608–13.

Catholic Theological Society of America. *A Report on the Status of Women in*

Church and Society: Considered in Light of the Question of Women's Ordination. Ed. Sara Butler. Mahwah, NJ: Darlington Seminary, 1978.

Cazden, Elizabeth. *Antoinette Brown Blackwell: A Biography.* Old Westbury, NY: The Feminist Press, 1982.

Chesler, Phyllis. *Women and Madness.* New York: Avon-Doubleday and Company, Inc., 1973.

Chodorow, Nancy. *The Reproduction of Mothering: Psychoanalysis and the Sociology of Gender.* Berkeley: University of California Press, 1978.

Christ, Carol P. *Diving Deep and Surfacing: Women Writers on Spiritual Quest.* Boston: Beacon Press, 1980.

Christ, Carol P. *Laughter of Aphrodite: Reflections on a Journey to the Goddess.* San Francisco: Harper & Row, 1987.

Christ, Carol P. and Judith Plaskow, eds. *Womanspirit Rising: A Feminist Reader in Religion.* New York: Harper & Row, 1979.

Clark, Elizabeth A. *Women in the Early Church.* Wilmington, DE: Michael Glazier, Inc., 1983, 1987.

Clark, Elizabeth A. and Herbert Richardson, eds. *Women and Religion: A Feminist Sourcebook of Christian Thought.* New York: Harper & Row, 1977.

Clark, Linda et al. *Image Breaking/Image Building: A Handbook for Creative Worship with Women in Christian Tradition.* New York: The Pilgrim Press, 1981.

Coll, Regina. *Women and Religion: A Reader for the Clergy.* New York: Paulist Press, 1982.

Collins, Adela Yarbro, ed. *Feminist Perspectives on Biblical Scholarship.* Chico, CA: Scholars Press, 1985.

Collins, Sheila. *A Different Heaven and Earth: A Feminist Perspective on Religion.* Valley Forge, PA: Judson Press, 1974.

Conley, Verena Andermatt. *Helene Cixous: Writing the Feminine.* Nebraska: University of Nebraska Press, 1984.

Conn, Joann Wolski, ed. *Women's Spirituality: Resources for Christian Development.* New York: Paulist Press, 1986.

Conn, Joann Wolski. "Contemporary Women's Spirituality: A Breakthrough of Power." *Proceedings of the Catholic Theological Society of America* 37 (June 10-13, 1982): 112-15.

Conn, Joann Wolski. "Toward a Contemplative Theology." *Proceedings of the Catholic Theological Society of America* 38 (June 15-18, 1983): 71-3.

Conn, Walter. "Two-handed Theology." *Proceedings of the Catholic Theological Society of America* 38 (June 15-18, 1983): 66-70.

Cooke, Bernard. "Non-Patriarchal Salvation." *Horizons* 10:1 (1983): 22-31.

Coriden, James, ed. *Sexism and Church Law*. Ramsey, NJ: Paulist Press, 1971.

Cornwall Collective. *Your Daughters Shall Prophesy: Feminist Alternatives in Theological Education*. New York: The Pilgrim Press, 1980.

Cott, Nancy F. *The Bonds of Womanhood: Woman's Sphere in New England 1780–1835*. New Haven, CT: Yale University Press, 1977.

Culley, Margot and Catherine Portuges, eds. *Gendered Subjects: The Dynamics of Feminist Teaching*. Boston: Routledge and Kegan Paul, 1985.

Daly, Mary. *Beyond God the Father: Toward a Philosophy of Women's Liberation*. Boston: Beacon Press, 1973.

Daly, Mary. *The Church and the Second Sex*. New York: Harper & Row, 1968, 1975.

Daly, Mary. *Gyn/Ecology: The Metaethics of Radical Feminism*. Boston: Beacon Press, 1978.

Daly, Mary. *Pure Lust: Elemental Feminist Philosophy*. Boston: Beacon Press, 1984.

Davaney, Sheila Greeve, ed. *Feminism and Process Thought: The Harvard Divinity School/Claremont Center for Process Studies Symposium Papers*. New York: The Edwin Mellen Press, 1981.

Davis, Angela Y. *Women, Race and Class*. New York: Vintage Books, 1983.

Davis, Elizabeth Gould. *The First Sex*. Baltimore: Penguin Books, Inc., 1972.

Degler, Carl. *At Odds: Women and Family in America from the Revolution to the Present*. New York: Oxford University Press, 1980.

Dinnerstein, Dorothy. *The Mermaid and the Minotaur: Sexual Arrangements and Human Malaise*. New York: Harper Colophon Books, 1976.

Doely, Sarah Bentley, ed. *Women's Liberation and the Church: The New Demand for Freedom in the Life of the Christian Church*. New York: Association Press, 1970.

Douglas, Ann. *The Feminization of American Culture*. New York: Avon Books, 1978.

Downing, Christine. *The Goddess: Mythological Images of the Feminine*. New York: Crossroad, 1981.

Duck, Ruth, ed. *Bread for the Journey: Resources for Worship*. New York: The Pilgrim Press, 1981.

Duck, Ruth and Michael G. Bausch, eds. *Everflowing Streams: Songs for Worship*. New York: The Pilgrim Press, 1981.

Durkin, Mary G. *The Suburban Woman: Her Changing Role in the Church*. New York: Crossroad–The Seabury Press, 1975.

Ebaugh, Helen Fuchs. *Out of the Cloister*. Austin: University of Texas Press, 1977.

Eisenstein, Zillah R., ed. *Capitalist Patriarchy and the Case for Socialist Feminism.* New York: Monthly Review Press, 1978.

Eisenstein, Zillah R. *Feminism and Sexual Equality: Crisis in Liberal America.* New York: Monthly Review Press, 1984.

Eisenstein, Zillah R. *The Radical Future of Liberal Feminism.* New York: Longman, Inc., 1981.

Eisenstein, Hester and Alice Jardine, eds. *The Future of Difference.* New Brunswick, NJ: Rutgers University Press, 1985.

Elizondo, Virgil and Norbert Greinacher, eds. *Women in a Man's Church. Concilium* 134. New York: Seabury·Press, 1980.

Elshtain, Jean Bethke. *Public Man, Private Woman: Women in Social and Political Thought.* Princeton, NJ: Princeton University Press, 1981.

Emswiler, Sharon Neufer and Thomas Neufer Emswiler. *Women and Worship: A Guide to Non-Sexist Hymns, Prayers and Liturgy.* New York: Harper & Row, 1974. Revised 1984.

Engel, Mary Potter. "Tambourines to the Glory of God: From the Monarchy of God the Father to the Monotheism of God the Great Mysterious." *Word and World* 7:2 (Spring 1987): 153-66.

Engelsman, Joan Chamberlain. *The Feminine Dimension of the Divine.* Philadelphia: Westminster Press, 1979.

Ewens, Mary. *The Role of the Nun in Nineteenth-Century America: Variations on the International Theme.* Diss. University of Minnesota, 1971. Ann Arbor: UMI, 1972. 71-72, 272. New York: Arno Press, 1978.

Farley, Margaret. *Personal Commitments.* San Francisco: Harper & Row, 1986.

Farley, Margaret. "Power and Powerlessness: A Case in Point." *Proceedings of the Catholic Theological Society of America* 37 (June 10-13, 1982): 116-18.

Farley, Margaret. "Sources of Sexual Inequality in the History of Christian Thought." *Journal of Religion* 56:2 (April 1976): 162.

Faxon, Alicia Craig. *Women and Jesus.* New York: United Church Press, 1973.

Ferder, Fran. *Called to Break Bread: A Psychological Investigation of 100 Women Who Feel Called to Priesthood in the Catholic Church.* Mt. Rainier, MD: Quixote Center, 1978.

Fiorenza, Elisabeth Schüssler. *Bread Not Stone: The Challenge of Feminist Biblical Interpretation.* Boston: Beacon Press, 1984.

Fiorenza, Elisabeth Schüssler. *In Memory of Her: A Feminist Theological Reconstruction of Christian Origins.* New York: Crossroad, 1983.

Fiorenza, Elisabeth Schüssler. "Sexism and Conversion." *Network Quarterly* 9:3 (May-June 1981): 15-22.

Fiorenza, Elisabeth Schüssler. "Why Not a Category of Friend/Friendship?" *Horizons* 2:1 (Spring 1975): 117–18.

Fiorenza, Elisabeth Schüssler and Mary Collins, eds. *Women: Invisible in Church and Theology. Concilium* 182. Edinburgh: T. and T. Clark, 1985.

Flexner, Eleanor. *Century of Struggle: The Women's Rights Movement in the United States.* New York: Atheneum, 1949, 1973.

Firestone, Shulamith. *The Dialectic of Sex: The Case for Feminist Revolution.* New York: William Morrow and Company, Inc., 1970.

Fischer, Clare Benedicks, Betsy Brenneman and Anne McGraw Bennett. *Women in a Strange Land: Search for a New Image.* Philadelphia: Fortress Press, 1975.

Fox-Genovese, Elizabeth. "For Feminist Interpretation." *Union Seminary Quarterly Review* XXXV:1 & 2 (Fall/Winter 1979–80): 5–14. (The entire issue is devoted to themes in feminist theology.)

Friday, Nancy. *My Mother, My Self: The Daughter's Search for Identity.* New York: Dell Publishing Co., Inc., 1977.

Friedlander, Judith et al., eds. *Women in Culture and Politics: A Century of Change.* Bloomington, IN: Indiana University Press, 1986.

Gallop, Jane. *The Daughter's Seduction: Feminism and Psychoanalysis.* Ithaca, NY: Cornell University Press, 1982.

Gardiner, Anne Marie, ed. *Women and Catholic Priesthood: An Expanded Vision: Proceedings of the Detroit Ordination Conference.* New York: Paulist Press, 1976.

Gayraud, Wilmore S. and James H. Cone, eds. *Black Theology: A Documentary History, 1966–1979.* Maryknoll, NY: Orbis Books, 1979.

Gelb, Joyce and Marian Lief Palley. *Women and Public Policies.* Princeton, NJ: Princeton University Press, 1982.

Giles, Mary E., ed. *The Feminist Mystic and Other Essays on Women and Spirituality.* New York: Crossroad, 1982.

Gilligan, Carol. *In a Different Voice: Psychological Theory and Women's Development.* Cambridge: Harvard University Press, 1982.

Goldenberg, Naomi Ruth. *Changing of the Gods: Feminism and the End of Traditional Religions.* Boston: Beacon Press, 1979.

Goldenberg, Naomi Ruth. *The End of God: Important Directions for a Feminist Critique of Religion in the Works of Sigmund Freud and Carl Jung.* Ottawa, Ontario: University of Ontario Press, 1982.

Gordon, Mary. "Coming to Terms with Mary." *Commonweal* CIX (January 25, 1982): 11.

Gottwald, Norman K., ed. *The Bible and Liberation: Political and Social Hermeneutics.* Maryknoll, NY: Orbis Books, 1983.

Greeley, Andrew M. *The Mary Myth: On the Femininity of God.* New York: Seabury Press, 1977.

Greenburg, Blu. *On Women and Judaism: A View from Tradition.* Philadelphia: The Jewish Publication Society, 1981.

Griffin, Susan. *Women and Nature: The Roaring Inside Her.* New York: Harper & Row, 1978.

Gross, Rita. *Beyond Androcentrism: New Essays on Women and Religion.* Missoula, MT: Scholars Press, 1977.

Gross, Rita and Nancy Auer Falk, eds. *Unspoken Worlds: Women's Religious Lives in Non-Western Cultures.* San Francisco: Harper & Row, 1980.

Gudorf, Christine E. "To Make a Seamless Garment, Use a Single Piece of Cloth." *Cross Currents* 34:4 (Winter 1984–85): 473–91.

Gudorf, Christine E. "Renewal or Repatriarchalization? Responses of the Roman Catholic Church to the Feminization of Religion." *Horizons* 10:2 (Fall 1983): 231–51.

Hageman, Alice L., ed. *Sexist Religion and Women in the Church: No More Silence!* New York: Association Press, 1974.

Halkes, Catharina J. M. *Gott hat nicht nur starke Söhne: Grundzuge einer feministischen Theologie.* Germany: Gutersloher Verlagshaus Gerd Mohn, Gutersloh, 1980.

Hamelsdorf, Ora and Sandra Adelsberg. *Jewish Women and Jewish Law.* Biblio Press, 1982.

Hammerton-Kelly, Norbert. *God the Father: Theology and Patriarchy in the Teaching of Jesus.* Philadelphia: Fortress Press, 1979. Reviewed by Phyllis Trible in *Theology Today* 37 (1980): 116–19.

Hardesty, Nancy. *Women Called to Witness: Evangelical Feminism in the 19th Century.* Nashville: Abingdon Press, 1984.

Harding, Sandra. *The Science Question in Feminism.* Ithaca, NY: Cornell University Press, 1985.

Harkness, Georgia. *Women in Church and Society.* Nashville: Abingdon Press, 1972.

Harrison, Beverly Wildung. *Making the Connections: Essays in Feminist Social Ethics.* Ed. Carol S. Robb. Boston: Beacon Press, 1985.

Harrison, Beverly Wildung. *Our Right to Choose: Toward a New Ethic of Abortion.* Boston: Beacon Press, 1983.

Haughton, Rosemary. *The Re-Creation of Eve.* Springfield, IL: Templegate Publishers, 1987.

Heilbrun, Carolyn G. *Reinventing Womanhood.* New York: W. W. Norton & Company, 1979.

Heschel, Susanna. *On Being a Jewish Feminist: A Reader.* New York: Shocken Books, 1983.

Hewitt, Emily C. and Suzanne R. Hiatt. *Women Priests: Yes or No?* New York: Seabury Press, 1973.

Heyer, Robert J., ed. *Women and Orders.* New York: Paulist Press, 1974.

Heyward, Isabel Carter. *Our Passion for Justice: Images of Power, Sexuality, and Liberation.* New York: The Pilgrim Press, 1984.

Heyward, Isabel Carter. *A Priest Forever: Formation of a Woman and a Priest.* New York: Harper & Row, 1976.

Heyward, Isabel Carter. *The Redemption of God: A Theology of Mutual Relation.* Lanham, MD: University Press of America, 1982.

Hill, Mary A. *Charlotte Perkins Gilman: The Making of a Radical Feminist 1860-1896.* Philadelphia: Temple University Press, 1980.

Hole, Judith and Ellen Levine. *Rebirth of Feminism.* New York: Quadrangle Books, 1971.

Hooks, Bell. *Ain't I a Woman: Black Women and Feminism.* Boston: South End Press, 1981.

Hopko, Thomas, ed. *Women and the Priesthood.* Crestwood, NY: St. Vladimir's Seminary Press, 1983.

Hubbard, Ruth and Marian Lowe, eds. *Woman's Nature: Rationalizations of Inequality.* Elmsford, NY: Pergamon Press, 1983.

Hull, Gloria T., Patricia Bell Scott and Barbara Smith, eds. *All the Women are White, All the Blacks are Men, But Some of Us are Brave: Black Women's Studies.* Old Westbury, NY: The Feminist Press, 1982.

Irwin, Joyce L. *Womanhood in Radical Protestantism 1525-1675.* New York: The Edwin Mellen Press, 1979.

Jacobus, Mary, ed. *Women Writing and Writing About Women.* London: Croom Helm, 1979.

Jaggar, Allison. *Feminist Politics and Human Nature.* Totowa, NJ: Rowan and Allanheld, 1983.

James, Janet Wilson, ed. *Women in American Religion.* Philadelphia: University of Pennsylvania Press, 1980.

Janeway, Elizabeth. *Man's World, Woman's Place: A Study in Social Mythology.* New York: Dell Publishing Co., 1971.

Jardine, Alice. *Gynesis: Configurations of Women and Modernity.* Ithaca, NY: Cornell University, 1985.

Jegen, Carol Frances, ed. *Mary According to Women.* Kansas City: Leaven, 1985.

Jewett, Paul K. *Man as Male and Female: A Study in Sexual Relationships from a Theological Point of View.* Grand Rapids, MI: William B. Eerdmans Publishing Company, 1975.

Jewett, Paul K. *The Ordination of Women.* Grand Rapids, MI: William B. Eerdmans Publishing Company, 1980.

Johnson, Elizabeth A. "The Incomprehensibility of God and the Image of

God Male and Female." *Theological Studies* 45:3 (September 1984): 441–80.

Johnson, Elizabeth A. "Jesus, the Wisdom of God: A Biblical Basis for Non-Androcentric Christology." *Ephemerides Theologicae Lovanienses* LX 1:4 (December 1985): 261–94.

Johnson, Elizabeth A. "The Marian Tradition and the Reality of Women." *Horizons* 12:1 (Spring 1985): 116–35.

Johnson, Elizabeth A. "Mary and Contemporary Christology: Rahner and Schillebeeckx." *Eglise et Theologie* 15 (1984): 155–82.

Johnson, Elizabeth A. "The Symbolic Character of Theological Statements About Mary." *Journal of Ecumenical Studies* 22:2 (Spring 1985): 312–36.

Jung, Patricia Beattie. "Give Her Justice." *America* 150 (April 14, 1984): 276–8.

Katoppo, Marianne. *Compassionate and Free: An Asian Woman's Theology.* New York: Orbis Books, 1980.

Katz, Jane B., ed. *I Am the Fire of Time: The Voices of Native American Women.* New York: E. P. Dutton, 1977.

Keller, Evelyn Fox. *Reflections on Gender and Science.* New Haven, CT: Yale University Press, 1985.

Kelly-Gadol, Joan. "The Social Relations of the Sexes: Methodological Implications of Women's History." *Signs* 1:4 (1976): 812–17.

Keohane, Nannerl O., Michelle Z. Rosaldo and Barbara C. Gelpi. *Feminist Theory: A Critique of Ideology.* Chicago: University of Chicago Press, 1982.

Kingston, Maxine Hong. *The Woman Warrior: Memoirs of a Girlhood Among Ghosts.* New York, Random House, 1976.

Kinnear, Mary. *Daughters of Time: Women in the Western Tradition.* Ann Arbor, MI: The University of Michigan Press, 1982.

Kolbenschlag, Madonna. *Kiss Sleeping Beauty Good-Bye: Breaking the Spell of Feminine Myths and Models.* Garden City, NY: Doubleday and Co., Inc., 1979.

Kolbenschlag, Madonna. "Women and Evangelization." *New Catholic World* 228:1364 (March/April 1985): 70–76.

Koltun, Elizabeth, ed. *The Jewish Woman: New Perspectives.* New York: Schocken Books, 1976.

Kristeva, Julia. *Powers of Horror: An Essay on Abjection.* Trans. Leon S. Roudiez. New York: Columbia University Press, 1982.

Kristeva, Julia. *The Kristeva Reader.* Ed. Toril Moi. New York: Columbia University Press, 1986.

Küng, Hans and Jurgen Moltmann, eds. *Mary in the Churches. Concilium* 168. New York: Seabury Press, 1983.

Lakeland, Paul. *Can Women be Priests? Theology Today Series* 34. Ed. Edward Yarnold, S. J. Hales Corners, WI: Clergy Book Service, 1975.

Lakoff, Robin. *Language and Woman's Place.* New York: Harper & Row, 1975.

Lamb, Matthew L. *Solidarity with Victims: Toward a Theology of Social Transformation.* New York: Crossroad, 1982.

Lambert, Jean C. "An F Factor? The New Testament in Some White Feminist Christian Theological Construction." *Journal of Feminist Studies in Religion* 1:2 (Fall 1985): 93–114.

Lane, Anne J., ed. *The Charlotte Perkins Gilman Reader.* New York: Pantheon Books–Random House Inc., 1980.

Langland, Elizabeth and Walter Grove, eds. *A Feminist Perspective in the Academy: The Difference It Makes.* Chicago: University of Chicago Press, 1983. (These essays were originally published in *Soundings* 64:4, Winter 1981.)

Lerner, Gerda, ed. *Black Women in White America.* New York: Vintage Books Edition, 1973.

Lerner, Gerda. *The Creation of Patriarchy.* New York: Oxford University Press, 1986.

Lerner, Gerda. *The Majority Finds Its Past.* New York: Oxford University Press, 1979.

Lorde, Audre. *Sister Outsider.* Trumansville, NY: Crossing Press, 1984.

Luke, Helen M. *Woman, Earth and Spirit: The Feminine in Symbol and Myth.* New York: Crossroad, 1984.

Lutheran Church of America. *Guidelines for Inclusive Language.* Available from LCA Office for Communication, 231 Madison Ave., New York, NY 10016.

McDonough, Elizabeth. "Women and the New Church Law." *Canon Law: Church Reality. Concilium* 185, eds. James Provost and Knut Wolf. Edinburgh: T. and T. Clark, 1986: 73–81.

McFague, Sallie. *Metaphorical Theology: Models of God in Religious Language.* Philadelphia: Fortress Press, 1982.

McFague, Sallie. *Models of God: Theology for an Ecological, Nuclear Age.* Philadelphia: Fortress Press, 1987.

McGrath, Albertus Magnus, O.P. *What a Modern Catholic Believes About Women.* Chicago: Thomas More Press, 1972.

McIntyre, Marie. *Female and Catholic: A Journal of Mind and Heart.* Mystic, CT: Twenty-Third Publications, 1986.

McLaughlin, Eleanor. " 'Christ My Mother': Feminine Naming and Metaphor in Medieval Spirituality." *St. Luke's Journal of Theology* 18 (1975): 356–86.

McMillan, Carol. *Women, Reason, and Nature: Some Philosophical Problems with Feminism.* Princeton, NJ: Princeton University Press, 1982.

Maguire, Daniel C. "The Exclusion of Women from Orders: A Moral Evaluation." *Cross Currents* 34:2 (Summer 1984): 141–52.

Maguire, Daniel C. "The Feminization of God and Ethics." *Christianity and Crisis* 42:4 (March 15, 1982): 59.

Maitland, Sara. *A Map of the New Country: Women and Christianity.* Boston: Pandora Press–Routledge and Kegan Paul, 1983.

Marks, Elaine and Isabelle de Courtivron, eds. *New French Feminisms.* New York: Schocken Books, 1981.

Martines, Lauro and Julia O'Faolain, eds. *Not in God's Image: Women in History from the Greeks to the Victorians.* New York: Harper Torchbooks, 1973.

Massey, Marilyn Chapin. *Feminine Soul: The Fate of an Ideal.* Boston: Beacon Press, 1985.

Merchant, Carolyn. *The Death of Nature: Women, Ecology, and the Scientific Revolution.* San Francisco: Harper & Row, 1980.

Metz, Johannes-Baptist and Edward Schillebeeckx, eds. *God as Father? Concilium* 143. New York: Seabury Press, 1981.

Meyer, Charles R. "Ordained Women in the Early Church." *Chicago Studies* 4:3 (Fall 1965): 285–309.

Micks, Marianne H. *Our Search for Identity: Humanity in the Image of God.* Philadelphia: Fortress Press, 1982.

Micks, Marianne H. and Charles P. Price, eds. *Toward a New Theology of Ordination: Essays on the Ordination of Women.* Somerville, MA: Greeno, Hadden and Co., 1976.

Miles, Margaret R. *Image as Insight: Visual Understanding in Western Christianity and Secular Culture.* Boston: Beacon Press, 1985.

Miller, Casey and Kate Swift. *Words and Women: New Language in New Times.* New York: Anchor Books–Doubleday & Co., Inc., 1976.

Miller, Jean Baker. *Psychoanalysis and Women.* Baltimore, MD: Penguin Books Inc., 1973.

Miller, Jean Baker. *Toward a New Psychology of Women.* Boston: Beacon Press, 1976.

Mitchell, Juliet. *Psychoanalysis and Feminism.* New York: Vintage Books–Random House, 1975.

Mitchell, Juliet. *Woman's Estate.* New York: Vintage Books–Random House, 1973.

Mollenkott, Virginia Ramey. *The Divine Feminine: The Biblical Imagery of God as Female.* New York: Crossroad, 1981.

Mollenkott, Virginia Ramey. *Women, Men and the Bible.* Nashville: Abingdon, 1977.

Moltmann-Wendel, Elisabeth, ed. *Frau und Religion: Gottes Erfahrungen im*

Patriarchat. Germany: Fischer Taschenbuch Verlag, 1983.

Moltmann-Wendell, Elisabeth. *Liberty, Equality, Sisterhood: On the Emancipation of Women in Church and Society.* Trans. Ruth C. Gritsch. Philadelphia: Fortress Press, 1978.

Moltmann-Wendel, Elisabeth and Jurgen Moltmann. *Humanity in God.* New York: The Pilgrim Press, 1983.

Monaghan, Patricia. *The Book of Goddesses and Heroines.* New York: E. P. Dutton, 1981.

Moraga, Cherrie and Gloria Anzaldua, eds. *This Bridge Called My Back: Writings by Radical Women of Color.* New York: Kitchen Table: Women of Color Press, 1981.

Morgan, Robin. *The Anatomy of Freedom: Feminism, Physics and Global Politics.* Garden City, NY: Anchor Books–Doubleday, 1984.

Morton, Nelle. *The Journey is Home.* Boston: Beacon Press, 1985.

Murray, Pauli. "Black, Feminist Theologies: Links, Parallels and Tensions." *Anglican Theological Review* 60 (January 1978). *Christianity and Crisis* 40 (1980): 85–96.

National Conference of Catholic Bishops. "Theological Reflections on the Ordination of Women." *Review for Religious* 32:2 (March 1973): 221. *Journal of Ecumenical Studies* 10 (1973): 695–99.

Neal, Marie Augusta. "Social Encyclicals: Role of Women." *Network Quarterly* 3:2 (Spring 1975).

Nelson, James B. *Embodiment: An Approach to Sexuality and Christian Theology.* Minneapolis, MN: Augsburg Publishing House, 1978.

Niethammer, Carolyn. *Daughters of the Earth: The Lives and Legends of American Indian Women.* New York: Collier Books, 1977.

Oakley, Ann. *Sex, Gender and Society.* New York: Harper & Row, 1972.

O'Brien, Mary. *The Politics of Reproduction.* Boston: Routledge and Kegan Paul, 1981.

Ochs, Carol. *Behind the Sex of God: Toward a New Consciousness—Transcending Matriarchy and Patriarchy.* Boston: Beacon Press, 1977.

Ochs, Carol. *Women and Spirituality.* Totowa, NJ: Rowman and Allanheld, 1983.

Ochshorn, Judith. *The Female Experience and the Nature of the Divine.* Bloomington, IN: Indiana University Press, 1981.

O'Connor, June. "Liberation Theologies and the Women's Movement." *Horizons* 1:2 (Spring 1975): 103–13.

O'Connor, June. "Sensuality, Spirituality, Sacramentality." *Union Seminary Quarterly Review* 40: 1–2 (May 1985): 59–70.

O'Flaherty, Wendy Doniger. *Women, Androgynes, and Other Mythical Beasts.* Chicago: University of Chicago Press, 1980.

Ohanneson, Joan. *Woman: Survivor in the Church.* Minneapolis, MN: Winston Press, 1980.

Okin, Susan Moller. *Women in Western Political Thought.* Princeton: Princeton University Press, 1979.

Olson, Karl. ed., *The Book of the Goddess Past and Present: An Introduction to Her Religion.* New York: Crossroad, 1983.

O'Neill, William. *Everyone Was Brave: The Rise and Fall of Feminism in America.* Chicago: Quadrangle Books, 1969.

Orthodox Church in America (Subcommittee of the Ecumenical Task Force). *Women and Men in the Church: A Study of the Community of Women and Men in the Church.* New York: Department of Religious Education Orthodox Church in America, 1980.

Ortner, Sherry B. and Harriet Whitehead, eds. *Sexual Meanings: The Cultural Construction of Gender and Sexuality.* Cambridge: Cambridge University Press, 1981.

Osiek, Carolyn. *Beyond Anger: On Being a Feminist in the Church.* New York: Paulist Press, 1986.

Otwell, John H. *And Sarah Laughed: The Status of Women in the Old Testament.* Philadelphia: Westminster, 1977.

Oxford-Carpenter, Rebecca. "Gender and the Trinity." *Theology Today* 41:1 (April 1984): 7–25.

Pagels, Elaine. *The Gnostic Gospels.* New York: Vintage Books–Random House, 1981.

Pagels, Elaine. "Paul and Women: A Response to Recent Discussion." *Journal of the American Academy of Religion* 42:3 (September 1974): 538–49.

Pagels, Elaine. "What Became of God the Mother? Conflicting Images of God in Early Christianity." *Signs* 2:2 (Winter 1976): 293–303.

Papa, Mary Bader. *Christian Feminism: Completing the Subtotal Woman.* Chicago: Fides/Claretian, 1981.

Parvey, Constance F., ed. *Ordination of Women in Ecumenical Perspective.* Geneva: World Council of Churches, 1980.

Patrick, Anne E. "Coming of Age: Women's Contributions to Contemporary Theology." *New Catholic World* 228:1364 (March/April 1985): 61–9.

Patrick, Anne E. "Conservative Case for the Ordination of Women." *New Catholic World* 218:1305 (May/June 1975): 108–11.

Patrick, Anne E. "Narrative and the Social Dynamics of Virtue." *Changing Values and Virtues.* Eds. Dietmar Mieth and Jacques Pohier. *Concilium* 191. Edinburgh: T. and T. Clark, 1987: 69–80.

Patrick, Anne E. "Toward Renewing the Life and Culture of Fallen Man: *Gaudium et Spes* as Catalyst for Catholic Feminist Theology." *Questions of Special Urgency: The Church in the Modern World Two*

Decades after Vatican II. Ed. Judith A. Dwyer. Washington D.C.: Georgetown University Press, 1986.

Paul, Diana. *Women in Buddhism.* Berkeley: Asian Humanities Press, 1979.

Pellauer, Mary. "Violence Against Women: The Theological Dimension." *Christianity and Crisis* 43 (May 30, 1983): 206, 208–12.

Petchesky, Rosalind Pollack. *Abortion and Woman's Choice: The State, Sexuality and Reproductive Freedom.* Boston: Northeastern University Press, 1985.

Phelps, Jamie. "A Black Perspective." *Proceedings of the Catholic Theological Society of America* 37 (June 10–13, 1982): 119–22.

Phillips, J. B. *Eve: The History of an Idea.* New York: Harper & Row, 1984.

Plaskow, Judith. *Sex, Sin and Grace: Women's Experience and the Theologies of Reinhold Niebuhr and Paul Tillich.* Washington, D.C.: University Press of America, 1980.

Plaskow, Judith and Joan Arnold Romero, eds. *Women and Religion: Papers of the Working Group on Women and Religion 1972–73, Revised Edition.* American Academy of Religion. Missoula, MT: The Scholars Press, 1974.

Plaskow, Judith. "Christian Feminism and Anti-Judaism." *Cross Currents* 28:3 (Fall 1978): 306–9.

Plaskow, Judith. "On Carol Christ on Margaret Atwood: Some Theological Reflections." *Signs* 2:2 (Winter 1976): 293–303.

Pomeroy, Sarah B. *Goddesses, Whores, Wives, and Slaves: Women in Classical Antiquity.* New York: Schocken Books, 1975.

Pope Paul VI. "Address to Committee for the International Women's Year." *Origins* 4:45 (May 1, 1975): 718–19.

Porterfield, Amanda. *Feminine Spirituality in America: From Sarah Edwards to Martha Graham.* Philadelphia: Temple University Press, 1980.

Poster, Mark. *Critical Theory of the Family.* New York: Continuum–Seabury Press, 1980.

Power, Eileen. *Medieval Women.* Cambridge, England: Cambridge University Press, 1975.

Procter-Smith, Marjorie. "Liturgical Anamnesis and Women's Memory." *Worship* 61:5 (September 1987): 405–24.

Rabuzzi, Kathryn Allen. *The Sacred and the Feminine: Toward a Theology of Housework.* New York: Seabury Press, 1982.

Rader, Rosemary. *Breaking Boundaries: Male/Female Friendship in Early Christian Communities.* New York: Paulist Press, 1983.

Rahner, Karl. "The Position of Women in the New Situation in Which the Church Finds Herself." *Theological Investigations.* Trans. David Bourke. New York: Herder and Herder, 1971. Vol. 8.

Rahner, Karl. "Women and the Priesthood." *Theological Investigations.*

Trans. Edward Quinn. New York: Crossroad, 1981. Vol. 20.

Raming, Ida. *The Exclusion of Women from the Priesthood: Divine Law on Sex Discrimination.* Trans. Norman R. Adams. Metuchen, NJ: Scarecrow Press, 1974.

Rich, Adrienne. *Of Woman Born: Motherhood as Experience and Institution,* New York: Bantam Books, 1977.

Rich, Adrienne. *On Lies, Secrets, and Silence: Selected Prose, 1966–1978.* New York: W. W. Norton & Co., 1979.

Richards, Janet Radcliffe. *The Sceptical Feminist: A Philosophical Inquiry.* London: Routledge and Kegan Paul, 1980.

Richardson, Nancy and Carol Robb. "Politics and Theology of Ministry with Women." *Radical Religion* 2 (1975).

Rigney, Barbara. *Lilith's Daughters: Women and Religion in Contemporary Fiction.* Madison, WI: University of Wisconsin Press, 1982.

Romero, Joan Arnold, chairperson (Working Group on Women and Religion). *Women and Religion 1973 Proceedings.* Florida: American Academy of Religion, 1973.

Röper, Anita. *Ist Gott ein Mann? Ein Gesprach mit Karl Rahner.* Dusseldorf: Patmos, 1979.

Rosaldo, Michelle Zimbalist and Louis Lamphere, eds. *Women, Culture and Society.* Stanford, CA: Stanford University, 1974.

Ross, Susan A. "The Future of Humanity: Feminist Perspectives." *Proceedings of the Catholic Theological Society of America* 41 (June 11–14, 1986): 157–59.

Rossi, Alice S., ed. *The Feminist Papers.* New York: Bantam Books, 1974.

Roszak, Betty and Theodore Roszak, eds. *Masculine/Feminine: Readings in Sexual Mythology and the Liberation of Women.* New York: Harper Colophon Books, 1969.

Ruether, Rosemary Radford. *Mary—The Feminine Face of the Church.* Philadelphia: Westminster Press, 1977.

Ruether, Rosemary Radford. *New Woman/New Earth: Sexist Ideologies and Human Liberation.* New York: Seabury Press, 1975.

Ruether, Rosemary Radford. *Religion and Sexism: Images of Women in the Jewish and Christian Traditions.* New York: Simon and Schuster, 1974.

Ruether, Rosemary Radford. *Sexism and God-Talk: Toward a Feminist Theology.* Boston: Beacon Press, 1983.

Ruether, Rosemary Radford. *To Change the World: Christology and Cultural Criticism.* New York: Crossroad, 1981.

Ruether, Rosemary Radford. *Womanguides: Readings Toward a Feminist Theology.* Boston: Beacon Press, 1985.

Ruether, Rosemary Radford. *Women-Church: Theology and Practice of Femi-*

nist Liturgical Communities. San Francisco: Harper & Row, 1986.

Ruether, Rosemary Radford and Rosemary Skinner Keller, eds. *Women and Religion in America: A Documentary History.* 3 vols. San Francisco: Harper & Row, 1981, 1983, 1986.

Ruether, Rosemary Radford and Eleanor McLaughlin, eds. *Women of Spirit: Female Leadership in the Jewish and Christian Traditions.* New York: Simon and Schuster, 1979.

Ruether, Rosemary Radford. "Female Symbols, Values, and Context." *Christianity and Crisis* 46:19 (January 12, 1987): 460–64.

Ruether, Rosemary Radford, "Godesses and Witches: Liberation and Countercultural Feminism." *Christian Century* (September 10-17, 1980): 842-47.

Ruether, Rosemary Radford. "A Religion for Women: Sources and Strategies." *Christianity and Crisis* 39:19 (December 10, 1980): 307–11.

Ruether, Rosemary Radford. "An Unrealized Revolution." *Christian and Crisis* 43:17 (October 31, 1983): 398–400.

Russell, Letty M. *Becoming Human.* Philadelphia: Westminster Press, 1982.

Russell, Letty M., ed. *Feminist Interpretation of the Bible.* Philadelphia: Westminster Press, 1985.

Russell, Letty M. *The Future of Partnership.* Philadelphia: Westminster Press, 1979.

Russell, Letty M. *Growth in Partnership.* Philadelphia: Westminster Press, 1981.

Russell, Letty M. *Household of Freedom: Authority in Feminist Theology.* Philadelphia: Westminster Press, 1987.

Russell, Letty M. *Human Liberation in a Feminist Perspective: A Theology.* Philadelphia: Westminster Press, 1974.

Russell, Letty M. *The Liberating Word: A Guide to Non-Sexist Interpretation of the Bible.* Philadelphia: Westminster Press, 1976.

Sacred Congregation for the Doctrine of the Faith. "Declaration on the Question of the Admission of Women to the Ministerial Priesthood." Vatican City, 1976. Reprinted in: *Women Priests,* eds. Swidler and Swidler, 319–46; *Origins* 6:3 (February 1977): 517–24; *New Women, New Church* 10:1 (January/February): 9–13.

Saiving, Valerie. "Androcentrism in Religious Studies." *Journal of Religion* 56:2 (April 1976): 177-97.

Saiving, Valerie. "The Human Situation: A Feminine View." *Journal of Religion* 40 (April 1960): 100–112.

Sanday, Peggy Reeves. *Female Power and Male Dominance: On the Origins of Sexual Inequality.* Cambridge: Cambridge University Press, 1981.

Sawicki, Marianne. *Faith and Sexism: Guidelines for Religious Educators.* New York: Crossroad–Seabury Press, 1979.

Scanzoni, Letha. *Sexuality.* Philadelphia: Westminster Press, 1984.

Scanzoni, Letha and Nancy Hardesty. *All We're Meant to Be.* Waco, TX: Word Books, 1975.

Schaberg, Jane. *The Illegitimacy of Jesus: A Feminist Theological Interpretation of the Infancy Narratives.* San Francisco: Harper & Row, 1987.

Schaef, Anne Wilson. *Women's Reality: An Emerging Female System in the White Male Society.* Minneapolis: Winston Press, 1981.

Schaffran, Janet and Pat Kozak. *More Than Words: Prayer and Ritual for Inclusive Communities.* Cleveland, OH: 1986.

Schaupp, Joan. *Woman: Image of the Holy Spirit.* New Jersey: Dimension Books, 1975.

Schmidt, Gail Ramshaw. *Christ in Sacred Speech: The Meaning of Liturgical Language.* Philadelphia: Fortress Press, 1986.

Schmidt, Gail Ramshaw. "De Divinis Nominibus: The Gender of God." *Worship* 56:2 (March 1982): 117–31.

Schneiders, Sandra M. *Women and the Word.* New York: Paulist Press, 1986.

Schneiders, Sandra M. "Women and Power in the Church: A New Testament Reflection." *Proceedings of the Catholic Theological Society of America* 37 (New York 1982): 127–28.

Scroggs, Robin. "Paul and the Eschatological Woman." *Journal of the American Academy of Religion* 40:3 (September 1972): 283–303.

Scroggs, Robin. "Paul and the Eschatological Woman: Revisited." *Journal of the American Academy of Religion* 42:3 (September 1974): 532–37.

Sharma, Arvind, ed. *Women in World Religions.* New York: State University of New York Press, 1987.

Sherman, Julia A. and Evelyn Torton Beck. *The Prism of Sex.* Madison: University of Wisconsin Press, 1979.

Singer, June. *Androgyny: Toward a New Theory of Sexuality.* New York: Doubleday, 1976.

Smith, Barbara, *Home Girls: A Black Feminist Anthology.* Brooklyn, NY: Kitchen Table: Women of Color Press, 1983.

Smith, June I., ed. *Women in Contemporary Muslim Societies.* Lewisburg, PA: Bucknell University Press, 1980.

Soelle, Dorothee. *Beyond Mere Obedience.* New York: The Pilgrim Press, 1982.

Soelle, Dorothee. *The Strength of the Weak: Toward a Christian Feminist Identity.* Trans. Robert Kimber and Rita Kimber. Philadelphia: Westminster Press, 1984.

Soelle, Dorothee. "Liberation and the Names of God." *Christianity and Crisis* 41:11 (June 22, 1981): 179–85.

Spender, Dale, ed. *Feminist Theorists: Three Centuries of Key Women Thinkers.* New York: Pantheon Books, 1983.

Spretnak, Charlene, ed. *The Politics of Women's Spirituality: Essays on the Rise of Spiritual Power within the Feminist Movement.* New York: Doubleday, 1982.

Stagg, Evelyn and Frank Stagg. *Women in the World of Jesus.* Philadelphia: The Westminster Press, 1978.

Stanton, Elizabeth Cady. *The Original Feminist Attack on the Bible (The Woman's Bible).* New York: Arno Press, Inc., 1974 reprint.

Starhawk (Simos, Miriam). *Dreaming the Dark: Magic, Sex and Politics.* Boston: Beacon Press, 1982.

Starhawk (Simos, Miriam). *The Spiral Dance: The Rebirth of the Ancient Religion of the Great Goddess.* San Francisco: Harper & Row, 1979.

Stendahl, Krister. *The Bible and the Role of Women.* Philadelphia: Fortress Press, 1966.

Stuhlmueller, C. P., Carroll. *Women and Priesthood: Future Directions, A Call to Dialogue from the Faculty of the Catholic Theological Union at Chicago.* Collegeville, MN: The Liturgical Press, 1978.

Suchocki, Marjorie. *God-Christ-Church: A Practical Guide to Process Theology.* New York: Crossroad, 1982.

Suleiman, Susan Rubin, ed. *The Female Body in Western Culture: Contemporary Perspectives.* Cambridge: Harvard University Press, 1986.

Swidler, Arlene, ed. *Sister Celebrations: Nine Worship Experiences.* Philadelphia: Fortress Press, 1974.

Swidler, Arlene. *Woman in a Man's Church.* New York: Paulist Press, 1972.

Swidler, Arlene and Walter E. Conn, eds. *Mainstreaming: Feminist Research for Teaching Religious Studies.* Lanham, MD: University Press of America, 1985.

Swidler, Leonard. *Biblical Affirmations of Women.* Philadelphia: Westminster Press, 1979.

Swidler, Leonard. "Jesus Was a Feminist." *New Catholic World* 214 (1971): 771-73.

Swidler, Leonard and Arlene Swidler, eds. *Women Priests: A Catholic Commentary on the Vatican Declaration.* New York: Paulist Press, 1977.

Tamez, Elsa. *Bible of the Oppressed.* Maryknoll, NY: Orbis, 1982.

Tavard, George H. *Women in Christian Tradition.* Notre Dame: University of Notre Dame Press, 1973.

Taves, Ann. "Mothers and Children and the Legacy of Mid-Nineteenth Century American Christianity." *Journal of Religion* 67:2 (April 1987): 203-19. (The entire issue is devoted to themes in feminist theology.)

Tavris, Carol and Carole Offir. *The Longest War: Sex Differences in Perspective.* New York: Harcourt, Brace, Jovanovich, Inc., 1977.

Tennis, Diane. *Is God the Only Reliable Father?.* Philadelphia: Westminster

Press, 1985.

Tennis, Diane. "The Loss of the Father God: Why Women Rage and Grieve." *Christianity and Crisis* 41:10 (June 8, 1981): 164–70.

Tennis, Diane. "Reflections on the Maleness of Jesus." *Cross Currents* 28 (1978): 137–40.

Tetlow, Elizabeth M. *Women and Ministry in the New Testament.* New York: Paulist Press, 1980.

Thistlethwaite, Susan Brooks. *Metaphors for a Contemporary Church.* New York: Pilgrim Press, 1983.

Thomas, Hilah F. and Rosemary Skinner Keller, eds. *Women in New Worlds: Historical Perspectives on the Wesleyan Tradition.* Nashville: Abingdon Press, 1981.

Timmerman, Joan. *The Mardi Gras Syndrome: Rethinking Christian Sexuality.* New York: Crossroad, 1984.

Timmerman, Joan. "Women in Theological Research." *Proceedings of the Catholic Theological Society of America* 38 (June 15–18, 1983): 63–65.

Tolbert, Mary Ann, ed. *Semeia 28: The Bible and Feminist Hermeneutics.* Society of Biblical Literature, 1983.

Trask, Haunani-Kay. *Eros and Power: The Promise of Feminist Theory.* Philadelphia: University of Pennsylvania Press, 1986.

Trible, Phyllis. *God and the Rhetoric of Sexuality.* Philadelphia: Fortress Press, 1978.

Trible, Phyllis. *Texts of Terror: Literary-Feminist Readings of Biblical Narratives.* Philadelphia: Fortress Press, 1984.

Trible, Phyllis. "DePatriarchalizing the Biblical Interpretation." *Journal of the American Academy of Religion* 41:1 (March 1973): 30–48.

Van der Meer, Haye. *Women Priests in the Catholic Church?* Philadelphia: Temple University Press, 1973. McBrien, Richard. Review. *Commonweal* 101:2 (October 11, 1974): 44–5.

Van Herik, Judith. *Freud on Femininity and Faith.* Berkeley: University of California Press, 1982.

Van Scoyoc, Nancy J. *Women, Change and the Church.* Nashville, TN: Abingdon, 1980.

Vaughn, Judith. *Sociality, Ethics, and Social Change: A Critical Appraisal of Reinhold Niebuhr's Ethics in the Light of Rosemary Radford Ruether's Works.* Lanham, MD: University Press of America, 1983.

Verdesi, Elisabeth Howell. *In But Still Out: Women in the Church.* Philadelphia: Westminster Press, 1973.

Vetterling-Braggin, Mary, Frederick A. Elliston and Jane English, eds. *Feminism and Philosophy.* Totowa, NJ: Littlefield, Adams, and Co., 1981.

Vetterling-Braggin, Mary, ed. *"Femininity," "Masculinity," and "Androgyny": A Modern Philosophical Discussion.* Totowa, NJ: Littlefield, Adams, and Co., 1982.

Vetterling-Braggin, Mary. *Sexist Language: A Modern Philosophical Analysis.* Boston: Littlefield, Adams, and Co., 1981.

Wahlberg, Rachel Conrad. *Jesus According to a Woman.* New York: Paulist Press, 1975.

Wahlberg, Rachel Conrad. *Jesus and the Freed Woman.* New York: Paulist Press, 1978.

Walker, Alice. *The Color Purple.* New York: Harcourt, Brace, Jovanovich, 1982.

Walker, Alice. *In Search of Our Mothers' Gardens: Womanist Prose.* San Diego: Harcourt, Brace, Jovanovich, 1983.

Ware, Ann Patrick, ed. *Midwives of the Future: American Sisters Tell Their Story.* Kansas City, MO: Leaven Press, 1985.

Warner, Marina. *Alone of All Her Sex: The Myth and the Cult of the Virgin Mary.* New York: Alfred A. Knopf, 1976.

Warner, Marina. *Joan of Arc: The Image of Female Heroism.* New York: Alfred A. Knopf, 1981.

Warren, Mary Anne. *The Nature of Woman: An Encyclopedia and Guide to the Literature.* California: Edgepress, 1980.

Washburn, Penelope. *Becoming Woman: The Quest for Wholeness in Female Experience.* New York: Harper & Row, 1977.

Washburn, Penelope. *Seasons of Women.* San Francisco: Harper & Row, 1979.

Watkins, Keith. *Faithful and Fair: Transcending Sexist Language in Worship.* Nashville: Abingdon Press, 1981.

Weaver, Mary Jo. *New Catholic Women: A Contemporary Challenge to Traditional Religious Authority.* San Francisco: Harper & Row, 1985.

Weidman, Judith, ed. *Christian Feminism: Visions of a New Humanity.* San Francisco: Harper & Row, 1984.

Weidman, Judith. *Women Ministers: How Women Are Redefining Traditional Roles.* New York: Harper & Row, 1981.

Welch, Sharon. *Communities of Resistance and Solidarity: A Feminist Theology of Liberation.* Maryknoll, NY: Orbis Books, 1985.

Williams, Delores S. "Womanist Theology: Black Women's Voices." *Christianity and Crisis* 47:3 (March 2, 1987): 66–70.

Wilson-Kastner, Patricia. *Faith, Feminism and the Christ.* Philadelphia: Fortress Press, 1983.

Wilson-Kastner, Patricia et al. *A Lost Tradition: Women Writers of the Early Church.* Lanham, MD: University Press of America, 1981.

Zapata, Dominga Maria. "The Role of the Hispanic Woman in the Church."

New Catholic World (July/August 1980): 172.

Zikmund, Barbara Brown. "The Trinity and Women's Experience." *Christian Century* 104:12 (April 15, 1987): 354–56.

Index